K

Case Studies in Information Technology Ethics

Second Edition

Case Studies in Information Technology Ethics

Richard A. Spinello

Boston College
Carroll School of Management

Upper Saddle River, New Jersey 07458

Library of Congress Cataloging-in-Publication Data

SPINELLO, RICHARD A.
Case studies in information technology ethics / by RICHARD A. SPINELLO.—2nd ed.
p. cm.
ISBN 0-13-099150-3
1. Information technology—Moral and ethical aspects—Case studies. I. Title.

T58.5 .S72 2003
174'.90904—dc21 2002070948

VP, Editorial Director: *Charlyce Jones Owen*
Acquisitions Editor: *Ross Miller*
Assistant Editor: *Wendy Yurash*
Editorial Assistant: *Carla Worner*
Editorial/Production Supervision: *Joanne Riker*
Prepress and Manufacturing Buyer: *Brian Mackey*
Marketing Manager: *Chris Ruel*
Marketing Assistant: *Scott Rich*
Cover Art Director: *Jayne Conte*
Cover Designer: *Bruce Kenselaar*

This book was set in 10.5/12.5 Palatino by Compset, Inc.
and was printed and bound by Courier Companies, Inc.
The cover was printed by Coral Graphics.

Printed in the United States of America

10 9 8 7 6 5 4 3

ISBN 0-13-099150-3

Pearson Education LTD, *London*
Pearson Education Australia PTY, Limited, *Sydney*
Pearson Education Singapore, Pte. Ltd
Pearson Education North Asia Ltd, *Hong Kong*
Pearson Education Canada, Ltd., *Toronto*
Pearson Educación de Mexico, S.A. de C.V.
Pearson Education—Japan, *Tokyo*
Pearson Education Malaysia, Pte. Ltd
Pearson Education, *Upper Saddle River, New Jersey*

In Memory of my Uncles,
Gene, Carmen, and John

Contents

Preface

Since this book was first published in 1996 under the original title *Case Studies in Information and Computer Ethics*, there have been many changes in this expanding field of study. Computer ethics courses began infiltrating the curriculum at many universities and there has been an outpouring of books and articles. The field is more mature now with its own journal, *Ethics and Information Technology*, published by Kluwer Academic Publishers, and its own scholarly organization, the International Society for Ethics and Information Technology (INSEIT). In keeping with this nomenclature, we have opted to change the title of this book to *Case Studies in Information Technology Ethics.*

Also, at that time of the first edition the World Wide Web was in its infancy and most electronic commerce business models were still on the drawing board—inchoate ideas in the minds of visionaries like Jeff Bezos of Amazon.com. During the ensuing period there was an explosion of growth on the Web followed by the great dot.com crash of 2000. But while the euphoria about the Net has faded, no one is dismissing the likelihood that this global network will be a main thoroughfare of commerce and community in the future.

This new edition puts considerable emphasis on the major ethical dilemmas provoked by the Web and the Internet, especially in the areas of privacy, free speech, and intellectual property. Several new sections have been added, including an entire chapter on free speech in cyberspace along with a chapter on fair competition and Internet access issues. Free speech issues have emerged as particularly contentious ones thanks to the availability of automated content controls such as filters; several cases in Chapter 2 will emphasize the disputed role of these technologies in controlling discourse in cyberspace. There is also much emphasis in this book on property and interconnectivity issues that stem from activities such as hyperlinking. The property cases deal with digital music and the Internet phenomenon of Napster, and they also examine controversial issues such as Web site linking and the proper use of metatags.

Other topics covered by this book include security, software reliability and liability, and, of course, the vital issue of privacy. The chapter on privacy includes a case on Web bug architectures as well as a new case on the controversy surrounding Toysmart.com's customer list. There is a new section in this chapter called "Privacy and Public Safety" that includes two case studies on the government's conflicting demands to protect privacy and provide security. The first case study focuses on the FBI's controversial Carnivore technology and the demands placed on Internet Service Providers to cooperate in Carnivore's deployment. The Carnivore case allows students to consider the difficult trade-offs that must be made between security and liberty. The second selection, "Crypto Wars," is an updated version of a case that appeared in the first edition. That case now reflects the liberalization of encryption export policy and other important changes. The privacy issues raised by both of these cases obviously have greater salience in the post-September 11 world.

Also new to this edition is a secondary focus on policy issues for those so inclined to present some of these cases from that perspective. Included in Chapter 1 is an overview of Larry Lessig's framework along with more general background material on how to frame policy debates about the Internet. The final chapter is especially suited for policy discussion with its cases on the information infrastructure. These cases involve the problems of open access on the Internet and the digital divide. Included in this chapter are two cases on Microsoft: a comprehensive review of the antitrust trial and a timely discussion on the potential for renewed antitrust problems with the release of the Windows XP operating system.

This book presents a total of 42 case studies; 22 of these cases are new and several of the remaining cases have been updated where appropriate. Some of these cases (such as the pair of Microsoft cases) look at the moral propriety of corporate policy, while others look at what constitute suitable and fair public policies. Still other cases are based on the actual experiences of managers and Information Technology (IT) professionals who work in the field of computer technology or have some responsibility for managing a company's information resources. A few cases represent hypothetical but realistic situations.

The purpose of these diverse cases, of course, remains the same: to help students, IT professionals, and managers to reflect on the vexing ethical dilemmas and problems that are emerging in the information age. In this fast-paced environment the rules seem to change quite rapidly and the standards of propriety are difficult to define. Many of the cases presented here are complex and multifaceted, and hence they defy facile solutions. But the problems posed are certainly not insoluble, and, as a guide to effective resolution, this book includes an overview of theoretical ethical frameworks. The frameworks presented include consequentialism, pluralism, and contractarianism. They enable us to analyze moral problems from the viewpoint of consequences, duties, and rights. If used properly, these "avenues" of ethical reasoning can be instrumental in helping us develop a cogent action plan within the bounds of ethical probity and social acceptabilty.

Finally, there is a selective but thorough bibliography that includes major books and articles in the field of information technology ethics. It is organized by the topics covered in this book and it will facilitate the process of future research on many of the issues raised in the case studies and the chapter introductions.

THE METHOD

The case study remains a popular instrument to provoke students to grapple with complicated moral problems and quandaries. Cases present such problems in a particular context, and as a result they require students to discern the ethical dimension of a situation among a plethora of intricate, perplexing, and sometimes conflicting information. Further, they compel students to frame the issues carefully and to develop a tenable and morally defensible action plan. Since these cases are based on real-life situations, they prepare students for the ethical dilemmas they will confront in their own professional careers. The expectation is that they will be able to deal with those dilemmas more responsibly and purposefully once they have developed this valuable skill of ethical analysis.

The most significant benefit of using the case study method is that it engages students and requires them to become active participants rather than passive observers. This method is a form of student-centered education that heavily involves students in the learning process. According to Charles I. Cragg, in "Because Wisdom Can't Be Told," (*Harvard Alumni Bulletin* October 19, 1940)

> The case system, properly used, initiates students into the ways of independent thought and responsible judgment. It faces them with situations which are not hypothetical but real. It places them in the active role, open to criticism from all sides. It puts the burden of understanding and judgment upon them. It provides them the occasion to deal constructively with their contemporaries and their elders.

The cases in this book have been designed to stimulate dialogue and reflection on a well-defined set of complex issues. They are timely and yet embody enduring controversies that will remain with us for many years. They can stand alone or be used with supplementary material such as background essays, articles, and even news clips available on video. Most of the cases have been tested at various seminars and classes at Boston College, and they have been chosen because they can function as excellent springboards to productive and lively discussions.

THE AUDIENCE

Interest in this provocative subject matter has certainly intensified in the last decade. As a result, new courses and workshops in information technology ethics have proliferated on college campuses, corporate education settings, and elsewhere. It is my hope that this updated case book will continue to be a valuable resource for such courses and seminars.

This book can be used profitably in advanced undergraduate and graduate programs in schools of business, engineering, and public policy. It is most suitable for courses devoted exclusively to information technology (or computer) ethics, but it could be used in engineering ethics courses where a major axis of discussion is information processing. It has also been designed for interdisciplinary courses that probe the business and legal environment of telecommunications and information technology such as "Seminar in Internet Law, Ethics, and Policy." Or it could be used profitably in generic policy or ethics courses offered in schools of business (for example, courses such as "Social Issues in Management"or "Moral Dilemmas of Management"). This text could even find a place in some humanities and philosophy courses that treat broader areas such as practical ethics or technology and society. Lastly, this collection of cases can be an important resource in corporate management education programs. Professional managers also need to be introduced to the array of issues presented in these case studies. In any of these contexts this text can be used by itself or it can serve as a companion piece to a narrative or book of readings on computer ethics.

Ultimately the goal of this book is to help instructors sensitize students and managers to the vital importance of the careful and responsible use of information technology. It raises many questions, challenges certain assumptions, and even provides a glimpse into the future. But above all, the primary objective is to heighten our ethical awareness in order to help ensure that technology will not be used to create a future inimical to human values or the fundamental principles of justice and fairness.

ACKNOWLEDGEMENTS

I have received considerable feedback from users of the first edition. I am indebted to my own students for their candid comments and have also profited immensely from the thoughtful evaluations of faculty members who have used this book in their courses. I have tried to incorporate as many of their suggestions as possible. In addition, I would like to thank several individuals who helped with this new edition. I am grateful for the commitment and cooperation of Ross Miller and Wendy Yurash from Prentice Hall. Helpful comments came from Prentice Hall's reviewers C. Dianne Martin of George Washington University and Stephanie L. Fitch of University of Missouri–Rolla. I am also grateful to Joanne Riker for her work in producing this book and for her patience in deciphering last minute edits and alterations. Thanks to Joyce O'Connor at the Carroll School of Management for providing some much needed administrative support. And finally I am grateful to Boston College for giving me a sabbatical; the free time has allowed me to complete this book along with several other related projects.

Richard A. Spinello
Hyde Park, Massachusetts

Case Studies in Information Technology Ethics

Frameworks for Ethical and Policy Analysis

This book presents a wide range of cases on the general topic of information technology and communications (ICT) ethics. While we do not want to frame the debates about these cases according to a particular set of moral assumptions, we cannot approach this material in a vacuum. Rather, we need some theoretical frameworks that will help us assess behavior in complex situations where critical ethical analysis is necessary. Hence in this chapter we present an overview of traditional ethical frameworks that offer some direction when the course of responsible conduct is not obvious.

In addition, many of the cases in this book focus on moral dilemmas and other social problems peculiar to the realm of cyberspace. These cases will inevitably trigger questions about the regulation of cyberspace. Is cyberspace "regulable" and, if so, *how* should it be regulated? In order to help us navigate this set of issues we introduce another framework: Larry Lessig's structural analysis of the regulatory landscape in cyberspace. In cyberspace we must contend with the potent regulatory impact of computer "code" and the complicated relationship between policy and technology.

For some of the cases in this book it will be useful to consider public policy implications along with an ethical assessment. It is quite important, for example, to make sound ethical judgments about privacy issues especially since in the United States there is a public policy void. But in the long run should we rely on the ethical goodwill of managers to do the right thing about privacy or do we need laws to fill that void? If so, those policies should be grounded in sound ethical reasoning and reflect the reality of basic human rights. The core values of ethics can help us evaluate the rationality and acceptability of public policies formulated to address social problems or market imperfections that arise in cyberspace.

MORAL FRAMEWORKS

Why Be Moral?

Before discussing these ethical frameworks, it is instructive to consider how we might answer the question, Why be moral? Why should engineers, computer professionals, information technology managers, and others be concerned with morality and doing the right thing? Why should they take into account the interests of others or aspire to ideals such as justice, honesty, and generosity?

Some would say that it's difficult enough to be a successful professional and to make sound management decisions without muddying the waters by worrying about morality. Also if the prospects of being caught are slim or nonexistent, then the temptations to flout the norms of morality are even greater. Others might note that morality can actually interfere with a prosperous career since we must compete against many professionals who are not always so moral. Recall Machiavelli's chilling admonition in *The Prince* that "a man who wishes to profess goodness at all times must fall to ruin among so many who are not good."[1]

Why, then, should one adopt the moral point of view? What can be gained by following one's moral duty or performing acts of self-sacrifice? The philosopher Immanuel Kant raises this important question in his famous essay *The Foundations of the Metaphysics of Morals* without providing a direct answer. Throughout this work, however, he expounds on the simple notion that if an individual's immoral acts, such as lying or promise breaking, were universalized, the world would be a terrible place. For Kant, the moral agent must constantly ask himself questions such as, What if everybody did what I did? What sort of world would it be? Therefore, in Kant's view, the moral law commands us to perform actions which can be universalized without contradiction.

A similar argument is advanced in Lon Fuller's seminal work *The Morality of Law*. He makes a critical distinction between the morality of duty and the morality of aspirations. He observes that the morality of duty espouses the "basic rules without which an ordered society is impossible, or without which an ordered society directed toward certain specific goals must fail in its mark."[2] Hence, unless we abide by the basic laws or duties of morality, we will fail to live up to the minimal requirements of social living. To a great extent our well-being depends upon the well-being of society and its well-being depends upon our willingness to act morally and responsibly. Clearly, then, to a large extent our moral behavior is in our own best interest. As Hobbes has written in the *Leviathan,* life without some sort of order and morality would be "solitary, poor, nasty, brutish, and short."[3]

Philosophers have argued for centuries that our human nature virtually compels us to be moral, since we cannot realize our potential as human beings unless we act morally. In other words, morality is essential for "human flourishing." Also, since we cannot achieve genuine human flourishing in isolation but only in community, we come back to the idea that since acting morally benefits the community, it will also benefit us. According to James Loughran, "Since man is and flourishes as 'person-in-community,' then whatever promotes community promotes personal life; and whatever promotes personal life promotes community."[4]

Beyond any doubt, engineers and managers bring credit to their profession and strengthen the bonds of their respective communities when they behave according to the highest moral standards. Their "flourishing" as individuals and as professionals depends upon the mutual cooperation and companionship that can occur only within a harmonious community setting. Hence the critical need to take morality seriously and to analyze ethical dilemmas with the same care that is devoted to technical or other managerial problems.

Traditional Ethical Theories

If one does decide to take morality seriously, it can sometimes be difficult to ascertain the "right" course of action. Some moral decisions are uncontroversial and they can be resolved at the level of moral common sense, but others need critical analysis. Let us consider several ethical theories and principles that can serve as general guidelines for those dilemmas requiring such critical analysis. Ethical theories present principles that will enable us to reach a justifiable normative judgment about the proper course of conduct. These theories explain and define what it means to act morally and thereby reveal to us the moral imperative that we must assume if we want to be a responsible and upright individual. As we shall see, these theories are by no means flawless nor are they able to function as formulas that give us simple answers to complex moral dilemmas. Rather, they are "avenues" or approaches to such problems that facilitate analysis and reflection on the issues at hand. They provide evocative concepts that can enrich our moral assessments of various scenarios.

For the most part we will be considering modern ethical theories, and these can be divided into two broad categories: teleological and deontological, the ethics of ends and the ethics of duty. The term "teleological" is derived from the Greek word *telos* which means end or goal. Teleological theories give priority to the good over the right and evaluate actions by the goal or consequences that they attain. In other words, the right is adjectival to the good and dependent upon it. Thus, right actions are those that produce the most good or optimize the consequences of one's choices, whereas wrong actions are those that do not contribute to the good. We will consider one example of a teleological approach to ethics, namely utilitarianism, a form of consequentialism.

Deontological theories, on the other hand, argue for the priority of the right over the good or the independence of the right from the good. "Deontological" is also derived from a Greek word, *deon*, which means obligation. According to a deontological framework, actions are intrinsically right or wrong regardless of the consequences which they produce. The "right" or ethically proper action might be deduced from a duty or a basic human right, but it is never contingent on the outcome or the consequences of an action. Deontological theories include both duty-based and rights-based approaches to ethical reasoning. These are sometimes referred to as pluralism and contractarianism, respectively.

Utilitarianism. The theory of utilitarianism is a teleological theory, and it is by far the most popular version of consequentialism. Classic utilitarianism was developed by two British philosophers, Jeremy Bentham (1748–1832) and John Stuart Mill (1806–1873). According to this theory the right course of action is to promote the general good. This general good can also be described in terms of "utility," and this principle of utility is the foundation of morality and the ultimate criterion of right and wrong. The term "utility" simply refers to the net benefits (or good) created by an action. According to

William Frankena, utilitarianism is the view that "the sole ultimate standard of right, wrong and obligation is the *principle of utility* or *beneficence,* which says quite strictly that the moral end to be sought in all that we do is *the greatest possible balance of good over evil* (or the least possible balance of evil over good)."[5] Thus an action or policy is right if it will produce the greatest net benefits or the lowest net costs (assuming that all of the alternatives impose some net cost).

It should be emphasized that utilitarianism is quite different from ethical egoism. An action is right not if it produces utility for the person performing that action but for *all* parties affected by the action. With this in mind we might reformulate the moral principle of utilitarianism as follows: *Persons ought to act in a way that promotes the maximum net expectable utility, that is, the greatest net benefits or the lowest net costs, for the broadest community affected by their actions.*

Utilitarianism assumes that we can somehow measure the benefits and harms produced by an action and thereby determine a sum of those benefits and harms. According to Manuel Velasquez, "the principle assumes that all benefits and costs of an action can be measured on a common numerical scale and then added or subtracted from each other."[6] For example, if a manager is weighing the goods of privacy versus security in the workplace, he or she might assign 300 positive units of utility to workplace privacy but 400 negative units to the security risks that accompany a corporate policy of strong privacy rights. How one assigns such measurements in a nonarbitrary way is a matter of some dispute.

In practice, therefore, utilitarianism requires one to develop and execute a sort of moral calculus. This is usually in the form of a cost-benefit analysis which can be employed in situations where there are several possible alternatives or courses of action. Once one has determined all of the possible alternatives, each alternative is evaluated in terms of its costs and benefits (both direct and indirect). Based on this analysis, one chooses the alternative that produces the greatest net expectable utility, that is, the one with the greatest net benefits (or the lowest net costs).

The core idea of utilitarianism that one should strive to optimize consequences in one's actions has considerable merit. Even philosophers who categorically reject utilitarianism and embrace other frameworks would admit that a basic requirement of ethical reasoning is attention to the probable consequences of one's decisions. According to John Rawls, a contemporary deontologist, "All ethical doctrines worth our attention take consequences into account when judging rightness."[7] This explains why utilitarianism is appealing to many as a natural, common-sense approach to morality. Many managers and professionals make decisions focusing on consequences and considering the costs and benefits of various alternatives. When these managers assert that they have a moral obligation to do something, they usually justify that obligation in terms of the net benefit yielded by that action.

It is no surprise therefore that various forms of utilitarian reasoning are quite common in business decisions. However, this form of reasoning can easily be distorted by self-serving managers. Consider a former president of Lockheed, who was accused in the early 1970s of paying $12 million in bribes to Japanese officials in order to persuade them to buy Lockheed's TriStar plane. This president advanced two arguments to defend these illicit payments: (a) They did not violate any American laws; (b) in the long run they were quite beneficial to many constituencies in the United States, since by securing the purchase of these planes they all reaped big rewards. This second line of reasoning at least implicitly invokes utilitarianism since this manager is arguing that his actions advanced the social good. To some extent, he may be correct. Stockholders certainly benefited through enhanced profits. At the same time, Lockheed's suppliers, its employees and their communities, and to some degree the entire U.S. economy benefited from this action. Moreover, the Japanese received an excellent airplane at a reasonable price. Of course, there were some costs to Lockheed's competitors and to others, but one could reasonably argue that these were most likely outweighed by the tangible benefits received by Lockheed's diverse stakeholders.[8] But did this manager really consider the dangers of bribery in a free enterprise system or the impairment of the overall level of trust in society caused by his actions? Did he conveniently underestimate the harms and overestimate the benefits?

The Lockheed example illustrates a key aspect of utilitarianism: What matters first and foremost are the consequences; how these consequences are achieved is only a secondary matter. This points to one of the most serious deficiencies with utilitarianism. It strongly implies that there are no intrinsically evil acts. To be sure, utilitarians would maintain that actions such as deceit, murder, or theft are usually morally wrong because of the harmful consequences that they bring about. But at the same time, these actions can be justified ethically if it can be proved decisively that they produce the greatest good or maximize net expectable utility. Presumably, then, even human or moral rights are not absolute, since a person's or group's rights could be taken away for the sake of maximizing utility. But are there not rights that transcend utilitarian calculations such as the rights to life and liberty? If we could somehow maximize happiness for a society by enslaving a small segment of that society, would that action really be justified morally?

As discussed, the utilitarian approach assumes that the goods involved in each alternative are commensurable. In other words, they can be measured and evaluated according to some common standard. But very often this is simply not the case, since the goods compared will at times be incommensurable. For example, how do we compare these two options: An automobile manufacturer can choose to install safer back seat belts in one of its most popular models at a cost of $87 million *or* it can refuse to do the installation, endure some bad publicity, but save $87 million. If the seat belts are installed, it is estimated that they would probably save about 10 lives a year. Should the company install the safer seat belts? If we attempt a cost-benefit analysis to answer this question, how can we compare lives saved with dollars and cents? Aren't these goods completely incommensurable? Or we might consider two abstract goods such as justice and truth. If these goods are at stake in a moral decision, how does the consequentialist choose between them? According to Germain Grisez, if a consequentialist admits that two goods are "fundamental and incommensurable, then the consequentialist also admits that the 'greatest net good' is meaningless whenever one must choose between promoting and protecting or impeding and damaging these two goods in some participations."[9]

The final difficulty with this popular theory is a practical and procedural one. Can managers and professionals objectively work through the sort of moral calculus demanded by consequentialism? Can these individuals avoid self-serving assumptions and various prejudices in the process of moral reasoning? Unfortunately, as we saw in the Lockheed example, consequentialist reasoning that does not overcome those assumptions can easily slide into a rationalization of unethical or selfish behavior. Moreover, the challenge of objectively considering carefully *all* the diffuse consequences of an action and estimating the costs and benefits can at times be quite formidable.

Duty-based Ethical Theory. We turn our attention now to deontological ethical theories which deny that the right is a function of the good, that is, whatever promotes net expectable utility. We will first consider pluralism or duty-based approaches as expressed in the philosophies of Immanuel Kant (1724–1804) and William D. Ross (1877–1940).

Kant's ethical theory is indeed a model of the deontological approach to morality which stresses fidelity to principle and duty. Kant's ethical philosophy is articulated and developed in his second critique, *The Critique of Practical Reason*, and in a much more concise work, *Foundations of the Metaphysics of Morals*. This philosophy is firmly opposed to utilitarianism and modern natural rights theories first developed by Hobbes and Locke. In the preface to *The Critique of Practical Reason* Kant indicates his intention to construct a "pure moral philosophy, perfectly cleared of everything which is only empirical, and which belongs to anthropology."[10] This pure moral philosophy is grounded not in the knowledge of our human nature but in a common idea of duty.

But what is this common idea of duty? To begin with, duty embodies the idea that one should do the right thing in the right spirit. In other words, according to Kant, "an action done from duty has moral worth, not in the purpose that is attained by it, but in the maxim according to which the action is determined."[11] Thus, an action's moral worth is not found in what it tries to accomplish but in the agent's intention and the summoning of one's energies to carry out that intention. Results, purpose, consequences cannot be taken into account to establish the validity of the moral law or to make exceptions to that law. For Kant, the moral individual must perform actions for the sake of duty *regardless of the consequences.*

What is the duty of a moral agent? In Kant's systematic philosophy our moral duty is simple: to follow the moral law which like the laws of science or physics must be rational. Also, like all rational laws, the moral law must be universal, since universality represents the common character of rationality and law. And this universal moral law is expressed as the *categorical imperative*: "I should never act except in such a way that I can also will that my maxim should become a universal law."[12] The imperative is "categorical" because it is absolute and does not allow for any exceptions.

A "maxim" is merely an implied general principle underlying a particular action. If, for example, I usually break my promises, then I act according to the maxim or principle that promise breaking is morally acceptable when it is in my best interests to do so. But can one take this individual maxim and transform it into a universal moral law? As a universal law this particular maxim would be expressed as follows: "It is permissible for everyone to break promises when it is in their best interests to do so." Such a law, however, is invalid since it contains a logical and pragmatic contradiction. There is a pragmatic (or practical) contradiction because the maxim is self-defeating if it is universalized. According to Christine Korsgaard, "your action would become ineffectual for the achievement of your purpose if everyone (tried to) use it for that purpose."[13] If I borrow some money from a friend and promise to pay her back, but this is a false promise, my objective, that is, getting some money from her, cannot be achieved by making a false promise in a world where this maxim has been universalized. According to Korsgaard,

"The efficacy of the false promise as a means of securing money depends on the fact that not everyone uses promises that way."[14]

Universal promise breaking also entails a logical contradiction (like a square circle), since if everyone broke promises, the entire institution of promising would collapse; there would be no such thing as a "promise" because in such a climate anyone making a promise would lack credibility. A world of universalized promise breaking is inconceivable. Thus, this maxim would destroy itself as soon as it was transformed into a universal law. If the universalized maxim for an action is clearly self-contradictory, as it is in this case, we can unequivocally conclude that the action is morally wrong.

Kant strongly implies that perfect duties, that is duties that we are always obliged to follow such as telling the truth or keeping a promise, entail both a logical and pragmatic contradiction. Violations of imperfect duties, however, are pragmatic contradictions.[15] Korsgaard explains that "perfect duties of virtue arise because we must refrain from particular actions *against* humanity in our own person or that of another."[16] Imperfect duties, on the other hand, are duties to develop one's talents where the individual has the latitude to fulfill this duty using many different means.

Kant's categorical imperative, then, is his ultimate ethical principle. It is a test of whether an action is right or wrong. Can the action in question pass the test of universalization? If not, the action is immoral and one has a duty to avoid it. The general principle of Kantian moral philosophy is that "self-contradictory universalized maxims are morally prohibited."[17] In order to be morally acceptable, an individual's action cannot be based on a principle (or maxim) that would be impossible for everyone else to follow.

Although there is only one categorical imperative or moral law, it can be expressed in several different ways. Kant's second formulation of this imperative is a pithy summary of his moral philosophy: "Act in such a way that you treat humanity, whether in your own person or in the person of another, always at the same time as an end and never simply as a means."[18] In other words, the principle of humanity as an end in itself serves as a limiting condition of every person's freedom of action. We cannot exploit other human beings and treat them exclusively as a means to our ends or purposes. Quite simply, the value of one's projects or objectives cannot supercede the worth of other human beings. For Kant, this principle can also be summed up in the word **respect**—the moral law can be reduced to the absolute principle of respect for other human beings who deserve respect because of their rationality and freedom, the hallmark of personhood for Kant.

Clearly, Kant's ethical theory has many virtues, but it is also controversial and fraught with serious problems because of its inflexibility and rigid absolutism. Specifically, do we really have absolute or perfect duties to keep promises or tell the truth? What if by lying to a criminal or a madman I can save the life of an innocent person? Am I still obliged to tell the truth under such circumstances? Kant would appear to say that the duty to tell the truth always prevails since lying cannot be universalized. But this seems to violate moral common sense, since we all recognize conditions when lying or deception is appropriate behavior. Consider the overwrought but helpful example of telling a lie to save someone from a ruthless murderer. In this case there is a conflict of universal laws: the law to tell the truth and the law to save a life in jeopardy. We must, of course, admit an exception to one of these laws. As A. C. Ewing points out,

> . . . in cases where two laws conflict it is hard to see how we can rationally decide between them except by considering the goodness or badness of the consequences. However important it is to tell the truth and however evil to lie, there are surely cases where much greater evils can still be averted by a lie, and is lying wrong then?[19]

Thus, it is difficult to avoid an appeal to consequences when two laws conflict, and this is problematic for a strict Kantian.

Also, it is worth pointing out that some philosophers such as Hegel have criticized Kant's categorical imperative because it is only a formal principle and, as such, it is empty and deficient. For Hegel, the moral law presented by Kant requires an empirical content, some genuine substance, and there is no content which can fit with its formal universality. But in some respects this criticism, which has been repeated by other philosophers, is somewhat unfair to Kant. There *is* a content to Kantian moral philosophy that is implicit in the categorical imperative. Recall that the second formulation of this imperative commands us to treat humanity as an end and never simply as a means. Thus, the dignity of the other as an end is the unconditioned principle and "content" of Kant's moral philosophy. It is true, of course, that the categorical imperative is a very general moral principle, but this is precisely what Kant intended. It is a compass or guide that provides us with a test for determining our concrete ethical duties. Indeed, it becomes clear that this emphasis on respect for persons endows Kant's ethics with a certain vitality. For Kant, the ethical life is never fully realized; rather, we are always striving to close the distance between our real moral situations and the ideal of the categorical imperative.

The British philosopher W. D. Ross has also developed a duty-based ethical theory in his book *The Right and the Good* which can be viewed as an extension of Kant's focus on a single, absolute duty. Ross claims that through reflection on our ordinary moral beliefs we can intuit the rules of morality. These moral rules or duties are ultimate and irreducible; hence, they are the first principles of moral reasoning. Ross, however, in contrast to Kant, refuses to accept these duties as absolute or prevailing without exception. Rather, he argues that they are *prima facie* duties which means that they are moral imperatives that should apply most of the time under normal circumstances. For Ross, the demands of morality are quite serious but not categorical.

In simplest terms, a *prima facie* obligation is a conditional one that can be superceded by a more important, higher obligation, usually under very exceptional circumstances. Thus, we do have a *prima facie* duty to be honest and truthful. But if a murderer comes to the door of your home looking for his wife whom you have hid in the basement, your obligation to tell the truth becomes subordinate to your obligation to protect human life. A moral principle can be sacrificed, but only for another moral principle, not just for arbitrary, pragmatic reasons. Although these *prima facie* duties must not be dismissed lightly or cavalierly, each of them has justified exceptions and in extraordinary circumstances they can be overridden by a higher duty.

According to Ross, there are seven basic moral duties that are binding on moral agents. These duties are as follows:

1. One ought to keep promises and tell the truth *(fidelity).*
2. One ought to right the wrongs that one has inflicted on others *(reparation).*
3. One ought to distribute goods justly *(justice).*
4. One ought to improve the lot of others with respect to virtue, intelligence, and happiness *(beneficence).*
5. One ought to improve oneself with respect to virtue and intelligence *(self-improvement).*
6. One ought to exhibit gratitude when appropriate *(gratitude).*
7. One ought to avoid injury to others *(noninjury).*

Ross does not maintain that this list of duties is complete or exhaustive, but he does believe that these duties are indisputable and self-evident. They are manifest to the mind through simple intuition. As he explains in *The Right and the Good*:

> I am assuming the correctness of some of our convictions as to *prima facie* duties, or more strictly, am claiming that we *know* them to be true. To me it

> seems self-evident as anything could be, that to make a promise, for instance, is to create a moral claim on us in someone else. Many readers will say that they do *not* know this to be true. If so, I certainly cannot prove it to them: I can only ask them to reflect again, in the hope that they will ultimately agree that they know it.[20]

As Ross indicates here, he makes no effort to provide any substantial rationalization or theoretical grounding of these duties. We might just say that they are common rules of morality, obvious to all rational humans because they have the general effect of reducing harm or evil to others.

There is one final issue regarding these *prima facie* duties which points to a deficiency in Ross' approach to morality: How do we handle cases where duties conflict? If two such duties are in conflict, Ross recommends that this basic principle should be followed: "That act is one's duty which is in accord with the more stringent *prima facie* obligation." If the situation is even more complex and there are more than two duties in conflict, then we must abide by a different guideline: "That act is one's duty which has the greatest balance of *prima facie* rightness over *prima facie* wrongness."[21]

Both of these principles, however, are somewhat vague and do not really facilitate resolving difficult conflicts between basic duties. They seem to raise more questions rather than help us reach answers. What is meant by Ross' use of the word "stringent"? What makes one obligation more compelling or stringent than another? Ross is silent on this critical issue, and this represents a serious flaw in his ethical philosophy. Likewise, Ross' second principle is riddled with ambiguity. He states that when various duties conflict, we should choose the duty that produces or yields the greatest proportion of "rightness." But this too begs the question and doesn't really offer us much assistance in deliberating over the question of which duty takes precedence.

Despite these shortcomings, however, Ross' theory has certain attractions. A focus on one's duty in a particular situation is an excellent starting point for determining the right course of action or resolving an ethical dilemma. Moreover, Ross' approach, unlike that of Kant's, provides for some flexibility, which to a certain extent better permits its application to complex moral problems where justified exceptions to basic duties are sometimes demanded.

Rights-Based Ethics. A third distinct approach to ethics focuses on individual rights and respect for those rights. This rights-based avenue of ethical thinking is another example of a deontological approach to ethics with its attention to moral principle instead of consequences. It is closely related to the duty-based approach since rights and duties are correlative. If one person has a right, another has a duty to respect that right. Kant argues that legitimate rights must be derived from moral duties:

> We know our own freedom (from which all moral laws and hence all rights as well as duties are derived) only through the moral [i.e., categorical] imperative, which is a proposition commanding duties; the capacity to obligate others to a duty, that is, the concept of a right, can be subsequently derived from this imperative.[22]

A right can be most simply defined as an *entitlement* to something. Thus, thanks to the First Amendment of the Constitution, all Americans are entitled to freedom of speech. This right is derived from and guaranteed by our legal system so it is a "legal right." There are also moral or human rights which are entitlements that all human beings should have by virtue of being human. Such rights are universal since they are grounded in human nature. Hence, unlike legal rights they are not confined to a particular legal jurisdiction. In addition, these human rights are equal rights; everyone, for example, shares equally in the right of free expression regardless of their nationality or status in society.

Philosophers make an important distinction between positive and negative rights. Negative rights imply freedom from outside interference in certain activities. Examples of negative rights include freedom of expression, the right to liberty, and the right to privacy. Thus, if one has a right to privacy in the workplace, an employer cannot interfere with one's private affairs. The challenge in that context is to determine what is "private." Obviously, the corollary of these rights is one's duty to avoid such interference. A positive right, on the other hand, implies a requirement that the holder of this right be provided "with whatever he or she needs to freely pursue his or her interests."[23] The rights to health care and education are examples of positive rights. If someone had a right to medical care, there would be a correlative duty on the part of some agent (probably the government) to provide that care in some fashion. In American society there has been far more emphasis on negative rights than on positive rights.

For some philosophers, the rights-based viewpoint is synonymous with *contractarianism* which has its roots in the social philosophy of philosophers such as Hobbes, Locke, and Rousseau. According to these philosophers, morality is grounded in the so-called social contract. This contract is necessitated because of the prepolitical state of nature which preceded civil society and in which there were absolute freedom and a constant state of war and strife. In order to overcome these intolerable conditions a civil government is established and all individuals enter into a tacit, implicit contract with that government to respect the other's desires for life and liberty. In return civil society agrees to respect and protect the basic rights of its citizens, specifically, the rights of life, liberty, property, and so forth. Society owes each individual protection of these rights in exchange for their obedience to the law. These are contractual rights that are usually synonymous with the legal rights guaranteed by the Constitution.

Several contractarians such as John Locke have argued for the social contract but also support the notion that our rights are fundamental and not dependent on this contract. Locke maintained that the rights of life, liberty, and property are natural, God-given rights that can never be abrogated by the state. What Hobbes, Locke, and other social contract philosophers have in common is their strong emphasis on *rights* as the fundament of morality. According to this perspective, moral reasoning should be governed by respect for individual rights and a philosophy of fairness. As Kenneth Goodpaster observes, "fairness is explained as a condition that prevails when all individuals are accorded equal respect as participants in social arrangements."[24] In short, then, contractarianism focuses on the need to respect an individual's legal, moral, and contractual rights as the basis of justice and fairness.

A rights-based analysis of moral problems should consider whether a particular course of action violates any of an individual's human or legal rights such as the right to privacy, the right to own property, or the right to the fruits of one's labor. As we shall see in subsequent chapters, the primary challenge confronting this sort of analysis emanates from the difficulty of establishing the parameters of these rights. It should be evident that like pluralism this approach to morality is markedly different from utilitarianism which regards rights or entitlements as subservient to the general welfare. For utilitarians, rights can be circumscribed if by doing so one can maximize the common good, but those who embrace contractarianism would categorically reject this claim.

Like utilitarianism and pluralism, an ethical theory based on rights has certain shortcomings. There is a tendency to argue for a proliferation of various rights without adequate consideration of how those rights can be morally grounded. In addition, rights-based approaches provide little guidance for reconciling conflicting rights, and this can make the practical application of this theory somewhat difficult. These shortcomings, however, by no means undermine this avenue of ethical reasoning, which has many important features including its special focus on basic human values such as equality and freedom.

Competing Frameworks

Is there any way to reconcile deontological and teleological frameworks which embody such fundamentally different notions about the relationship between the right and the good? Do individuals need to make a fundamental choice about which theory is conceptually or practically superior? Both theories have positive features. The teleological approach is predicated on a common-sense idea that we must first know the good in order to determine what is right. The appeal of a deontological theory, on the other hand, is the emphasis on the nature of the act itself instead of the goal it promotes or the consequences which it yields. It also emphasizes general principles of social morality such as honesty and beneficence. Some philosophers have suggested that while these theories differ profoundly, they can actually complement one another.

According to Cody and Lynn,

> At the risk of oversimplifying the work of philosophers, [managerial] ethics are formed by the clash of two basic viewpoints: utilitarianism versus deontological. The utilitarian believes that the end sought justifies the means to that end. The deontologist believes that certain absolute principles (e.g., honesty) should be obeyed, regardless of the consequences. In real life, none of us is exclusively utilitarian or deontological. Our personal values reflect a mix of these viewpoints, depending on the issue. Sometimes we act solely as a matter of principle (deontological) and sometimes we act practically (utilitarian). Frequently, our ethical choices are explained by a compromise between the two.[25]

Thus, it may not be necessary to choose one theory over another, since one can regard these theories as complementary. They represent divergent perspectives that illuminate different aspects of a complex moral situation. From a purely pragmatic perspective these theories can be used in conjunction with one another to analyze a moral dilemma in a comprehensive and thorough manner. We can approach these dilemmas and see our alternatives through a filter of basic moral norms, but also view those alternatives in relationship to the consequences they are likely to produce.

Justice Issues

In some cases one's analysis of an ethical problem is incomplete without some evaluation of justice concerns. While these issues may emerge in a treatment of utility, rights, or duties, they can sometimes be overlooked and an important moral perspective is lost. According to

Gerald Cavanaugh and his co-authors, "a failure to consider justice explicitly and separately leads to a kind of moral myopia—an inability to visualize all of the ethical issues in a situation."[26] In addition to a focus on whether an act maximizes consequences or respects the rights of individuals, one should also explicitly ask whether the act or policy is consistent with the norms of justice. But what are the norms of justice?

First, we must clarify that our focus is distributive justice, the comparative treatment of human beings. All theories of distributive justice have in common the minimal, formal requirement that equals must be treated equally, while unequals must be treated unequally. According to Frankena, the paradigm case of injustice "is that in which there are two similar individuals in similar circumstances and one of them is treated better or worse than the other."[27] This conception of distributive justice has its roots in Aristotle, who argued that "what is just is in some way proportionate, and what is unjust is counter-proportionate."[28] Studies reveal that this Aristotelian notion of proportionality which demands that equals are to be treated equally is also widely accepted in non-Western cultures.[29]

If this principle of proportionality is followed, people will be treated fairly and consistently. For example, if Susan, Ted, and Elaine are working for XYZ Consulting Co., and they are all doing the same work with no *relevant* differences between them or between the work they are doing, then Susan Ted, and Elaine should receive the same hourly wage and benefits. Justice does not imply that people must be treated identically, but it means "making the same relative contribution to the goodness of their lives . . . or asking the same relative sacrifice."[30] Justice is often equated with fairness, since when individuals are treated equally and consistently, they are also being treated fairly.

This formal theory of distributive justice does not explain the ways in which equals should be treated equally, and it provides no criteria for determining what constitutes equality. According to Tom Beauchamp and James Childress, the theory "merely asserts that whatever respects are under consideration as relevant, persons equal in those respects should be treated equally; that is, no person should be treated unequally, despite all differences with other persons, unless some difference between them is relevant to the treatment at stake."[31] This formal theory of justice, however, does not indicate those "relevant respects" that determine the basis for equality of treatment. Most would argue that under ordinary circumstances age should not be a relevant difference in allocating jobs, but there is certainly not a universal consensus on this issue. More robust theories of justice which consider who should get what incorporate a material principle, that is, some criterion for how material goods should be distributed. A discussion of the varied material principles of justice is beyond the scope of this analysis. Suffice it to say that one of the most popular principles is that *benefits should be distributed in proportion to the value of the contribution an individual makes to society*. This is often called the capitalist version of justice and it stands in contrast to more egalitarian principles which stipulate that *every person should be given exactly equal shares of society's benefits and burdens*. There have been long and spirited debates about the superiority of different justice principles, but we will avoid the perils associated with entering into that debate.

Finally, it should be remarked that the basic requirement of justice, equality of treatment, is a *prima facie* moral obligation, which, like the *prima facie* duties of Ross could be overridden for a higher moral duty. There may be rare circumstances where unequal treatment could be tolerated for a higher moral purpose, provided that there is ample moral justification for such a course of action.

A General Framework for Ethical Analysis

We have presented here three different ethical frameworks and noted the general polarity between teleological and deontological approaches to morality. The former is a pragmatic morality of ends while the latter stresses fidelity to principle in the form of rights or duties. But despite these differences, each approach represents a unique perspective from which one can assess and deliberate over moral issues. All theories seek to elevate the level of moral discourse from preoccupation with "feelings" or a purely intuitive reaction to a reasoned and thoughtful consideration of the right course of action and thereby improve the clarity and substance of an ethical judgment.

How do we incorporate these ethical questions into a thoughtful analysis of the cases in this book? Perhaps the best way to proceed is to follow a general three-step approach. This approach begins appropriately at the level of one's intuitive feeling about a case, since often we can intuit right and wrong based on our past experiences or a well-formed conscience. If a particular moral decision is uncontroversial, it may not be necessary to go beyond this level of analysis. But most moral problems that arise in the field of information technology are controversial, so there is a need for more critical analysis. The second step tests that intuition according to several basic ethical principles (utility, duties, rights, and justice), and the process concludes with a consideration of public policy implications (if any).

There are, of course, other questions which can be raised and many different methods of analyzing case studies. This broad framework, however, represents a plausible starting point which can certainly be embellished and supplemented depending upon one's interests and perspectives.

Three Steps for Ethical Analysis—Intuition, Critical Normative Evaluation, Public Policy Implications

- What are your first impressions or thoughtful reactions to the ethical issues triggered by the case—in other words, what does your *moral intuition* say about the action or policy under consideration: Is it right or wrong?
- Consider the issue from the viewpoint of *ethical theory* and review the following questions in order to develop a coherent rationale that defends your normative conclusion about the case: Does the action (or policy) optimize the consequences and generate the greatest net expectable utility for all parties involved? Does this course of action violate any ethical duties or infringe upon any basic human rights? If moral duties are in conflict, what is the higher duty? Is this conduct consistent with the norms of justice?
- Finally, consider the possible *public policy implications* of this case and of your normative conclusion. Should the recommended behavior be prescribed through legislation or specific regulations?

POLICY FRAMEWORKS

The final stage of our three-step analysis involves a consideration of the policy implications of one's normative conclusion. Moral decisions are often necessitated by public policy vacuums. For example, while it may be perfectly legal to randomly read employee e-mail without warning, there are moral questions about such a dubious practice, and one may conclude on the basis of moral reasoning that employee e-mail should not be subjected to surveillance under normal circumstances. But should there also be a law to fill this policy vacuum and, if so, how should such a law be formulated? Many of the cases we will consider in this book have significant public policy implications. In addition to exploring moral issues, therefore, it will also be instructive to review how particular social problems should be addressed in a public policy forum.

Policy and Information Technology: Conceptual Framework. Governments provide a vital role in any organized society. Among other goals such as national security, they seek to ensure some economic security or a basic level of social welfare through well-designed public policies. A public policy "is a plan of action undertaken by government officials to achieve some broad public purpose affecting a substantial segment of a nation's citizens."[32]

At its most basic level a policy framework considers the interactions which take place among the elements of this triad: the marketplace, public policy, and organizations (especially corporations). The norm for the marketplace is perfect competition where there is perfect information, an inability for a single seller to manipulate prices, an absence of transaction costs, and so forth. Markets sometimes fail, however, and this gives rise to certain imperfections. Externalities, such as environmental pollution, are one type of imperfection. An externality (or "spillover") involves costs borne involuntarily by society that are not reflected in the price of the good whose production has generated those costs. According to Ronald Coase, these externalities or social costs are the result of the "actions of business firms which have harmful effects on others."[33] Another imperfection is imperfect information. When there are information asymmetries, that is, when buyers lack the information they need to make informed purchasing decisions, goods or services may be over or underproduced. Finally, natural monopolies or oligopolies represent a third market failure, since they tend to charge prices in excess of marginal cost or cause other damage, which can lead to a misallocation of society's resources. Microsoft is a prime example of such monopoly power.

Policy makers often attempt to intervene and fix these market imperfections. They may develop antitrust policies to make markets more competitive or impose product and labeling regulations to prevent deception of consumers. Thus, policy instruments most often "serve to compensate for some market imperfection."[34] The U.S. Justice Department's antitrust suit against Microsoft was an effort to resolve the apparent ill effects of its monopoly power.

Organizations such as corporations interact with markets, where they sell their goods and services, and with public policy makers. They attempt to influence policies to their advantage. Through the political process they may try to prevent the implementation of public policies perceived as damaging or costly and promote policies like patents and copyright that raise barriers to entry and help maximize profits. According to Willis Emmons, "competition among organizations to shape public policy with respect to a particular market should be viewed not as a one time event but as an ongoing process."[35] Many e-commerce companies in the United States, for example, have lobbied (so far successfully) against comprehensive privacy regulations, which they regard as too costly.

Corporate America, at least as a collective, is generally hostile to government intervention, though individual corporations often demand that government constrain the actions of their rivals. There are different philosophies among policy makers and economists about how active government should be. Some economists like A. C. Pigou have argued for heavy government intervention: Government can "control the play of economic forces in such wise as to promote the economic welfare, and, through that, the total welfare, of their citizens as a whole."[36] Others, like Coase, put more faith in markets to rectify imperfections without the aid of government interference. According to Coase, there is room for the markets to resolve harmful effects and externalities, and even where the market does not work, government regulations may not lead to an optimal outcome due to "inefficiencies inherent in a governmental organization."[37]

In cyberspace this interaction of policy and markets is further complicated by the role of technology. In order to comprehend the regulatory options in the emerging information infrastructure it is necessary to appreciate the nature of Internet protocols and software and their impact on value decisions. We turn now to Professor Larry Lessig's framework which explicitly takes these issues into account.

Lessig's Paradigm. Larry Lessig's book *Code and Other Laws of Cyberspace* seeks to answer the question, What things regulate us? What forces constrain our behavior? Lessig argues that in the physical world we are regulated by four fundamental forces: law, norms, the market, and architecture.

Laws, according to Lessig, are rules imposed by the government which are enforced through *ex post* sanctions. There are, for example, laws that dictate the speed limit and other rules for driving. If we break these laws, we can be subjected to fines or other penalties levied by the government after the incident has occurred.

Social norms, on the other hand, are expressions of the community. Most communities have a well-defined sense of normalcy which is reflected in their norms or standards of behavior. Cigar smokers are not usually welcome at most community functions. There may be no laws against cigar smoking in a particular setting, but those who try to smoke cigars will most likely be stigmatized and ostracized by others.

The third regulative force is the market. The market regulates through the price it sets for goods and services and through the wages it sets for various types of labor. One might aspire to own a BMW, but unless one has about $40,000, such ownership will not be possible. Unlike norms and laws, market forces are not an expression of the community, and they are imposed immediately (not in *ex post* fashion)—you will not drive the BMW off the lot unless you can pay for it.

The final modality of regulation is known as architecture. The world consists of many physical constraints on our behavior—some of these are natural (such as the mountains of Afghanistan) while others are human constructs (such as buildings and bridges). A room without windows imposes certain constraints since no one can see outside. Once again "enforcement" is not *ex post,* but at the same time the constraint is imposed. Moreover, architecture is "self-enforcing"—it does not require the intermediation of an agent who makes an arrest or who expels someone from the community. According to Lessig, "the constraints of architecture are self-executing in a way that the constraints of law, norms, and the market are not."[38]

As in real space, so in cyberspace; these same four modalities of regulation apply. There are laws that restrict our behavior: copyright and patent laws that control access to content like digital music, or regulations that protect children's privacy. Cyberspace also has its own set of norms: Spam is not illegal, but spammers are usually shunned by the cyberspace community. The market, too, plays a role in influencing behavior. The more advertising revenues a Web site generates, the greater its ability to attract more users and develop a sustainable competitive advantage.

But arguably the most powerful regulative force in cyberspace is the analogue for architecture which Lessig calls "code." According to Lessig, "the software and hardware that makes cyberspace what it is constitute a set of constraints on how you can behave. The substance of these constraints may vary, but they are experienced as conditions on your access to cyberspace."[39]

This provocative passage invites several remarks. Consider the many ways in which code controls behavior. Cookie technology, which deposits small files on one's hard drive, enables data to be automatically collected at a Web site without a user's knowledge, and that changes the Web environment to one where there is less privacy. Filters like X-Stop or CyberPatrol restrict pornographic content; encryption programs help protect confidentiality when messages are transmitted in cyberspace; and digital rights management systems tightly enclose digital files in order to protect copyrights. Thus, in many respects, the "code is the law." Lessig explains that "the architectures of cyberspace are as important as the law in defining and defeating the liberties of the Net."[40]

Lessig, however, is concerned about the regulative force of code because while laws are transparent, code is obscure. Restrictions are embodied in lines of source code which are concealed from the public eye. Also, if code is law and code is deployed by software programmers, it follows that those programmers are in a certain sense "lawgivers." This is an obvious problem since, unlike democratically elected officials, they are not accountable to the public. Moreover, laws are not being formulated through the normal channels associated with a deliberative democracy.

It is also important to note that while law regulates primarily through direct regulation, imposing a penalty for a particular crime, it can also regulate indirectly. According to Lessig, "the government can coopt the other structures of cyberspace, so that they constrain to the government's end."[41] Some would argue that this is the situation with the Children's Internet Protection Act (see Case 2.1), where the government is using the law to help ensure that schools and libraries adopt blocking mechanisms to filter out pornographic material. This seems to be an example of how government "can regulate the architectures of cyberspace, so that cyberspace becomes more regulable."[42] Code has emerged as a formidable regulatory force in cyberspace, but this should not imply that the law is now impotent.

The value of Lessig's simple framework is undeniable. It illuminates the sovereignty of code and underscores the complexity of engaging in moral analysis about the conundrums of cyberspace. In many case studies involving the Internet it will be instructive to review how behavior is currently constrained—is it through norms, laws, or code? Is this how it should be constrained? Do we need new or revised laws? Should code play a role in regulating this behavior? What's the proper interaction between the law and the underlying information technologies? How do the technologies of cyberspace alter the set of policy options? The Lessig framework is a valuable starting point for thinking through the ethical and policy implications of the many issues suggested by the cases in this book.

NOTES

1. N. Machiavelli, *The Prince,* trans. Mark Musa (New York: St. Martin's Press, 1964), Chap. XV, p. 127.

2. L. Fuller, *The Morality of Law* (New Haven, CT: Yale University Press, 1964), pp. 5–6.
3. Hobbes, *Leviathan,* ed. Michael Oakeshott (London: Collier-Macmillan, Ltd., 1969), p. 100.
4. J. Loughran, S.J., "Reasons for Being Just," *The Value of Justice: Essays on the Theory and Practice of Social Virtue* (New York: Fordham University Press, 1979), p. 55.
5. W. Frankena, *Ethics* (Upper Saddle River, NJ: Prentice Hall, 1963), p. 29.
6. M. Velasquez, *Business Ethics: Concepts and Cases,* 3d ed. (Upper Saddle River, NJ: Prentice Hall, 1992), p. 61.
7. J. Rawls, *A Theory of Justice* (Cambridge, MA: Harvard University Press, 1971), p. 30.
8. See the discussion of Lockheed in J. Boatright, *Ethics and the Conduct of Business* (Upper Saddle River, NJ: Prentice Hall, 1993), pp. 42–43.
9. G. Grisez, "Against Consequentialism," 23 *American Journal of Jurisprudence* 39 (1978).
10. I. Kant, *The Critique of Practical Reason* (London: Longmans Green and Co, 1909), p. 3.
11. I. Kant, *Foundations for the Metaphysics of Morals* (Indianapolis, IN: Hackett Publishing Company, 1981), pp.12–13.
12. Ibid., p. 14.
13. C. Korsgaard, *Creating the Kingdom of Ends* (Cambridge: Cambridge University Press, 1996), p. 78.
14. Ibid., p. 92.
15. N. Bowie, *Business Ethics: A Kantian Perspective* (Oxford: Blackwell Publishers, 1999), p. 26
16. Korsgaard, *Creating the Kingdom of Ends,* p. 21.
17. Bowie, *Business Ethics,* p. 14.
18. Kant, *Foundations,* p. 36.
19. A. C. Ewing, *Ethics* (New York: Free Press, 1965), p. 58.
20. W. D. Ross, *The Right and the Good,* quoted in R. Fox and J. CeMarco, *Moral Reasoning* (Fort Worth, TX: Holt Rinehart, 1990), p. 142.
21. Ibid., p. 144.
22. I. Kant, *The Metaphysical Elements of Justice,* trans. J. Ladd (Indianapolis, IN: Bobbs-Merrill, 1965), p. 45.
23. Velasquez, *Business Ethics,* p. 76.
24. K. Goodpaster, "Some Avenues for Ethical Analysis in General Management," in K. Goodpaster, J. Matthews, and L. Nash, *Policies and Persons,* 1st ed. (New York: McGraw-Hill, 1985), p. 497.
25. W. Cody and R. Lynn, *Honest Government: An Ethics Guide for Public Service* (Westport, CT: Praeger, 1992), p. 6.
26. G. Cavanaugh, D. Moberg, and M. Velasquez, "Making Business Ethics Practical," *Business Ethics Quarterly* 5, no. 3 (1995), pp. 399–418.
27. Frankena, *Ethics,* p. 39.

28. Aristotle, *Nicomachean Ethics*, trans. T. Irwin (Indianapolis, IN: Hackett Publishing, 1985), Bk. V, chap. 4.
29. K. Leung and S. Iwawaki, "Cultural Collectivism and Distributive Behavior," *Journal of Cross-Cultural Psychology* 19 (1988), pp. 35–49.
30. Frankena, *Ethics*, p. 41.
31. T. Beauchamp and J. Childress, *Principles of Biomedical Ethics*, 4th ed. (New York: Oxford University Press, 1994) pp. 328–329.
32. J. Post et al., *Business and Society*, 10th ed. (New York: McGraw-Hill, 2002), p. 154.
33. R. Coase, "The Problem of Social Cost," *Journal of Law and Economics* 3 (1960), pp. 1–44.
34. W. Emmons, "Public Policy and the Manager" (Cambridge, MA: Harvard Business School Publications, 1993), p. 3.
35. Ibid., p. 8.
36. A. Pigou, *The Economics of Welfare*, 4th ed. (London: Macmillan, 1962), pp. 129–130.
37. R. Coase. "Economics and Public Policy," in *Large Corporations in a Changing Society*, ed. J. Weston (New York: New York University Press, 1974), p. 183.
38. L. Lessig, *Code and Other Laws of Cyberspace* (New York: Basic Books, 1999), p. 236.
39. Ibid., p. 89.
40. L. Lessig, "The Code Is the Law," *Industry Standard* (19–26 April 1999), p. 16.
41. L. Lessig, "The Laws of Cyberspace," unpublished paper presented at Taiwan Net Conference, Taipei, March 1998.
42. Ibid.

2

Free Expression in Cyberspace

INTRODUCTION

The cases in this chapter revolve around the theme of free expression in cyberspace. The Internet magnifies the capabilities of most citizens in democratic regimes to exercise their free speech rights. There are low entry barriers for anyone who wants to provide or disseminate information. The democratic potential of this new medium is unprecedented, since it gives many new voices extraordinary "reach" to communicate their ideas and redistribute information. According to Michael Godwin, "the Net has brought to fruition the freedom of speech that [Justice] Brandeis wrote about—free speech that gets heard, free speech that makes a difference."[1] Unfortunately, a byproduct of this expansion of free expression is a proliferation of many unwelcome and upsetting forms of speech—pornography, hate speech, online threats, and spam.

In the United States there are few rights more cherished than the right of free expression guaranteed under the First Amendment to the Constitution. But that right is not absolute. Obscenity (such as child pornography), threatening speech that incites violence, defamation, and libel are some of the forms of speech that the First Amendment does not protect. Some of the more difficult cases in this chapter involve determining whether a particular form of expression fits into these categories.

The first case in the chapter is a substantial excerpt from a piece of legislation known as the Children's Internet Protection Act (CHIPA). This bill was signed into law on December 21, 2000 and it took effect in April 2001. It represents the government's efforts to use private surrogates, libraries, and schools to regulate speech available to minors. But is this type of legislation an appropriate response to the problem of cyberporn? Should schools and libraries adopt filters for this purpose and should the federal government withhold e-rate funds if they fail to do so? The debate about the use of filters as a basis for content control has intensified. Opponents maintain that filters are inaccurate and repressive, while proponents say that they are the optimal solution to the problem, that is, protecting children from pornographic text and images. The second case in the chapter, *Multnomah Public Library et al. v. U.S.*, presents an overview of a constitutional challenge to CHIPA brought forward by a number of libraries and library associations. The Multnomah plaintiffs may have precedence on their side. In a now famous case, *Mainstream Loudon v. Loudon County* (2 F.Supp2d 781 [E.D. Va 1998]), a federal judge ruled that the mandatory use of filters in public libraries is unconstitutional.

A closely related case is "Censorship at New England University." In this scenario university officials must make a decision about censoring sexually explicit user groups on the university's Internet connection. How does the university balance protection of free speech rights with the need to preserve and honor its cultural and moral values?

The setting of the next case is also a university, but the problem is very different. Aside from pornography there are other forms of troubling online speech such as threats. But in cyberspace it can sometimes be difficult to separate a real threat from idle fantasy. Such was the problem in the convoluted episode of Jake Baker. Baker was a University of Michigan student accused of threatening a female classmate. But were his Internet ramblings, however disturbing, just a form of fantasy? As one untangles this case a crucial question becomes paramount: When does online communication inflict enough harm so that it no longer deserves protection under the First Amendment?

In the next case, "Encryption Source Code and the First Amendment," based on the *Junger v. Daley* lawsuit, the speech issue is considered from a different angle: What forms of speech are included in an individual's right to free speech? Does it, for example, include computer source code? In this unusual case Junger claims that the encryption source code which he has written should be regarded as within the ambit of his free speech rights, while the government disagrees. The key question in this case hinges on whether or not encryption source code is expressive enough to be eligible for First Amendment protection.

The chapter concludes with two cases that focus on the international dimension of the speech problem that introduces a new layer of complications. In the first case, "CompuServe Deutschland," a manager of CompuServe's German subsidiary is arrested for failing to block out pornographic and hate speech sites for this Internet Service Provider's (ISP) German customers. Should ISPs act as censors in this situation, and should the German government exercise its sovereignty over an American company? The second case deals with the government of Saudi Arabia which is searching for a new filtering system to protect its citizens from unwholesome Web sites and other types of dangerous speech. Should American companies that produce this blocking technology help the Saudi government in its efforts to censor speech throughout its country? Do software companies have any responsibility for how their products are utilized once they are sold?

Case 2.1 Excerpts from the Children's Internet Protection Act of 2000 (CHIPA)

TITLE XVII—*CHILDREN'S INTERNET PROTECTION ACT*

SEC. 1701. SHORT TITLE.

This title may be cited as the "Children's Internet Protection Act."

SEC. 1702. DISCLAIMERS.

(a) **DISCLAIMER REGARDING CONTENT.**—Nothing in this title or the amendments made by this title shall be construed to prohibit a local educational agency, elementary or secondary school, or library from blocking access on the Internet on computers owned or operated by that agency, school, or library to any content other than content covered by this title or the amendments made by this title.

(b) **DISCLAIMER REGARDING PRIVACY.**—Nothing in this title or the amendments made by this title shall be construed to require the tracking of Internet use by any identifiable minor or adult user.

SEC. 1703. STUDY OF TECHNOLOGY PROTECTION MEASURES.
(a) **IN GENERAL.**—Not later than 18 months after the date of the enactment of this Act, the National Telecommunications and Information Administration shall initiate a notice and comment proceeding for purposes of—
(1) evaluating whether or not currently available technology protection measures, including commercial Internet blocking and filtering software, adequately addresses the needs of educational institutions;
(2) making recommendations on how to foster the development of measures that meet such needs; and
(3) evaluating the development and effectiveness of local Internet safety policies that are currently in operation after community input.

(b) **DEFINITIONS.**—In this section:
(1) **TECHNOLOGY PROTECTION MEASURE.**—The term "technology protection measure" means a specific technology that blocks or filters Internet access to visual depictions that are—
(A) obscene, as that term is defined in section 1460 of title 18, United States Code;
(B) child pornography, as that term is defined in section 2256 of title 18, United States Code; or
(C) harmful to minors.

(2) **HARMFUL TO MINORS.**—The term "harmful to minors" means any picture, image, graphic image file, or other visual depiction that—
(A) taken as a whole and with respect to minors, appeals to a prurient interest in nudity, sex, or excretion;
(B) depicts, describes, or represents, in a patently offensive way with respect to what is suitable for minors, an actual or simulated sexual act or sexual contact, actual or simulated normal or perverted sexual acts, or a lewd exhibition of the genitals; and
(C) taken as a whole, lacks serious literary, artistic, political, or scientific value as to minors.

(3) **SEXUAL ACT; SEXUAL CONTACT.**—The terms "sexual act" and "sexual contact" have the meanings given such terms in section 2246 of title 18, United States Code.

—Subtitle A—Federal Funding for Educational Institution Computers

SEC. 1711. LIMITATION ON AVAILABILITY OF CERTAIN FUNDS FOR SCHOOLS.
Title III of the Elementary and Secondary Education Act of 1965 (20 U.S.C. 6801 et seq.) is amended by adding at the end the following:

PART F—LIMITATION ON AVAILABILITY OF CERTAIN FUNDS FOR SCHOOLS

SEC. 3601. LIMITATION ON AVAILABILITY OF CERTAIN FUNDS FOR SCHOOLS.

(a) INTERNET SAFETY.—

(1) IN GENERAL.—No funds made available under this title to a local educational agency for an elementary or secondary school that does not receive services at discount rates under section 254(h)(5) of the Communications Act of 1934, as added by section 1721 of Children's Internet Protection Act, may be used to purchase computers used to access the Internet, or to pay for direct costs associated with accessing the Internet, for such school unless the school, school board, local educational agency, or other authority with responsibility for administration of such school both—

(A)(i) has in place a policy of Internet safety for minors that includes the operation of a technology protection measure with respect to any of its computers with Internet access that protects against access through such computers to visual depictions that are—

(I) obscene;

(II) child pornography; or

(III) harmful to minors; and

(ii) is enforcing the operation of such technology protection measure during any use of such computers by minors; and

(B)(i) has in place a policy of Internet safety that includes the operation of a technology protection measure with respect to any of its computers with Internet access that protects against access through such computers to visual depictions that are—

(I) obscene; or

(II) child pornography; and

(ii) is enforcing the operation of such technology protection measure during any use of such computers.

(2) TIMING AND APPLICABILITY OF IMPLEMENTATION.—

(A) IN GENERAL.—The local educational agency with responsibility for a school covered by paragraph (1) shall certify the compliance of such school with the requirements of paragraph (1) as part of the application process for the next program funding year under this Act following the effective date of this section, and for each subsequent program funding year thereafter.

(B) PROCESS.—

(i) SCHOOLS WITH INTERNET SAFETY POLICIES AND TECHNOLOGY PROTECTION MEASURES IN PLACE.—A local educational agency with responsibility for a school covered by paragraph (1) that has in place an Internet safety policy meeting the requirements of paragraph (1) shall certify its compliance with paragraph (1) during each annual program application cycle under this Act.
(ii) SCHOOLS WITHOUT INTERNET SAFETY POLICIES AND TECHNOLOGY PROTECTION MEASURES IN PLACE.—A local educational agency with responsibility for a school covered by paragraph (1) that does not have in place an Internet safety policy meeting the requirements of paragraph (1)—
(I) for the first program year after the effective date of this section in which the local educational agency is applying for funds for such school under this Act, shall certify that it is undertaking such actions, including any necessary procurement procedures, to put in place an Internet safety policy that meets such requirements; and
(II) for the second program year after the effective date of this section in which the local educational agency is applying for funds for such school under this Act, shall certify that such school is in compliance with such requirements.
Any school covered by paragraph (1) for which the local educational agency concerned is unable to certify compliance with such requirements in such second program year shall be ineligible for all funding under this title for such second program year and all subsequent program years until such time as such school comes into compliance with such requirements.

(3) DISABLING DURING CERTAIN USE.—An administrator, supervisor, or person authorized by the responsible authority under paragraph (1) may disable the technology protection measure concerned to enable access for bona fide research or other lawful purposes.

(4) NONCOMPLIANCE.—
(A) USE OF GENERAL EDUCATION PROVISIONS ACT REMEDIES.—
Whenever the Secretary has reason to believe that any recipient of funds under this title is failing to comply substantially with the requirements of this subsection, the Secretary may—
(i) withhold further payments to the recipient under this title,
(ii) issue a complaint to compel compliance of the recipient through a cease and desist order, or
(iii) enter into a compliance agreement with a recipient to bring it into compliance with such requirements, in same manner as the Secretary is

authorized to take such actions under sections 455,456, and 457, respectively, of the General Education Provisions Act (20 U.S.C. 1234d).
(B) RECOVERY OF FUNDS PROHIBITED.—The actions authorized by subparagraph (A) are the exclusive remedies available with respect to the failure of a school to comply substantially with a provision of this subsection, and the Secretary shall not seek a recovery of funds from the recipient for such failure.
(C) RECOMMENCEMENT OF PAYMENTS.—Whenever the Secretary determines (whether by certification or other appropriate evidence) that a recipient of funds who is subject to the withholding of payments under subparagraph (A)(i) has cured the failure providing the basis for the withholding of payments, the Secretary shall cease the withholding of payments to the recipient under that subparagraph.

(5) DEFINITIONS.—In this section:
(A) **COMPUTER.**—The term 'computer' includes any hardware, software, or other technology attached or connected to, installed in, or otherwise used in connection with a computer.
(B) **ACCESS TO INTERNET.**—A computer shall be considered to have access to the Internet if such computer is equipped with a modem or is connected to a computer network which has access to the Internet.
(C) **ACQUISITION OR OPERATION.**—An elementary or secondary school shall be considered to have received funds under this title for the acquisition or operation of any computer if such funds are used in any manner, directly or indirectly—
(i) to purchase, lease, or otherwise acquire or obtain the use of such computer; or
(ii) to obtain services, supplies, software, or other actions or materials to support, or in connection with, the operation of such computer.
(D) **MINOR.**—The term 'minor' means an individual who has not attained the age of 17.
(E) **CHILD PORNOGRAPHY.**—The term 'child pornography' has the meaning given such term in section 2256 of title 18, United States Code.
(F) **HARMFUL TO MINORS.**—The term 'harmful to minors' means any picture, image, graphic image file, or other visual depiction that—
(i) taken as a whole and with respect to minors, appeals to a prurient interest in nudity, sex, or excretion;
(ii) depicts, describes, or represents, in a patently offensive way with respect to what is suitable for minors, an actual or simulated sexual act or sexual contact, actual or simulated normal or perverted sexual acts, or a lewd exhibition of the genitals; and

(iii) taken as a whole, lacks serious literary, artistic, political, or scientific value as to minors.
(G) **OBSCENE.**—The term 'obscene' has the meaning given such term in section 1460 of title 18, United States Code.
(H) **SEXUAL ACT; SEXUAL CONTACT.**—The terms 'sexual act' and 'sexual contact' have the meanings given such terms in section 2246 of title 18, United States Code.

SEC. 1712. LIMITATION ON AVAILABILITY OF CERTAIN FUNDS FOR LIBRARIES.
(a) AMENDMENT.—Section 224 of the Museum and Library Services Act (20 U.S.C. 9134(b)) is amended—
(1) in subsection (b)—
(A) by redesignating paragraph (6) as paragraph (7); and
(B) by inserting after paragraph (5) the following new paragraph:
"(6) provide assurances that the State will comply with subsection (f); and"; and
(2) by adding at the end the following new subsection:

(f) INTERNET SAFETY.—

(1) IN GENERAL.—No funds made available under this Act for a library described in section 213(2)(A) or (B) that does not receive services at discount rates under section 254(h)(6) of the Communications Act of 1934, as added by section 1721 of this Children's Internet Protection Act, may be used to purchase computers used to access the Internet, or to pay for direct costs associated with accessing the Internet, for such library unless—
(A) such library—
(i) has in place a policy of Internet safety for minors that includes the operation of a technology protection measure with respect to any of its computers with Internet access that protects against access through such computers to visual depictions that are—
(I) obscene;
(II) child pornography; or
(III) harmful to minors; and
(ii) is enforcing the operation of such technology protection measure during any use of such computers by minors; and
(B) such library—
(i) has in place a policy of Internet safety that includes the operation of a technology protection measure with respect to any of its computers with Internet access that protects against access through such computers to visual depictions that are—

(I) obscene; or
(II) child pornography; and
(ii) is enforcing the operation of such technology protection measure during any use of such computers.

(2) ACCESS TO OTHER MATERIALS.—Nothing in this subsection shall be construed to prohibit a library from limiting Internet access to or otherwise protecting against materials other than those referred to in subclauses (I), (II), and (III) of paragraph (1)(A)(i).

(3) DISABLING DURING CERTAIN USE.—*An administrator, supervisor, or other authority may disable a technology protection measure under paragraph (1) to enable access for bona fide research or other lawful purposes.* [emphasis added]

(4) TIMING AND APPLICABILITY OF IMPLEMENTATION.—
(A) IN GENERAL.—A library covered by paragraph (1) shall certify the compliance of such library with the requirements of paragraph (1) as part of the application process for the next program funding year under this Act following the effective date of this subsection, and for each subsequent program funding year thereafter.
(B) PROCESS.—
(i) **LIBRARIES WITH INTERNET SAFETY POLICIES AND TECHNOLOGY PROTECTION MEASURES IN PLACE.**—A library covered by paragraph (1) that has in place an Internet safety policy meeting the requirements of paragraph (1) shall certify its compliance with paragraph (1) during each annual program application cycle under this Act.
(ii) **LIBRARIES WITHOUT INTERNET SAFETY POLICIES AND TECHNOLOGY PROTECTION MEASURES IN PLACE.**—A library covered by paragraph (1) that does not have in place an Internet safety policy meeting the requirements of paragraph (1)—
(I) for the first program year after the effective date of this subsection in which the library applies for funds under this Act, shall certify that it is undertaking such actions, including any necessary procurement procedures, to put in place an Internet safety policy that meets such requirements; and
(II) for the second program year after the effective date of this subsection in which the library applies for funds under this Act, shall certify that such library is in compliance with such requirements.
Any library covered by paragraph (1) that is unable to certify compliance with such requirements in such second program year shall be ineligible for all funding under this Act for such second program year and all

subsequent program years until such time as such library comes into compliance with such requirements.

(5) NONCOMPLIANCE.
(A) **USE OF GENERAL EDUCATION PROVISIONS ACT REMEDIES.—**
Whenever the Director of the Institute of Museum and Library Services has reason to believe that any recipient of funds under this Act is failing to comply substantially with the requirements of this subsection, the Director may—
(i) withhold further payments to the recipient under this Act,
(ii) issue a complaint to compel compliance of the recipient through a cease and desist order, or
(iii) enter into a compliance agreement with a recipient to bring it into compliance with such requirements.
(B) **RECOVERY OF FUNDS PROHIBITED.**—The actions authorized by subparagraph (A) are the exclusive remedies available with respect to the failure of a library to comply substantially with a provision of this subsection, and the Director shall not seek a recovery of funds from the recipient for such failure.
(C) **RECOMMENCEMENT OF PAYMENTS.**—Whenever the Director determines (whether by certification or other appropriate evidence) that a recipient of funds who is subject to the withholding of payments under subparagraph (A)(i) has cured the failure providing the basis for the withholding of payments, the Director shall cease the withholding of payments to the recipient under that subparagraph.

(7) DEFINITIONS.—In this section:
(A) **CHILD PORNOGRAPHY.**—The term 'child pornography' has the meaning given such term in section 2256 of title 18, United States Code.
(B) **HARMFUL TO MINORS.**—The term 'harmful to minors' means any picture, image, graphic image file, or other visual depiction that—
(i) taken as a whole and with respect to minors, appeals to a prurient interest in nudity, sex, or excretion;
(ii) depicts, describes, or represents, in a patently offensive way with respect to what is suitable for minors, an actual or simulated sexual act or sexual contact, actual or simulated normal or perverted sexual acts, or a lewd exhibition of the genitals; and
(iii) taken as a whole, lacks serious literary, artistic, political, or scientific value as to minors.
(C) **MINOR.**—The term 'minor' means an individual who has not attained the age of 17.

(D) **OBSCENE.**—The term 'obscene' has the meaning given such term in section 1460 of title 18, United States Code.
(E) **SEXUAL ACT; SEXUAL CONTACT.**—The terms 'sexual act' and 'sexual contact' have the meanings given such terms in section 2246 of title 18, United States Code."

(b) EFFECTIVE DATE.—The amendment made by this section shall take effect 120 days after the date of the enactment of this Act.

—Subtitle B—Universal Service Discounts

SEC. 1721. REQUIREMENT FOR SCHOOLS AND LIBRARIES TO ENFORCE INTERNET SAFETY POLICIES WITH TECHNOLOGY PROTECTION MEASURES FOR COMPUTERS WITH INTERNET ACCESS AS CONDITION OF UNIVERSAL SERVICE DISCOUNTS.
(a) SCHOOLS.—Section 254(h) of the Communications Act of 1934 (47 U.S.C.254(h)) is amended—
(1) by redesignating paragraph (5) as paragraph (7); and
(2) by inserting after paragraph (4) the following new paragraph (5):
(5) **REQUIREMENTS FOR CERTAIN SCHOOLS WITH COMPUTERS HAVING INTERNET ACCESS.—**

(A) INTERNET SAFETY.—
(i) **IN GENERAL.**—Except as provided in clause (ii), an elementary or secondary school having computers with Internet access may not receive services at discount rates under paragraph (1)(B) unless the school, school board, local educational agency, or other authority with responsibility for administration of the school—
(I) submits to the Commission the certifications described in subparagraphs (B) and (C);
(II) submits to the Commission a certification that an Internet safety policy has been adopted and implemented for the school under subsection (l); and
(III) ensures the use of such computers in accordance with the certifications.
(ii) **APPLICABILITY.**—The prohibition in clause (i) shall not apply with respect to a school that receives services at discount rates under paragraph (1)(B) only for purposes other than the provision of Internet access, Internet service, or internal connections.
(iii) **PUBLIC NOTICE; HEARING.**—An elementary or secondary school described in clause (i), or the school board, local educational agency, or other authority with responsibility for administration of the school, shall provide reasonable public notice and hold at least 1 public

hearing or meeting to address the proposed Internet safety policy. In the case of an elementary or secondary school other than an elementary or secondary school as defined in section 14101 of the Elementary and Secondary Education Act of 1965 (20 U.S.C. 8801), the notice and hearing required by this clause may be limited to those members of the public with a relationship to the school.

(B) CERTIFICATION WITH RESPECT TO MINORS.—A certification under this subparagraph is a certification that the school, school board, local educational agency, or other authority with responsibility for administration of the school—
(i) is enforcing a policy of Internet safety for minors that includes monitoring the online activities of minors and the operation of a technology protection measure with respect to any of its computers with Internet access that protects against access through such computers to visual depictions that are—
(I) obscene;
(II) child pornography; or
(III) harmful to minors; and
(ii) is enforcing the operation of such technology protection measure during any use of such computers by minors.

(C) CERTIFICATION WITH RESPECT TO ADULTS.—A certification under this paragraph is a certification that the school, school board, local educational agency, or other authority with responsibility for administration of the school—
(i) is enforcing a policy of Internet safety that includes the operation of a technology protection measure with respect to any of its computers with Internet access that protects against access through such computers to visual depictions that are—
(I) obscene; or
(II) child pornography; and
(ii) is enforcing the operation of such technology protection measure during any use of such computers.

(D) DISABLING DURING ADULT USE.—An administrator, supervisor, or other person authorized by the certifying authority under subparagraph (A)(i) may disable the technology protection measure concerned, during use by an adult, to enable access for bona fide research or other lawful purpose.

(E) TIMING OF IMPLEMENTATION.—[similar to above]

(F) NONCOMPLIANCE.—[similar to above]

(b) LIBRARIES.—Such section 254(h) is further amended by inserting after paragraph (5), as amended by subsection (a) of this section, the following new paragraph:

(6) **REQUIREMENTS FOR CERTAIN LIBRARIES WITH COMPUTERS HAVING INTERNET ACCESS.**—

(A) INTERNET SAFETY:

(i) **IN GENERAL.**—Except as provided in clause (ii), a library having one or more computers with Internet access may not receive services at discount rates under paragraph

(1)(B) unless the library—

(I) submits to the Commission the certifications described in subparagraphs (B) and (C); and

(II) submits to the Commission a certification that an Internet safety policy has been adopted and implemented for the library under subsection (l); and

(III) ensures the use of such computers in accordance with the certifications.

(ii) **APPLICABILITY.**—The prohibition in clause (i) shall not apply with respect to a library that receives services at discount rates under paragraph (1)(B) only for purposes other than the provision of Internet access, Internet service, or internal connections.

(iii) **PUBLIC NOTICE; HEARING.**—A library described in clause (i) shall provide reasonable public notice and hold at least 1 public hearing or meeting to address the proposed Internet safety policy.

(B) CERTIFICATION WITH RESPECT TO MINORS.—A certification under this subparagraph is a certification that the library—

(i) is enforcing a policy of Internet safety that includes the operation of a technology protection measure with respect to any of its computers with Internet access that protects against access through such computers to visual depictions that are—

(I) obscene;

(II) child pornography; or

(III) harmful to minors; and

(ii) is enforcing the operation of such technology protection measure during any use of such computers by minors.

(C) CERTIFICATION WITH RESPECT TO ADULTS.—A certification under this paragraph is a certification that the library—

(i) is enforcing a policy of Internet safety that includes the operation of a technology protection measure with respect to any of its computers with Internet access that protects against access through such computers to visual depictions that are—

(I) obscene; or
(II) child pornography; and
(ii) is enforcing the operation of such technology protection measure during any use of such computers.

(D) DISABLING DURING ADULT USE.—An administrator, supervisor, or other person authorized by the certifying authority under subparagraph (A)(i) may disable the technology protection measure concerned, during use by an adult, to enable access for bona fide research or other lawful purpose.

(E) TIMING OF IMPLEMENTATION—[similar to above]

(F) NONCOMPLIANCE.—[similar to above]

(c) DEFINITIONS.—Paragraph (7) of such section, as redesignated by subsection (a)(1) of this section, is amended by adding at the end the following:

(D) **MINOR**.—The term 'minor' means any individual who has not attained the age of 17 years.
(E) **OBSCENE**.—The term 'obscene' has the meaning given such term in section 1460 of title 18, United States Code.
(F) **CHILD PORNOGRAPHY**.—The term 'child pornography' has the meaning given such term in section 2256 of title 18, United States Code.
(G) **HARMFUL TO MINORS**.—The term 'harmful to minors' means any picture, image, graphic image file, or other visual depiction that—
(i) taken as a whole and with respect to minors, appeals to a prurient interest in nudity, sex, or excretion;
(ii) depicts, describes, or represents, in a patently offensive way with respect to what is suitable for minors, an actual or simulated sexual act or sexual contact, actual or simulated normal or perverted sexual acts, or a lewd exhibition of the genitals; and
(iii) taken as a whole, lacks serious literary, artistic, political, or scientific value as to minors.
(H) **SEXUAL ACT; SEXUAL CONTACT**.—The terms 'sexual act' and 'sexual contact' have the meanings given such terms in section 2246 of title 18, United States Code.
(I) **TECHNOLOGY PROTECTION MEASURE**.—The term 'technology protection measure' means a specific technology that blocks or filters Internet access to the material covered by a certification under paragraph (5) or (6) to which such certification relates.

Case 2.2 *Multnomah Public Library et al. v. U.S.*

Free speech advocates were quite dismayed by the Children's Internet Protection Act (CHIPA). Lawsuits were promptly threatened by the American Civil Liberties Union (ACLU), People for the American Way Foundation, and the American Library Association (ALA), attacking the constitutionality of the law. In the wake of criticism, Senator John McCain, one of the bill's authors, rose to CHIPA's defense. According to McCain, "This legislation allows local communities to decide what technology they want to use and what to filter out so that our children's minds aren't polluted."[2]

While many agreed with this sentiment, opposition to CHIPA continued to build, especially among librarians. In April 2001, a group of libraries and library associations (including Multnomah County Public Library, the Connecticut Library Association, the Maine Library Association, and the Santa Cruz Public Library Joint Powers Authority) filed the first lawsuit against this legislation. This suit, *Multnomah Public Library et al. v. U.S.* was filed in the United States District Court for the Eastern District of Pennsylvania where other prominent free speech cases have been heard. The plaintiffs also included several Internet authors and publishers.

The Multnomah County Library is Oregon's largest public library, serving about 20 percent of the state's population. It offers Internet access at all of its branches and it estimates that about 18,000 users per week access the Internet at the central library. The Multnomah Library offers all patrons the option of using a blocking program when they log on to the Net, but no patrons (including minors) are required to utilize this software.

CHIPA requires all public libraries that participate in the federal e-rate program to install filters or other blocking mechanisms in order to prevent access to material that is obscene, child pornographic, or harmful to minors. The e-rate program requires local telecommunications carriers to charge libraries "rates less than the amounts charged for similar services to other parties to ensure affordable access to and use of such services by such entities."[3] Thus, e-rate is simply a discounted rate charged to libraries by telecommunications carriers. According to the plaintiffs, in 2000 and 2001 approximately 4,500 libraries and 800 consortia were approved for e-rate funding of $250 million. Multnomah receives about $100,000 per year in e-rate discounts. All libraries which want to continue with their e-rate discounts must certify compliance with CHIPA or indicate that they are taking appropriate steps to install blocking measures. Libraries that fail to comply "shall not be eligible for services at discount rates."[4] Similarly, CHIPA applies to libraries that receive funds to purchase computers or Internet access under the Library

Services and Technology Act (LSTA). However, libraries that have received LSTA funds are not required to return those funds if they fail to comply with CHIPA (1712(B)).

The *Multnomah* lawsuit enumerates several key objections to CHIPA. The main objection centers on the fallibility of filtering mechanisms which can often produce incongruous results:

> As Congress itself concluded, every available technology protection measure blocks access to a wide range of socially valuable online speech. This technology cannot be "fixed" to block only speech that is unprotected by the Constitution. Computer programs cannot make distinctions between protected and unprotected speech. By forcing public libraries to install such technology, CHIPA will suppress ideas and viewpoints that are constitutionally protected from reaching willing patrons. CHIPA thus imposes a prior restraint on protected speech in violation of the Constitution.[5]

In addition, the lawsuit argues, blocking mechanisms are too arbitrary and imprecise, and they will not be able to block offensive Web sites that should be blocked. Technology protection measures cannot block access to *all* the material that is obscene, child pornographic, or harmful to minors, as those categories were defined by CHIPA. (See section 1721(c).)

The lawsuit states several other reasons for opposition to CHIPA. The law applies to adults as well as to children. Filters can be circumvented for an adult only if that individual can demonstrate the need to access a certain Web site for a "bona fide research purpose." There is no further elaboration on this standard. Also, it may not be practical to temporarily disable a blocking program. CHIPA therefore forces libraries to make available for adults a level of speech fit for children. The plaintiffs also complain about the proprietary nature of the list of blocked sites used by filtering vendors. For proprietary reasons these companies do not reveal which specific Web sites are on their list of blocked sites. But the plaintiffs see a big problem in this methodology: "CHIPA will thus force libraries to install a system of private, prior blind censorship that will transform Internet access at libraries from an equalizing and democratizing opportunity to a randomly censored medium that will no longer serve the communities that need it most."[6]

The lawsuit also argues that CHIPA will have a negative impact on its library patrons, particularly those patrons whose only Internet access is through a library. CHIPA will prevent these patrons from making their own choices about the information they want to access on the Internet. Further, the cost of installing and maintaining the technology measures will be burdensome for many libraries. As a result, the implementation of CHIPA "will inevitably reduce the amount of money available to library plaintiffs for purchase of a wide range of books and other information resources, including Internet access."[7]

In general, the plaintiffs in this lawsuit reject CHIPA because it "distorts" the traditional role of the library, which is to provide open and unfettered access to the broadest range of content. More and more of that content is now to be found on the Internet, especially the Web. According to the Supreme Court in *Reno v. ACLU,* "The Web . . . is comparable, from the reader's viewpoint, to a vast library including millions of readily available and indexed publications."[8] Hence this constitutionally flawed legislation interferes with rights of information providers, and it subverts the library's primary mission as a purveyor of information resources.

Case 2.3 Censorship at New England University

Dean Jenkins glanced out his second story window at the antique clock on the restored façade of the tower building across the quad. It was already 6:00 P.M. It had been another long day for the dean of administration. Several student and faculty groups had visited his office to protest the decision to censor some of the newsgroups and Web sites available over the Internet at the university. He had also received today a protest letter from the local chapter of the ACLU and was pilloried in an editorial of the school newspaper for "selling out" on the First Amendment. His mind was sluggish, but he decided to stay in the office a bit longer and catch up on some paperwork. Tomorrow he would be visiting the president's office to discuss the situation and determine a future course of action.

NEW ENGLAND UNIVERSITY

New England University (NEU), located in the greater Boston area, was founded in the late 1940s in order to provide an affordable private education to students in New England and its environs. Many of its first students were veterans of World War II attending the college on the GI Bill. It was always seen as a respectable alternative to Harvard, MIT, Wellesley, and other more elitist and expensive private universities in the area. Its liberal arts undergraduate program enrolled about 1,800 students and its school of management enrolled about 600 students. The university also enrolled over 1,000 students in its continuing education and graduate programs. About 90 percent of the undergraduates were residential students while the remainder were commuters.

The school had been quite successful in recruiting students thanks to the outstanding reputation of its faculty. Its specialty areas included the sciences, especially biology and biochemistry, geology, and several of its management departments such as marketing and information technology. In recent years, however, due to demographic pressures in the New England area, it had to contend with a marginal drop in applications. The school was always able to fill the freshman class with quality students, but this objective was becoming more difficult to achieve.

For many years NEU had been in the forefront of technology. From the early 1980s the school was linked to the Internet so that its faculty could exchange research information with colleagues at other universities. As the Internet became more popular it attracted the attention of more and more faculty and university employees. Students were also encouraged to make use of the Internet's ample resources. While many students had their own computers, the university had established several computer labs where students could go to type their papers, conduct research, and so forth. Students were also allowed to use these computers to connect to the Internet in order to complete assignments. This was a common exercise for students taking certain computer science courses. In addition, computer science classes or group exercises were frequently held in these labs.

The entire student body had access to the computer labs which were monitored by student employees. These individuals would keep an eye on things while they were reading or doing homework. They were also responsible for certain maintenance tasks and for reporting any technical problems to the information technology services department.

A MINOR CRISIS

University administrators were certainly cognizant of the pornographic material available on the Internet, but they had never heard of any overt problems or reports of abuse in their school. However, in October, during the middle of the first semester, the school had to contend with what NEU's president described as a "minor crisis." A group of male students downloaded some images from a pornographic Web site and left them for display on the computers in one of the computer labs. They did this deliberately just before a freshman computer science class was to use the lab that day for several programming exercises. When the instructor and the students entered the room, they noticed the pornographic material on several of the workstations. The pictures were quite graphic and degrading, and some of the young women in the class became quite distraught. The pictures were quickly deleted from the screens, but the damage had been done. The instructor reported the incident to the dean of students who set out to find the students who were responsible for this misbehavior. Since there were several witnesses, this was not too difficult.

Several of the women students voiced their profound concerns to the dean of students who was investigating the incident. One woman said that the pictures were so disturbing that she had trouble sleeping for several nights and that she had "bombed" an exam in the class she took after the lab. She claimed that she was too distressed to concentrate on the material. Several other students maintained that they felt "harassed." The dean apologized and assured them that whoever was responsible would be punished severely. He also promised that he would try to ensure that this would not happen again.

Several days later the dean of students, Dr. Shirley Pellegrisi, met with Dean Jenkins to discuss this complicated matter. She told him that the male students responsible for this "prank" had been apprehended and were being suspended for the remainder of the semester. They could return to school in the spring semester. Some of her colleagues felt that this punishment was too harsh, but Dr. Pellegrisi was convinced that this matter was quite serious, and she wanted to send a strong message to the other students. The purpose of this meeting with Jenkins was to discuss preventative measures. What could the school do to protect its students, especially females, from being subjected to unwanted pornographic images in public facilities?

After several long discussions with her and other key administrators, Jenkins decided to restrict the university's access to the Internet. NEU would block sexually oriented newsgroups and pornographic Web sites from its Internet servers since some of these newsgroups and Web sites are dedicated to the posting of explicit digitized pornographic images. The university was concerned with the moral ramifications of allowing such images to be displayed in public places on campus, and it was also worried about its organizational liability. In light of this incident, if it did not take such action the school might be legally liable for any future incidents involving the display of indecent material. The university's executive vice president and president shared Jenkins's concerns and they reluctantly concurred with his decision. The decision was put into effect immediately and was implemented by the university's administrator for information technology systems.

THE AFTERMATH

Dean Jenkins and his colleagues, however, were not prepared for the aftermath of that decision. After its announcement in the school newspaper he received many e-mail messages and phone calls from angry faculty who protested that censorship was not the way to deal with this problem since it suppressed the right to free speech. They agreed, of course, that the culprits should be firmly punished and that such strong action would itself serve as a deterrent for those students who might be foolish enough to think of doing this again. Several of the female faculty members sent letters supporting the dean's decision, but about 90 percent of the faculty feedback was negative. The students were less vehement, but they too were clearly opposed to the university's censorship of Internet pornography.

The protests and criticisms culminated in today's meetings with two faculty committees, both of which asked Dean Jenkins to reconsider his "unfortunate and untimely" decision. At the same time, the problem was beginning to escalate thanks to the mounting negative publicity. The press had picked up on the story and articles on NEU had appeared in several computer papers along with the local newspapers. Also, Dean Jenkins's secretary had received a call earlier in the day from the producer of a local television newsmagazine. They were interested in doing a story about this bold but controversial decision to filter out the sex newsgroups; the producer did indicate that the show would try to present both sides of this volatile issue.

Jenkins knew that at tomorrow's meeting with the president and the university's general counsel it would be necessary to reassess this decision. Should NEU back down and reverse its decision or should it hold firm even in the face of this severe criticism and escalating turmoil?

Case 2.4 Jake Baker

Abraham Jacob Alkhabaz, also known as Jake Baker, was an undergraduate student at the University of Michigan during the mid-1990s. In addition to pursuing his studies, Jake also contributed sexually explicit and sadistic short stories to a popular USENET[9] bulletin board. One of these stories, however, led to some legal difficulties for Baker. In that story he described how he and a friend had kidnapped, tortured, and murdered a young woman, who was given the name of one of Baker's classmates. The snuff story was pure fiction, but the fact that it named a real student seemed to make it more offensive and troubling. At the same time Baker initiated a series of e-mail communications with another Internet user who went by the name of Arthur Gonda. He and Gonda indulged in various sexual fantasies and plotted online about how they could kidnap and torture other young women in the Ann Arbor area. Here is one piece of e-mail sent by Baker:

> I've been trying to think of secluded spots, but my area of knowledge of Ann Arbor, is mostly limited to the campus. I don't want any blood in my room. Though, I have come upon an excellent method to abduct a bitch. As I said before, my room is right across from the girls bathroom. Wait until late at night, grab her when she goes to unlock the door, knock her unconscious, and put her into one of these portable lockers, forget the word for it, or even a duffel bag. And hurry her out to the car and take her away. What do you think?

One of these bizarre rape stories, posted to the newsgroup alt.sex.stories, was discovered by an alumnus of the university living in Moscow. Upset that the story had the "umich.edu" tag, he brought the stories to the attention of University of Michigan officials, who promptly undertook an investigation. The stories were traced to Baker and he was expelled from campus on February 3, 1995 for naming a University of Michigan student as the victim of his erotic on-line fantasy. The case immediately attracted widespread publicity—Baker's expulsion was front page news in the Ann Arbor papers.[10]

But Baker's real troubles were just beginning. Several days later on February 9, FBI agents arrested Baker for transmitting threats across state lines. According to federal authorities, the "transmissions described Baker's desire to commit acts of abduction, bondage, torture, mutilation, sodomy, rape, and murder of young women." He was considered to be a dangerous threat to society and denied bail by the judge handling the case. According to Judge Friedman, "I would not want my daughter on the streets of Ann Arbor or Ohio with a man in the condition he is in now."[11]

Baker was arrested for violation of federal law, specifically, 18 U.S.C. §875 (c):

> Whoever transmits in interstate or foreign commerce any communication containing any threat to kidnap any person or any threat to injure the person of another, shall be fined under this title or imprisoned not more than five years, or both.

This statute is usually interpreted narrowly in order to avoid conflicts with someone's First Amendment rights.

In March, after he was finally released on bail, a federal grand jury opted not to indict Baker for his USENET posting that named the University of Michigan student. Instead he was indicted only for the graphic e-mail exchanges with Gonda which did not specify any women. Nonetheless he was charged with transmitting a "threat to injure another person." Baker's lawyers argued that his statements did not amount to "true threats," and that, however offensive, they were all protected under the First Amendment.

It was the court's responsibility to engage in First Amendment analysis to determine whether Baker's speech was protected or whether it should be proscribed as a "true threat." Supporters of Baker argued that he should not be punished for his thoughts and desires, however offensive they may be. They also observed that the messages were not publicly published but sent privately via e-mail. Baker, they argued, was indulging in fantasy and maybe even in fantasy role playing, activities which are not out of the ordinary in interactive communications such as e-mail.

Others maintained that Baker's speech may simply have gone too far. In an *amicus curiae* brief filed by the National Coalition against Sexual Support, Catherine McKinnon wrote: "When a social environment is created, such as the Internet, in which it becomes acceptable to share materials like the pornography of record, getting caught may appear less likely, perception of social disapprobation is reduced, controls disinhibited, and the possibility of aggressive acts correspondingly increases."[12]

The question then is whether or not Baker's e-mails constituted a threat. In these e-mails Baker set forth his plans for abducting and raping women and sometimes alluded to specific times and places. Would a reasonable person reading these e-mails consider them to be threatening? Was Baker just a troubled individual or was he a risk to the female students at the University of Michigan?

Case 2.5 Encryption Source Code and the First Amendment

Peter Junger is a law professor at Case Western University in Cleveland, Ohio. He maintains a Web site that includes course material, and he sought to post on that Web site encryption source code that he had written to illustrate how this technology worked. Data encryption is nothing more than the use of a secret code to ensure that confidentiality is not breached when a message is communicated.[13] It works by relying on an algorithm that translates a plain text message such as "we will invade tomorrow" into some sort of unintelligible ciphertext. The only way that this ciphertext can be translated into something intelligible is by means of a key, which is available only to the recipient of the message. There are many commercial software products that enable users to encrypt their messages, but Junger had written his own encryption program.

In 1997 Junger submitted an inquiry to the Department of Commerce concerning the status of encryption software source code that he intended to post to his Web site. In keeping with the law against exporting certain encryption code, which had originally been classified by the United States as munitions, Junger was informed that a license would be required before he could post this source code. According to *Junger v. Daley*, "almost any posting of software on the Internet is an export."[14] But Professor Junger had been allowed to publish encryption programs in his textbook *Computers and the Law*.

The federal government has long sought to control the dissemination of encryption software and products for obvious reasons. If strong encryption, that is, encryption with a virtually uncrackable 128-bit key, is employed by criminals or terrorists, it will stymie the surveillance efforts of law enforcement officials.

In response to this demand for an export license, Professor Junger challenged this decision in federal district court. He argued that the government's restriction was tantamount to prior restraint on his free speech rights. This case raises the larger question of whether the source code[15] of computer software is a form of expression deserving First Amendment protection. The district court determined that encryption source code is not protected by the First Amendment because it is not really expressive speech. According to the court, the export regulation is a content-neutral regulation that did not violate Junger's free speech rights. The district court also found that encryption source code in digital form was "inherently functional . . . indistinguishable from dedicated computer hardware that does encryption."[16]

Junger promptly appealed this decision, and the appeal was heard by the Sixth Circuit Court of Appeals. During this process export regulations were liberalized by the Clinton administration, but encryption software in electronic form was still considered subject to reporting requirements. In a surprising turn of events, the appeals court reversed the decision of the lower court, ruling that the First Amendment does indeed protect computer source code. The court admitted that the issue of First Amendment protection was a difficult one, since source code is both expressive and functional. It is expressive like a literary work, but it also functions like a virtual "machine" that processes data or computes numbers. The district court had reasoned that the functional characteristics of this source code "overshadowed" its expressive features. But as the appeals court opined, "the fact that a medium of expression has a functional capacity should not preclude constitutional protection." The court also pointed to the "versatile scope" of the First Amendment, which has fully protected "the artwork of Jackson Pollack, the music of Arnold Schoenberg, or the Jabberwocky verse of Lewis Carroll."[17]

Based on this reasoning, the Sixth Circuit reversed the district court on the matter of First Amendment protection and it remanded the case for further consideration in light of the amended export regulations (see Case 5.7, "Crypto Wars").

The federal government clearly has an interest in regulating and restricting certain forms of speech such as encryption source code. The appeals court recognized this but concluded that the government had not made the case that the national security issues at stake implied the need to curb the free exchange of encryption source code. Can such a case be made? Should national security interests outweigh the interests of free speech in this case?

Case 2.6 CompuServe Deutschland

In 1997 a CompuServe executive was indicted in Germany for violating local pornography laws. The indictment accused him of failing to block access to pornographic images that were available on the Internet through CompuServe Internet service. The case captured international attention as it triggered issues of free speech and "cyberjurisdiction." Civil libertarians in America and Europe expressed deep concerns about the possible precedent set by this case.

DER FALL SOMM

CompuServe USA is an on-line service provider linking people and businesses to the Internet. At the time of this case it had approximately four million subscribers. The company has since been purchased by America Online. CompuServe is a global organization, and it operated a subsidiary in Germany known as CompuServe Deutschland. CompuServe Deutschland provided local dialup access to CompuServe USA's facilities for German subscribers, who have access to proprietary content and Internet services. Felix Somm was the managing director of this subsidiary. Its offices were located in Munich, which is the capital of the conservative state of Bavaria in southeastern Germany.

The problem began in December 1995 when the German police raided CompuServe's Munich offices because of alleged violations of decency laws. The German police gave Somm a list of 282 USENET newsgroups which contained violent sexual images, child pornography, and bestiality (such as alt.sex.erotica). This content was stored on CompuServe USA's newsgroup servers, and it was accessible to all of CompuServe's subscribers including those in Germany. In response, CompuServe temporarily blocked access to all of these sites. The blocking program affected all of its customers including those outside of Germany. This caused an uproar among its users since, although some of these sites featured pornography, others contained discussions on AIDS and breast cancer. CompuServe USA then unblocked the sites for its users and provided parents with a filtering software package known as CyberPatrol.

An investigation ensued and eventually criminal charges were brought against Somm in April 1997. He was accused of "trafficking" in pornography and neo-Nazi propaganda. According to the prosecutor's office, he "knowingly allowed images of child pornography, violent sex, and sex with animals from newsgroups . . . to be made accessible to customers of CompuServe Germany."[18] According to authorities, CompuServe and Somm did not do enough to block German citizens from getting access to material that is illegal in Germany. The Somm case ("der fall Somm," as it was called in the German press) generated widespread publicity, especially in Europe. CompuServe vigorously defended itself against these allegations, contending that it was not responsible for the content of the many Internet sites accessed by CompuServe users. The company also maintained that it did not have the technical capability to monitor those users or to censor the diverse content of cyberspace.

FREE SPEECH IN GERMANY

Like the constitutions of most other democratic governments, the German constitution guarantees the right to free speech. According to Article 5, "[each person] has the right to freely express and disseminate his opinion in speech, writing and picture." However, the German Federal Constitution Court (the FCC) imposes broad restrictions on that right. According to Kristina Reed, "because speech is valued according to its utility in promoting personal development, the FCC balances the interest of free speech with civility norms under an objective ordering of values."[19] If the FCC judges that a community value takes precedence over this right, it may conclude that the law protecting that value is constitutional. Some forms of art such as pornography, for example, must be restricted for the sake of human dignity concerns.

German law, therefore, is more conservative than American law in regard to the scope of free speech rights. As a result, the CompuServe case presents a difficult jurisdictional problem. Should German law be permitted to restrict global Internet access and content? Do these specific laws apply in a universal medium such as the Internet or the World Wide Web?

THE VERDICT

The Somm case went to trial and a verdict was handed down in May 1998. Judge Wilhelm Hubbert found that Somm (together with CompuServe) violated Germany's criminal code by making various illegal forms of pornography publicly available. Moreover, according to the court, CompuServe had the technical capability to block access to these newsgroups but chose not to implement that technology. Its failure to do so, in the eyes of the court, was motivated purely by commercial gain. According to the judge, CompuServe had allowed "protecting the young . . . to take second place to maximizing profits." In the court's opinion, the defendant, Somm, knew this, but he too shared the same profit motive. Somm was therefore an accessory, since CompuServe Deutschland provided access to CompuServe USA's services for German subscribers and it willingly shared in the revenues and profits of CompuServe USA.

Judge Hubbert gave Somm a two-year suspended sentence and fined him DM100,000. The decision sent a signal to other Internet service providers operating in Germany: They are accountable for the Internet content accessible to their users and must take steps to block access to any objectionable material that violates German laws. The case was immediately appealed to the Bavarian State Court.

Case 2.7 Veil of Censorship

It was late Thursday afternoon as Websense executives gathered for a short meeting to discuss the next steps in winning a lucrative new contract. Websense, a San Diego Company specializing in content filtering software, was elated at the prospect of a major new customer, the Saudi Arabian government. They had just begun a product trial with the government and were now strategizing on how to prevail amid tough rivals vying for the chance to showcase their products through this sale. The Saudi government was benchmarking software packages that would efficiently block access to unauthorized Web sites. These sites included pornographic sites along with those that might offend the sensibilities of its citizens, that is, content critical of the Islamic religion or the Saudi regime. Political dissent is not tolerated in Saudi Arabia and government officials wanted to be sure that the Web would not provide a forum for such dissent.

Websense was competing for this contract with Secure Computing of San Jose, California. Secure Computing's contract was due to expire in 2003 and Websense felt they might have an opportunity to win the new contract for this Internet-filtering software. Websense already supplied this type of software to a list of prominent Fortune 500 companies, but it's tricky to make this software work at a country-wide level and the Websense managers were meeting to discuss the progress of the trial and some of the logistical problems that could be encountered.

Citizens of this rich Arab nation have become accustomed to using the Internet either in their own homes or in public places like hotels in the capital city of Riyadh. But all Internet traffic is funnelled through a main server in Riyadh and unwelcome content is not allowed through. If a Saudi user seeks access to a Web site on the prohibited list, the following message is displayed: "Access to the requested URL is denied!" The government believes that unfettered access to the World Wide Web would introduce too many sinister voices into the Saudi culture.

Saudi Arabia, of course, is not the only country to censor the Internet in such heavy-handed fashion. Although China has embraced digital technology and has tried to extend Internet usage among its citizens, it seeks to keep out the "foreign 'flies'—from liberalism to democracy to pornography—that will come in with the Internet."[20] China too relies on filtering software to accomplish this aim and that software blocks many mass media Web sites such as those operated by the BBC, CNN, and the Washington Post.

For Websense and other companies aggressively pursuing the Saudi contract for content filtering software, there are some ethical concerns. Should they provide the tools that make possible censorship of this broad scope? Do they share any moral liability in the Saudi government's efforts to suppress free speech on such a massive scale? These companies argue that they are selling a neutral piece of technology, a tool at the disposal of foreign governments. How that tool is used is not their responsibility. Critics argue that the censorship enabled by these filtering products goes too far. For example, the Web site of the Committee for the Defense of Human rights in the Arabian Peninsula (www.cdrhap.com) has been included on that list of Web sites suppressed in Saudi Arabia. Should Websense consider these concerns?

NOTES

1. M. Godwin, *CyberRights: Defending Free Speech in the Digital Age* (New York: Random House, 1998), p. 19.
2. C. Kaplan, "Free-Speech Advocates Fight Filtering Software in Public Schools," *CyberLaw Journal* (19 January 2001).
3. Telecommunications Act of 1996, 47 U.S.C. §254(h).
4. CHIPA, §1721 b.
5. Plaintiff's Complaint, *Multnomah Public Library et al. v. U.S.*, 402 E.D. Pa. (2001).
6. Ibid.
7. Ibid.
8. *Reno v. ACLU*, 117 Sup. Ct. 2335 (1997).
9. USENET is a protocol for exchanging messages on the Internet that are intended for public viewing; those messages are organized into newsgroups which are in turn organized into subjects (such as "sex").
10. J. Branam, "U-M Expelling Student for Internet Fantasy," *Ann Arbor News*, 3 February 1995, p. A1.
11. J. White, "Student Judged 'Too Dangerous' to be Released," *Michigan Daily*, 13 February 1995, p. A1.
12. C. McKinnon, Brief Amicus Curiae, *U.S. v. Alkahbaz*, 104 F.3d 1492, 6th Cir. (1997).
13. See Case 5.7 for more background on the nature of encryption technology and for a discussion of how export regulations have been changed.
14. *Junger v. Daley*, 8 F. Supp. 2d 708, N.D. Ohio (1998).
15. Source code consists of a computer program's instructions written in a high-level language such as C++, JAVA, or PL/1. A compiler is used to translate that source code into object code, the binary format executed by the computer.
16. *Junger v. Daley* (1998).
17. *Junger v. Daley*, 209 F. 3d 481 6th Cir. (2000).
18. Quoted in S. Biegel, "Indictment of CompuServe Official in Germany Brings Volatile Issues of CyberJurisdiction into Focus," http://www.gseis.ucla.edu/iclp/apr.html.
19. K. Reed, *From the Great Firewall of China to the Berlin Firewall: The Cost of Content Regulation on Internet Commerce*, 12 Transnational Lawyer 543 (1999).
20. "Wired China," *Economist* (22 July 2000), p. 25.

3

Intellectual Property Issues I: Software Ownership

INTRODUCTION

The case studies in this chapter concern the moral question of software ownership and the scope of intellectual property rights. During the last decade or so there has been a steady erosion of respect for intellectual property laws. Many end users and professionals seem to have few qualms about making illegal copies of commercial software. In a *Computerworld* poll, 53 percent of the information professionals surveyed indicated that they had made unauthorized copies of software programs.[1] Most of these individuals rationalized their behavior by saying that they were just "trying out" or sampling the software in question. Others claimed that because software is often so bug-ridden, they wanted to test it before making a purchase.

Some scholars, like Helen Nissenbaum, even question a "strong no-copy" position, arguing that copying software programs between friends or colleagues may be morally permissible. She challenges the conventional wisdom and propriety of the no-copy position because it "emphasizes the moral claims and interests of software producers while failing to consider other morally relevant claims—most notably, those of the private end-user."[2]

Discussions on software piracy bring us into the realm of intellectual property issues, but before we review that topic it is instructive to consider briefly the whole conception of property. Most contemporary analyses equate the notions of "ownership" and "property." Hence the statements "I own that house" and "That house is my property" are equivalent, since they convey the same information. Further, those analyses define ownership as "the greatest possible interest in a thing which a mature system of law recognizes."[3] More simply, ownership of property implies that the owner has certain rights and liabilities with respect to this property, including the rights to use, manage, possess, exclude, and derive income.

Intellectual property rights seem to imply that someone has the right to certain concepts, knowledge, or ideas. There are serious difficulties, however, with the notion that one has property rights in an idea, since this would mean the "right" to exclude others from using and building upon those ideas. Rather, it is generally recognized that one has property rights in the way one expresses ideas, whether it be in the form of a book, a play, or a software program. Thus, the distinction between an idea and its expression serves as a fundamental basis for making legal and moral decisions about intellectual property protection.

There are four major forms of intellectual property protection:

- Copyright protection for literary works; according to copyright law, a property right is granted to "original works of authorship in any tangible medium of expression."[4]
- Patent protection for machines, inventions, and processes.
- Trademark protection for brand names and product symbols.
- Trade secrecy protection for proprietary corporate information.

Software is eligible for several forms of protection. Finished software programs and works in progress can be classified as trade secrets. Companies usually implement this form of protection by means of nondisclosure agreements which prevent employees from using these ideas, prototypes, software code, and the like for their own personal gain or while they are employed at another company. One difficulty with trade secrets is that once a "secret" is in the public domain, it is no longer protected and can be used by others with impunity.

Since the landmark case of *Diehr v. Diamond*, patents have also become a legally acceptable way of protecting software programs. Patents normally have a 17-year duration and provide exclusive rights to the patent holder to use and profit from the product or process in question. The final and most popular means of protecting intellectual property rights in software is the use of the copyright. This became possible in 1980 when Congress passed the Computer Software Act. This legislation clarified that federal copyright laws protect both the source code and the object code of a program.[5]

Various moral arguments can also be invoked to buttress the legal claim of limited property rights. The labor-desert theory, inspired by John Locke, argues that labor and effort engender at least some sort of property rights. Those who work, who invest their time and energy in a project, have a right to the fruits of their labor. Thus, if software companies invest heavy resources and labor in creating a product, they should have a limited moral right to the returns which will be generated by this investment by controlling the use of that product. To a certain extent, American copyright and patent laws are grounded in this Lockean conception of property, since they confer long, heavily protected monopolies for product innovations that preclude competitors from cloning or otherwise imitating the protected product. Utilitarian reasoning is also used to justify intellectual property protection: "Intellectual property rights induce creators to develop works they would not otherwise produce without this protection, and this contributes to the general good of society."[6]

Finally it should not be overlooked that a copyright is not absolute. The U.S. Copyright Act allows copying of copyrighted material for some purposes such as news reporting and literary criticism. This is called "fair use." (The factors considered in making a fair use decision are enumerated in Cases 4.1 and 4.2.)

What we have been describing is the traditional Western conception of *private* property rights. It should be remarked, however, that other countries and traditions adopt a very different approach to property. In general, they put more emphasis on common property whereby some sort of access is granted to all. This is especially true with intellectual property which is conceived by many developing countries as common property. According to Paul Steidlmeier, "developing countries argue that individual claims on intellectual property are subordinated to more fundamental claims of social well-being . . . [and] that while people may have a right to the fruit of their labor, they have a duty to reward society which practically made the very fruitfulness of labor possible."[7] This divergence of opinion on intellectual property between American businesses and some of their competitors throughout the world has sometimes been the source of intractable legal and moral disputes.

Another source of moral controversy is the difficulty of differentiating between the property rights of employers and their employees. For example, what portion of an information asset or a software program belongs exclusively to one's present employer and which portion constitutes part of the employee's general knowledge and expertise that can be utilized without impunity in another organization? Does the employee's creative work on a project engender any sort of property rights or are these always surrendered to the employer?

We begin this chapter with a relatively straightforward case called "Piracy on the Internet." It describes a well-publicized incident in which software products were disseminated on the Internet without permission. There may be agreement that a serious moral transgression has occurred, but there is less consensus on the locus of responsibility and a fitting penalty for this misdeed in cyberspace. This case also provides a vehicle for discussing the unconventional viewpoint that software should not be considered as anyone's property.

The next three hypothetical cases involve scenarios where individuals must make key decisions about copying software programs. In "It's Never Right to Copy Software," a young teacher in a poor school district must decide about making unauthorized copies of a software program; unless he does so, the school's new computers will be virtually useless. This case asks the question implied by its title: Is the moral injunction against making illegal copies of software programs absolute or does it allow for exceptions, especially in these extenuating circumstances?

But in the other two cases the question of ownership seems less clear. In "Whose Program Is This?" an employee takes portions of a successful accounts payable program to her new position. Does her labor on this effort confer any right to appropriate some of this program for her own use, especially when there appears to be no adverse consequences for her employer? And in the case entitled "Doric Conversion Technologies, Inc." a software program is no longer marketed by a company, but is it acceptable for its developer to use this discarded program for his own personal gain?

The last case study, "Note on Software Compatibility and Reverse Engineering," focuses on two major legal controversies in the software industry which have significant ethical implications. Both disputes deal with the general theme of compatibility. The user community is looking for standards in software, yet standardization sometimes conflicts with the notion of intellectual property protection which may permit a particular company to have exclusive rights to a technology that is emerging as an industry de facto standard. Can we have common standards and some degree of compatibility without pulverizing the laws that are designed to protect intellectual property? The debate about standards comes to the forefront in the legal dispute of *Lotus v. Borland*, where the primary issue is on how much similarity should be allowed between user interfaces. The second conflict which is discussed in this note took place between Sega Ltd. and Accolade, Inc., two participants in the video game industry. The central question here is the following: What can a vendor do to obtain information needed to write software programs that will work on another vendor's hardware platform? In other words, to what extent should reverse engineering be permitted?

Case 3.1 Piracy on the Internet

In March 1994 the U.S. Attorney in Boston announced that charges would be filed against an MIT student, David LaMacchia, for computer fraud. It was alleged that this 20-year-old student operated a computer bulletin board on the Internet which distributed copies of various copyrighted software programs. LaMacchia was not accused of actually uploading or downloading any of the programs. The indictment also made it clear that he did not collect any money or materially profit from this activity in any way.

The problem of "piracy" and pilfered software programs has become quite serious and expensive. The software industry currently estimates that it loses almost $12 billion a year through various types of piracy. Moreover, downloading from bulletin boards and Web sites are considered to be the most common and costly forms of software piracy. Shortly after LaMacchia's indictment, Daniel A. Goldman, a student at Brown University, was arrested for alleged computer fraud. He too was accused of disseminating copyrighted software over the Internet. And since that time there have been many similar incidents of alleged piracy.

In the MIT case, authorities acted quickly in order to send an unambiguous signal that they would not allow computer bulletin boards to function as repositories and distributors of stolen software. Given the growing number of users on the Internet, copying could happen on a scale that would greatly magnify losses for software companies. LaMacchia's bulletin board was known as CYNOSURE. It was in operation from November 1993 through January 1995. It was estimated that approximately $1 million of software was illegally copied from CYNOSURE during this time frame. It remains unclear who uploaded the software for purposes of its illicit dissemination to various users. Both the uploading and downloading took place through an "anonymous server" in Finland which deleted the addresses of the users involved.

There were many oddities and ambiguities about this case, making it difficult for the U.S. Attorney to get a conviction. The most unusual fact was LaMacchia's refusal to collect any money for the software that was allegedly disseminated. If the young student did not wish to profit from this activity, what was his motivation?

Some sources at MIT speculated at the time that he was motivated by earnest beliefs about software ownership, rejecting the notion that companies should have ownership rights in the commercial software which they have developed. This position is also espoused by Richard Stallman, president of the Free Software Foundation. Stallman, who has never perpetrated or advocated actions like those of LaMacchia, has argued for many years that ownership of software programs is obstructive. He maintains that software should be in the public domain, freely available to anyone who wants to use it. He regards stiff software licensing fees as a disincentive to acquire programs and thus he concludes that legal ownership of software programs obstructs their utility; expensive, proprietary programs are enjoyed by too few users. Ownership also obstructs software modification and development. According to Stallman,

> Software development used to be an evolutionary process, where a person would take a program and rewrite parts of it for one new feature, and then another person would rewrite parts to add another feature; this could continue over a period of twenty years. . . . The existence of owners prevents this kind of evolution, making it necessary to start from scratch when developing a program.[8]

Stallman concludes that since the ownership of programs is so obstructive and yields such negative consequences, "society shouldn't have owners for programs."[9]

LaMacchia seemed to share this philosophy and apparently decided to do something about it by becoming a "Robin Hood" figure on the Internet, redistributing the ownership rights of copyrighted software programs from large corporations such as Microsoft to individual users.

Regardless of his motivation and the validity of these arguments, LaMacchia's actions were strongly condemned by many in the user community. Software companies praised the indictment as long overdue in the ongoing struggle to combat piracy, but this sentiment was by no means universal. Some civil liberties experts underscored LaMacchia's defense that he did not actually copy the software himself. Hence, what exactly was the crime or transgression that had been committed? According to Anthes, "the student's defense revolves around the assertion that a bulletin board is just a conduit for information and the notion that organizations such as telephone companies, book stores and newspapers cannot be prosecuted when information they convey is used illegally by others."[10] On the other hand, one could surely argue that he facilitated the use of the Internet as a conduit of criminal activity, that is, the illegal distribution of copyrighted software.

Another protest over the arrest of Mr. LaMacchia was voiced by constitutional law expert and Harvard Law School Professor Lawrence Tribe. Tribe argued that the case should not be pursued particularly since there was no attempt to profit from the distribution of the software. He and other civil libertarians regarded this incident as a free speech case. Tribe noted at the time that an indictment would be problematic since it could "chill the open transmission of information in cyberspace."

This unusual and controversial case was carefully watched by major software companies who had a significant stake in this decision. They were hoping that a conviction would deter future attempts to engage in piracy on the Internet. But U.S. District Court Judge Richard Stearns disappointed them. He concluded that LaMacchia could not be prosecuted for copyright infringement under the wire-fraud statute (which has since been modified). But the judge excoriated LaMacchia's behavior, describing his actions as "heedlessly irresponsible and, at worst, as nihilistic, self-indulgent and lacking in any fundamental sense of values."[11]

Case 3.2 "It's Never Right to Copy Software"

Roger Gleason breezed into the third floor teacher's room to get some coffee before his 8:45 A.M. meeting with the principal. The room was unusually serene since the first period of classes was already underway. He appreciated the opportunity for some quiet time to prepare for his meeting.

Roger was a mathematics teacher at City High School, an inner-city school with a reputation for academic excellence. City High typically sent 60 to 70 percent of its graduates to college and had a dropout rate of less than 10 percent. It was located on the fringe of an impoverished neighborhood where it drew the majority of its students. Most of these students came from families who received some sort of public assistance such as welfare. Despite its location and continuing budgetary constraints, the school was especially well known for its math and science departments which were among the best in the entire school district.

Roger was reassigned to this school several years ago from one of the suburban schools in the district. Roger was ambitious and felt that this assignment would enhance his career. He also felt privileged to be at a school with such a strong reputation for excellence in mathematics. During his second year here he volunteered to head the math team and under his tutelage it advanced to the semifinals in a statewide math contest.

Teaching at this school, however, was not without its challenges. Many incoming students came from inferior grammar schools and, despite their innate abilities, were grossly underprepared for high school, particularly in the areas of mathematics and English. As a result, conscientious teachers like Roger were called upon to put in extra hours in order to do remedial work with many students. Many of the faculty were quite willing to expend this extra effort, and, in Roger's view, this sense of commitment and caring gave the school its special ethos and distinctive character.

Roger was especially elated these days since he had learned several days ago that a significant gift to the math department would be forthcoming. A local company had decided to donate 22 used personal computers; they were Power Macintosh systems with 100 megabytes of memory. They were scheduled to be delivered within the next few weeks.

The administrators at City High were equally pleased about this magnanimous gesture. The computer science curriculum at the school was severely limited due to the lack of equipment. The school had a meager budget for such items. The science labs were also ill-equipped, and sometimes chemistry teachers were forced to improvise. For many scientific experiments chemistry teachers would use plastic bottles in place of beakers.

Since the principal had actually been anticipating this gift for some time, she met with the department on several occasions in order to elicit their recommendation for how these computers should be utilized. The consensus of the department was that some of the computers should be used to set up a special computer laboratory with at least 14 of the 22 systems. These machines would be available for students who needed tutorial assistance with freshman algebra, geometry, or other subjects. It was difficult for the teaching staff to keep up with the demands for such assistance and this lab might help solve the problem. It was also decided that Roger should be appointed as the coordinator of the new math computer lab. The principal concurred with both of these decisions. Roger was happy to assume this new responsibility even though it would require more of his time. But he enjoyed helping students and he saw this as an opportunity to take more of a leadership role in the school.

Roger finished his coffee and headed down the hall to the principal's office. The principal, Mary Lou Duffy, was a 30-year veteran of the school system. This was the beginning of her seventh year at City High School. She was well liked by both faculty and students. She had a reputation for being a no-nonsense, pragmatic, and results-oriented administrator, but she had an amiable and engaging personality. Her stature in the school district gave her some clout with the school board, and many on the board admired the way she would lobby for the needs of City High with vigor and diplomacy.

As usual, she was right on time for the meeting with Roger. After the exchange of the usual pleasantries, Mary Lou invited Roger into her office and promptly began the meeting: "I wanted to get together to talk about your role as the new lab coordinator. This lab is a great addition to the school and I'm grateful that you have decided to take this position. Your background with computers clearly makes you the most qualified person to run this lab." Roger thanked her for this vote of confidence and inquired about a budget. "I wasn't planning on much of a budget," she said, "since, as you know, our resources here are quite constrained. But what do you need?" "Well," Roger answered, "our primary need is for educational software for these new computers. I would like to get enough software for at least 10 of these machines. The best program is probably MATH-TUTOR, a series of diskettes that cover algebra, geometry, and even some calculus. This will be invaluable for our students who often need so much extra help in these areas." Roger sensed some skepticism, and so he elaborated on his request: "Having these machines function as 'electronic tutors' will take a big burden off our faculty; if they don't have to do remedial work, they will have more time to prepare their classes and introduce innovative material. Also, the students will be able to work at their own pace. They can spend as much time as they need on practicing problems."

After Roger finished talking, Mary Lou rose up in the chair from behind her desk. She checked a file and sat back down. "I notice that we already own one copy of this software. Isn't that right?" she asked Roger. Roger explained that the school did have one licensed copy of this software installed on one of the hardware systems in the computer resource center where the programming classes were now taught. "Well, then," responded Mary Lou, "why not just make copies for the 10 machines. No one will ever know." Roger looked surprised and there was some hesitancy in his voice. "But that's stealing, isn't it? I know that we don't have a lot of money around here, but it's never right to copy software programs." Mary Lou was a bit taken aback by this response, but she was insistent. "Roger, I appreciate your concern, but let's be practical. We just cannot afford to spend all that money for 10 copies of fairly expensive software. As I recall, these programs currently sell for $695. That means almost $7,000!" "Well what about asking the software company to make a donation or give us a break on the price?" Roger asked. Mary Lou shook her head. "We tried that a year ago and the company refused. They have a firm policy of no giveaways."

Roger was silent for a few moments as he mulled over the options. There did not appear to be a viable solution to this problem aside from copying the software. Mary Lou glanced at her watch and noticed that it was time for her next appointment. "Why don't you think it over a bit," she said. "You *are* the coordinator, so if you refuse to do this, I'll accept that. But keep in mind that I can't give you any money for software and without software these machines won't do us much good. At any rate, let me know by tomorrow what you have decided."

As Roger was ushered from the office, he wondered whether he was being too naive. As he taught his math classes that day he couldn't help focusing more intensely on the deprivation of his students and their bleak surroundings. What a stark contrast to the company that produced this software. He recalled reading somewhere that their profits last year exceeded $100 million. But then again, he thought, does this justify taking someone else's property?

Roger vacillated like this throughout the day. But he was determined to make a decision and move on to planning the other activities associated with starting up this computer lab. When he finished his classes he went straight to his tiny cubicle in the math department. After an hour or so his colleagues had all departed. Roger picked up the phone and began to dial the principal's extension.

Case 3.3 Whose Program Is This?

Ellen Pederson glanced out the rain-streaked windows at the few remaining cars in the dimly lit parking lot. She was once again putting in extra hours to finish an assignment on schedule. She was anxious to leave but knew she would need to work a few more hours if she was to make the crucial Friday deadline.

Ellen worked for the Apollo Group, a prestigious organization that specialized in providing employment counseling to executives. Apollo was also a headhunting firm that worked with Fortune 500 corporations to help them find the "right" executive for certain key positions. Ellen began her career at Apollo three years ago in the Information Systems (IS) department. When she joined Apollo after graduate school she began working as a programmer on various computer systems for the organization. The department had just expanded and its charge at that time was to construct applications that would provide client information to Apollo account executives, keep track of accounts receivable and accounts payable, and provide a meaningful decision support system for the company's top executives. As Apollo took on more clients and its revenues reached the $250 million mark, the need for these systems was considered critical.

Shortly after Ellen was hired, the IS department quickly moved into action in order to meet these objectives. It purchased a relational database, a 4GL, and other software tools in order to implement the systems requested by the Apollo executives. The company had an IBM mainframe computer system which would be the repository of the applications. Users were equipped with workstations and IBM PCs with ready access to the company's internal network along with the mainframe system.

Ellen's primary responsibility became the development of an on-line accounts payable system which became known as U-PAY. Users could go on line, select the vendor from an approved list, and then key in a description of the product or services provided, the amount of the purchase, and any other pertinent information. The system would automatically generate a purchase order or check requisition while encumbering funds from the department's budget. Payments could also be generated for individuals such as consultants who were not on the payroll but were rendering some service to the company. All approvals were handled on-line as well. Once accounts payable received the approved check requisition, it issued a check for the appropriate amount and sent it along to the vendor or the external consultant. The system had many advantages: It expedited the payments to Apollo's many adjunct consultants along with its numerous vendors and it also prevented budget overruns which had been a problem in past years.

Ellen had worked on this system for over two years before it was unveiled last August. It was an immediate sensation in the company. Unfortunately, Ellen's boss took much of the credit for the project despite the fact that his input was really confined to its design stage. Ellen was the project leader who put in the long hours to make this application a reality. She did receive a decent pay increase and a small bonus for her substantial efforts, but she was quite chagrined that she did not receive the credit or recognition for this project that she deserved. Now she was working on designing a major new database system along with some enhancements to U-PAY.

As Ellen became more disenchanted at Apollo, she began to look around for a new job. The market for programmers with her skills and experience was pretty strong despite a mild national recession. As a result, Ellen quickly secured several interviews. One of the interviews was with Apollo's chief competitor located in a nearby city. They were far behind Apollo in their systems development work and were impressed with Ellen's achievement. On her second interview at this company, the director of information systems asked to see some of her work. Ellen showed him a demo of U-PAY along with some of the code she had written for the system. U-PAY was written for the most part in the computer language PL/1. The director was convinced that Ellen was a consummate PL/1 programmer and he was quite eager to have her on his staff. He offered her an annual salary of $80,000 (she was making only $63,000 at Apollo) along with the title of associate director.

During this final meeting when this generous offer was made, the director indicated to Ellen that her first assignment would be to build a system "similar to U-PAY." He also pointed out that since she had already done this at Apollo, she should be able to expedite this project and complete it within a "pretty short time frame." The more he discussed this topic the more Ellen realized the implication of his remarks. The only way a project of this scope could be completed in such a short period of time would be to borrow heavily from her previous work. To be sure, if Ellen used the same design specs she used at Apollo and certain modules of PL/1 code, she could indeed finish the project within a year or so.

When the meeting ended she thanked the director for his offer and told him that she would get back to him with an answer within 24 hours. Ellen was delighted about the high salary and the new title, but she did have some reservations about "borrowing" so much of the work she had done at Apollo. She decided, however, to accept the offer. She also mentioned to her new boss that she would definitely be able to meet his timetable for a new accounts payable system.

Before giving her termination notice at Apollo Ellen made copies of the U-PAY design specs and the PL/1 source code that she and her team had written. Her superiors were sorry to see her go but they did not make a counteroffer. Ellen was not surprised. She would be quite happy to leave this ungrateful employer.

As she worked late this rainy night just three days before her final day at Apollo, she thought of her decision to take with her the design specifications and source code of the U-PAY system. Occasionally she felt some guilt over this decision, but her guilt was assuaged by her firm conviction that this was *her* work and that she had as much right to it as Apollo. Also, she would not be depriving Apollo of anything. This was a generic application that did not involve any competitive information. As long as Apollo had an efficient U-PAY system, what difference did it make if another company, even a competitor, had the same thing? Where was the harm? Also, she knew full well that this was a common practice among software engineers. She wasn't the only one leveraging the knowledge and experience that had been gained at a former employer. After all, she reasoned, that is the way the game is played these days.

Ellen sipped her Diet Coke as she continued coding the latest series of enhancements to the revised U-PAY system. She was looking forward to her last day on Friday and the going away lunch that her colleagues had planned for her.

Case 3.4 Doric Conversion Technologies, Inc.

Peter Johnson was late for the software engineering staff meeting in the main conference room. Staff meetings were held each Monday at 3:00 P.M. and despite his best efforts Peter always seemed to be late, much to the annoyance of the vice president of product development who routinely ran this meeting.

But this time Peter had a good reason for his tardiness. He had been engaged in a heated exchange with someone in the marketing department about discontinuing an important software product. As he entered the conference room, the meeting fell silent. Peter took his seat and the VP's assistant shot a manila folder across the glimmer of the table. It contained the agenda and supporting documentation for what looked like another long and tedious meeting. As things got underway again, Peter kept thinking about his latest run-in with marketing.

Doric Conversion Technologies was a major producer of conversion tools for mainframe and minicomputer software products. Under Peter's leadership, Doric had recently developed a conversion tool for a prominent database company that converted data and programs from version 4 to version 5 of its Data Base Productivity (DBP) software package. Version 5 of this popular DBP product represented a major upgrade. As a result, programs and applications written in version 4 could not be used for version 5 without being subjected to a conversion utility. Doric's product, which was sold directly to DBP customers, was designed to provide for a conversion of their applications expediently and efficiently.

This product had been on the market for one and a half years and had been a reasonable commercial success. Approximately 58 percent of the DBP customer base had converted to version 5 and almost all of them had purchased the Doric conversion tool. The database company's customer base was approximately 4,500 clients. This meant that Doric had sold about 2,600 copies of its conversion utility at a price of $8,500 each.

Cynthia Wilson was Doric's marketing director, and she was responsible for marketing and selling Doric's rather full product line. She typically had the final say in the company about product longevity. The company sold many types of conversion products that usually had a short life cycle. Cynthia was convinced that the life cycle of this product had just about run its course. If Doric customers had not converted by now, she reasoned, most of them would be quite loath to convert to version 5 in the near future because they lacked either the resources or interest to invest in this upgrade. In her view, it was not worthwhile to continue marketing, selling, or supporting this product.

The implementation of these conversion utilities such as the one for DBP was usually complicated and hence required help from the Doric technical support staff. Cynthia intended to inform DBP customers this week that support for this conversion utility would be eliminated within the next month. This might provide a major incentive for those few clients who had not yet converted. After that point she was unwilling to supply even limited support for this product. In addition, the company had almost run out of manuals and she did not want to assume the expense of a reprint.

Peter was convinced that the termination of this product was premature. He pointed out that similar Doric tools were given a much longer life cycle and that many DBP customers would buy the product eventually; many "old-time" users he spoke with told him that they would be making the conversion but could not do so at the present time. Thus, Peter believed that the prospects were promising for selling the conversion tool to a fairly large portion of the remaining 1,900 users of DBP who were still running version 4. Potential revenues could be millions of dollars. In his meeting with Cynthia he advocated a more intense marketing approach in collaboration with the database company. But his plan for more aggressive marketing was rejected by Cynthia and her boss. Her preference was to invest Doric's scarce marketing and customer support resources in newer and potentially more profitable products. Further, there was a great deal of turnover in the customer support department and she did not want to spend time teaching new analysts about the DBP conversion tool.

As Peter listened to his fellow engineers ramble on during the staff meeting, he had an idea about how to deal with this problem and take advantage of an opportunity that was being carelessly discarded by Doric. Peter reasoned that he could sell the product himself. Perhaps he could start his own company that would initially be devoted to the sale of this conversion program. He could market the product on his own and provide the necessary support. "After all," he thought, "I was the key person in developing this product and I know more about it than almost anyone else at Doric." Peter had been the project manager for this conversion tool and had supervised the engineering team responsible for its development. Also, as with most of Doric's other products, this particular product had no copyright or patent protection. The company's executives felt that this was unnecessary (and expensive) given the product's limited usefulness and short life cycle. Employees did sign nondisclosure agreements which prevented them from using Doric's technology for their own personal gain either while employed at Doric or for two years after they departed from the company. The following is an excerpt from that agreement:

> I hereby assign to the Company my entire right title and interest in any processes, techniques, know-how (whether in written, schematic or any other form) or idea, patentable or not, including without limitation any software and software documentation, made or conceived or reduced to practice or learned by me, either alone or jointly with others, during the period of my employment.

However, through an oversight, Peter and many other veteran employees of Doric never signed such an agreement. As a consequence, there did not appear to be any legal restrictions against appropriating this product and selling it on his own.

After the meeting ended, Peter returned to his small and crowded corner office overlooking Tottem Pond. The more he thought about this proposal, the more convinced he became that it was quite feasible. Peter figured that he could make necessary preparations for this during the next month while Doric was still selling and supporting the product.

And once it was officially discontinued, he would resign from Doric and sell the product through his own company. Of course, DBP clients could still buy the product from Doric after this point, but they would not get support or documentation. As a consequence the product would not be very useful under these circumstances. But Peter's company would provide both ample documentation and the necessary support. Thus, he would be competing with Doric but the provision of these vital services would give him a significant advantage.

Despite his upbeat attitude about the prospects for success, Peter did have some ethical reservations about this grand plan. He was apprehensive about telling Doric of his intentions, since he was fairly sure that they would not give him permission to execute this idea. When a colleague had approached the company about a similar scheme a year ago, the president emphatically refused to even consider his proposal. On the other hand, why should he allow this product to languish when it could still generate appreciable revenues? Was there anything really wrong with selling a product that Doric had abandoned? Peter needed to address these questions more carefully before making a final decision about this risky venture.

Case 3.5 Note on Software Compatibility and Reverse Engineering

> . . . the public at large remains free to discover and exploit the trade secret through reverse engineering of products in the public domain or by independent development.[12]

INTRODUCTION

In his popular bestseller *Being Digital,* Nicholas Negroponte echoes the widespread frustration with current copyright and patent protection for software programs: "Copyright law is totally out of date. It is a Gutenberg artifact. Since it is a reactive process, it will probably have to break down completely before it is corrected."[13] This sentiment is shared by users and producers alike who have been surprised by recent landmark judicial rulings in cases such as *Lotus v. Borland* or *Apple v. Microsoft*.

The software industry itself is sharply divided on the scope of intellectual property protection. On the one side are those who underscore the need for open standards and for compatibility between various hardware systems and software programs. Hence they advocate limited and narrow intellectual property protection. Many users and new entrants in the industry would fall in this category.

On the other hand, established software companies oppose this view, claiming that such narrow protection will ultimately stifle investment in new product development. As a result they "work to prevent innovators from making compatible software and hardware; not wanting standards, they fight to maintain rigidly proprietary systems and equipment, an approach that locks out competition."[14] This was the position adopted by Lotus in their protracted intellectual property dispute with Borland, a company which sought to market a spreadsheet similar to Lotus 1-2-3 called Quattro Pro. Companies such as Lotus do not want similar products and they regard reverse engineering and the development of compatible products as equivalent to theft of their property. Hence they seek broad copyright protection.

It is clear that federal copyright law protects not only the *source code* (the lines of computer code written in a high-level language such as COBOL, BASIC, or C), but also the *object code* (the binary code created when the source code is compiled) of programs. Thus, copyright infringement would occur if a programmer copied lines of source code and then sold them as his own program. Likewise, infringement occurs if someone makes duplicate copies of the finished product instead of purchasing or licensing their own copy. What is less clear is whether or not copyright laws are infringed if someone copies the logic, command sequence, general design, or "look and feel" of the program but embodies this in his or her own source code. The key question is this: What is protected beyond the actual source code? If a software program is developed that looks and functions like another software program even though no source code has been copied, has there been any copyright infringement? Also, what methods can be employed, short of copying source code, to ensure that one's software program will work on a specific hardware system?

The crux of the debate, then, can be expressed in terms of *compatibility*, that is, compatibility between two versions of a software product (such as a spreadsheet or database) and compatibility between software and a hardware platform. The key moral question seems to be whether or not there is an inherent contradiction between product compatibility and copyright protection. Among the specific issues that have been in dispute, two stand out as especially prominent:

1. How much similarity can there be between two programs in the screen interface and the command structure?

2. To what lengths can companies go to develop programs that are interoperable with a hardware system? Are companies entitled to reverse-engineer a product?

We will consider two specific disputes which illustrate both of these issues: the *Lotus v. Borland* case and the *Sega Ltd. v. Accolade, Inc.* case. Both of these cases provoke difficult questions about fairness, and the scope of intellectual property protection for software products.

LOTUS V. BORLAND

Borland International, Inc., located in Scotts Valley, California, was a major software producer known for its database and spreadsheet products along with programming tools and languages. It was founded in 1984 by entrepreneur Phillipe Kahn and grew quite rapidly. By 1991 its sales had increased to $226 million, up from $91 million in 1989. Also, in 1991 Borland acquired Ashton-Tate, the producer of the popular dBASE product, and this gave it a dominant position in the PC database market. During the mid-1990s, as the result of some management mistakes, Borland began to struggle. In 1994 its revenues declined sharply, and it posted a $45 million loss.

In the early 1990s Borland introduced a much delayed version of its spreadsheet product called Quattro Pro (QP). The product was available for DOS or Windows operating systems. But QP mimicked some of the commands used in the Lotus 1-2-3 spreadsheet. Borland assumed that it could copy functional features of other products (such as 1-2-3) without infringing on any copyright protection. Lotus, however, a pioneer in the $1 billion spreadsheet market, almost immediately sued Borland for copyright infringement. The Cambridge, Massachusetts company had once been the dominant player in the spreadsheet marketplace for many years; its market share in spreadsheets for DOS operating systems was about 89 percent. Hence the company had sought to defend its turf from the encroachment of Borland's new product.

At issue in this case was the protectability of Lotus's command structures. Lotus alleged in its lawsuit that Borland copied its command menus. Those menus included basic commands such as Print, Quit, File, Save, and so on. It maintained that the order of these commands in its pull-down menus was a creative decision that should be copyrightable. In addition, Quattro Pro accepted the same keystrokes as Lotus 1-2-3, and this meant that QP had the same "feel" as the Lotus program. For instance in both programs the "@" key is used to initiate a formula.

Thus, "Lotus was the first software developer to make an explicit look and feel claim in a copyright litigation about user interfaces."[15]

The other famous "look and feel" case was *Apple v. Microsoft.* In that case Apple alleged that the Microsoft Windows user interface copied the look and feel of the Apple Computer user interface. Apple contended in its lawsuit that Windows was a blatant infringement of its copyrights, especially the copyright covering the on-screen display of overlapping windows. Further, Apple argued that the graphic elements of its popular user interface (such as the use of the trash can icon) should be afforded protection from imitative products such as Windows. Apple lost a series of federal trial court rulings and in February 1995 the Supreme Court refused to hear the case, thereby handing Apple a final defeat in this hotly contested copyright suit.

In contrast to Apple Computer, Lotus was triumphant in the first round of its legal confrontation with Borland. In July 1992 Judge Robert E. Keeton enjoined Borland from selling its Quattro Pro product with its Lotus 1-2-3 compatible menus. According to the judge's opinion, "Borland copied copyrightable elements of 1-2-3 that constitute a substantial part of that program. Lotus has sued and Borland is liable."[16] Emboldened by this court victory Lotus immediately went on the offensive. It ran ads in major newspapers and trade publications with the headline

There's nothing innovative
about copying.
Lotus innovated. Borland copied.

Lotus defended its lawsuit in this ad, observing that Borland's copying was analogous to someone plagiarizing *The Grapes of Wrath,* changing the ending, and calling it a new novel. For Lotus, Borland's copying of its commands and keystrokes was tantamount to the pilfering of its creative work. Borland, on the other hand, maintained that the arrangement of commands was functional "because it was done to accord with predicted frequency of use."[17] The company also contended that it was unfair to disallow interface similarities and thereby undermine product compatibility that is a significant convenience for end users.

In March 1995, Borland was vindicated as a federal appeals court overturned Judge Keeton's ruling on behalf of Lotus. It ruled that Quattro Pro did not infringe Lotus's copyright on its 1-2-3 product by copying menus of computer commands. The court ruled that the commands are "methods of operation" and hence cannot be copyrighted. The ruling came just in time for this beleaguered company, since most analysts predicted that Borland would be forced to file for bankruptcy if it had to pay damages to Lotus. Lotus was in a quandary about whether or not to appeal this ruling to the U.S. Supreme Court, but ultimately its lawyers convinced the company that it would have good chance of winning such an appeal. The case was appealed and in January 1996, much to the dismay of Lotus, the U.S. Supreme Court affirmed Borland's victory in an unusual 4–4 vote. However, according to Hayes, "that decision won't provide formal national guidelines . . . of which parts of a software application can be imitated by competitors, [because] the Supreme Court was deadlocked [and] the ruling will only be binding in the 1st Circuit where the case was originally filed."[18]

Clearly, the message of the ruling is that commands themselves and the order and sequence of those commands are not subject to copyright protection. The decision, coming so quickly on the heels of the *Apple* ruling, was also another setback for the position that the look and feel of a program should be protected under copyright law.

But there are some lingering and unresolved questions here. Is it fair and equitable to imitate another program's command structure or is this analogous to plagiarism as Lotus has claimed? This ruling has made it easier for the software industry to develop compatible software and common interfaces. But is such compatibility in any way a form of theft as some companies contend? Finally, how does society achieve a balance between the interests of innovators and the needs of copiers, and how should this be embodied in the law?

REVERSE ENGINEERING: *SEGA V. ACCOLADE*

The controversial technique of reverse engineering has become especially popular in the video game industry. The stakes are high since a top video game can generate hundreds of millions of dollars in revenues and profits. For example, in 1994 sales for the video game Mortal Kombat II were $220 million, even though the game was only introduced in October in time for Christmas sales. According to the *Economist*, the worldwide home video game market was about $20 billion, "of which about two-thirds represents the games themselves and one-third the machines they are played on."[19] Thus there is a powerful incentive to develop a hit game on as many hardware platforms as possible.

The industry is dominated by two Japanese companies, Nintendo and Sega. Both companies have developed proprietary systems so that game cartridges that do not conform to the right specifications will not work on their consoles. Both companies relied on lockout mechanisms to preclude the use of unauthorized cartridges.

But in this industry there is a perceived "right" to reverse-engineer whenever there is no other way to get specifications that will allow a company to develop a game that is compatible with a specific hardware platform. The only other alternative is to pay stiff licensing fees to hardware vendors. Thus, for instance, Atari decided that it would manufacture and market Nintendo-compatible games without a license from Nintendo. And Accolade decided to do the same thing for Sega hardware.

Before considering the methods developed to implement this decision it is instructive to discuss the equity of reverse engineering. Is it acceptable, for example, that Atari sell Nintendo-compatible games without a Nintendo license? Atari and Accolade would obviously answer this question in the affirmative and the basis of their rationale is the desirability of free competition and the benefits open competition brings to the consumer. But Nintendo believed that it should be able to establish the terms for those companies that were developing the games for its consoles. Nintendo and Sega wanted only quality games to run on their consoles and hence sought to control the selection of their game developers. Many of those developers, however, regarded the exclusivity clause as too restrictive (for a two-year period the game developer agreed not to adapt the game for other hardware systems.) Hence the impasse and a resort to reverse-engineering techniques.

There are several ways to "reverse-engineer" a product. The general method involves the use of a reverse compiler that can reproduce at least some semblance of the original source code from the object code. Some legal scholars, such as Anthony Clapes, have expressed reservations about such techniques. According to Clapes, "We must recognize that 'reverse engineering' is a term that makes no real sense when applied to software."[20] The technique used in this case is called disassembly whereby the object code is translated into a readable language. The object code is decompiled using a special program, and in the process a copy of the translated object code must be made. One bone of contention in copyright disputes is whether making this intermediate copy is legitimate. Or does it constitute copyright infringement?

This question was surely at the core of the tense dispute between Accolade Inc. and Sega Enterprises, Ltd. Accolade, Inc., located in San Jose, California, is a major producer of video games. Its most popular game was known as Ishido: The Way of Stones. It had made games for Sega equipment for some time and had never experienced compatibility problems. But its games would not work with Sega's new Genesis consoles due to the lockout mechanism. In order to remedy this problem the company disassembled a Genesis console and reverse-engineered a few of Sega's game cartridges in order to decipher the key to the lockout mechanism.

Through disassembly of Sega's object code Accolade discovered the correct setup code and learned how to circumvent the lockout security mechanism that prevented foreign cartridges from working in the Sega console. With this vital information in hand Accolade was able to program its games to be compatible with Genesis systems.

Sega quickly sued Accolade, claiming that Accolade's disassembly had infringed its copyright. Sega sought and won an immediate preliminary injunction. According to *Business Week* in April 1992, "the U.S. District Court in San Francisco issued a preliminary injunction . . . that pulled six Accolade Inc.'s video games off the market and kept it from introducing eight more."[21] Judge Barbara Caulfield ruled that this type of reverse engineering predicated on disassembly was an infringement of property rights. Judge Caulfield also rejected Accolade's claim that this disassembly was fair use, since it was the only way to achieve compatibility. She pointed out that only certain forms of reverse engineering are permissible, especially the technique known as "peeling a chip."[22] In this time-consuming method a company can essentially peel off the top layer of the microchip and then make a copy of the object code. Some critics of this ruling noted that Accolade would still have to disassemble that object code in order to find the key to the lockout mechanism. They also argued that if the ruling stood, it would establish an unhealthy trend of restricting access to various hardware platforms which would seriously impair the software industry.

Accolade, of course, appealed this decision, arguing that its copying of the object code was not copyright infringement since the final product was not similar to the game console. It further argued that any disassembly of the Sega console was fair use. Accolade's attorneys also argued that when a product embodies an interface standard that cannot be circumvented, software developers must have the right to use whatever method is necessary to make their products interoperable with that standard.

The Ninth Circuit Court of Appeals found these arguments to be compelling and it ruled in favor of Accolade, overturning Judge Caulfield's decision. In so doing it also ruled in favor of a wider scope of reverse-engineering techniques. The court concluded that "disassembly of a computer program in order to gain an understanding of the unprotected functional elements of the program was a fair use when the person seeking the understanding has a legitimate reason for doing so and when no other means of access to the unprotected element exists. . . ."[23]

Despite this decision in *Sega v. Accolade*, the debate continues in some circles on the suitability of reverse engineering. Sega argued that they were not fairly treated by the Appeals Court. In their brief for the appeal Sega had claimed that "Accolade took a 'free ride' on [Sega's] hugely expensive research and development efforts. . . ."[24] How plausible was this argument? Is reverse engineering as pernicious as Anthony Clapes and the protectionists maintain? Should software products be better protected against the advances of competitors anxious to peek at proprietary code? If so, how can we have greater compatibility and common standards? Further, what are the economic implications of tighter property protections and restrictions on reverse engineering?

Finally, there are moral as well as legal issues at stake here. Is it *ethically proper* to engage in reverse engineering, to disassemble a console's object code to make compatible products so as to avoid paying the owner any licensing fees or other compensation? Moreover, what are the limits of such reverse-engineering techniques—should programmers be allowed to use *any* reverse-engineering techniques or are there moral constraints that should prevail here?

NOTES

1. M. Betts, "Dirty Rotten Scoundrels," *Computerworld* (22 May 1995), p. 1
2. H. Nissenbaum, "Should I Copy My Neighbor's Software," in *Computers, Ethics, and Social Values*, ed. D. Johnson and H. Nissenbaum (Upper Saddle River, NJ: Prentice Hall, 1995), pp. 201–213.
3. A.M. Honore, "Ownership," in A.G. Guest, ed., *Oxford Essays in Jurisprudence* (Oxford: Oxford University Press, 1961), p. 108.
4. 17 U.S.C.S. §102 (2001).
5. Source code represents the lines of computer code written in a high-level language such as COBOL, PL-1, PASCAL, etc.; the object code is the machine-readable binary code created when the source code is compiled.
6. R. Spinello, "An Ethical Evaluation of Web Site Linking," *Computers and Society* 30, no. 4 (December 2000), pp. 25–32.
7. P. Steidlmeier, "The Moral Legitimacy of Intellectual Property Claims: American Business and Developing Country Perspectives," *Journal of Business Ethics* (December 1993), pp. 161–162.
8. R. Stallman, "Why Software Should be Free," publication of the Free Software Foundation, Inc., 1990.
9. Ibid.
10. G. Anthes, "Piracy on the Rise; Companies Fear Liability," *Computerworld* (18 April 1994), p. 12
11. B. Carton, "Judge Drops Charges Against Student Who Ran Service for Software Pirates," *The Wall Street Journal*, (30 December 1994), p. B3.

12. *Bonito Boats, Inc. v. Thunder Craft Boats, Inc.*, 109 Sup. Ct. 971 (1989).
13. N. Negroponte, *Being Digital* (New York: Alfred A. Knopf, 1995), p. 58.
14. G. Davis, "War of the Words: Intellectual Property Laws and Standardization," *IEEE Micro* (December 1993), p. 19.
15. P. Samuelson, "The Ups and Downs of Look and Feel," *Communications of the ACM* (April 1993), p. 34.
16. *Lotus Development Corp. v. Borland International, Inc.*, 799 F. Supp. 203 D. Mass. (1992).
17. Samuelson, "Ups and Downs," p. 34.
18. F. Hayes, "Borland Victory Leaves a Murky Wake," *Computerworld* (January 22, 1996), p. 4.
19. "The Christmas Video Game Massacre," *Economist* (19 November 1994), p. 71.
20. A. Clapes, *The Softwars* (Westport, CT: Quorum Books, 1993), p. 145.
21. R. Brandt, "Bit by Bit, Software Protection is Eroding," *Business Week,* 20 July 1992, p. 87.
22. Cf. *Sega Enterprises, Ltd. v. Accolade, Inc.*, 785 F. Supp. 1392 (N.D. Cal.) rev'd. 977 F. 2d 1510 9th Cir. (1992).
23. Ibid.
24. Quoted in J. Band and M. Katoh, *Interfaces on Trial* (Boulder, CO: Westview Press, 1995), p. 194.

4

Intellectual Property Issues II: Digital Music, Interconnectivity, and Trespass

INTRODUCTION

This second chapter devoted to the theme of intellectual property issues covers some of the salient property disputes that have occurred so far in cyberspace. The broad themes suggested by these cases include the nature and scope of intellectual property rights on the Web, "virtual" trespass, fair use, and copyright infringement. Many of the issues discussed in these cases arise thanks to the phenomenon of interconnectivity, the ease by which users can connect and link to different sites on the World Wide Web.

According to some legal scholars, one of the disturbing trends in Internet litigation cases is the frequent allegation of trespass. Some organizations are quick to claim that they are victims of trespass whenever they detect unwelcome activities on their respective Web sites. According to Dan Burk, an "unqualified exclusionary right in the form of trespass" will cause serious problems for the free flow of information in cyberspace. Under such an exclusionary rule, "the imposition of myriad proprietary rights effectively fragments the network, allowing sites that have been physically connected to the network to segregate themselves legally from the network."[1] On the other hand, Web sites do exhibit some qualities of intellectual property, and property rights have traditionally included a "right to exclude."

We begin this chapter with a consideration of digital music and the now infamous Napster case. Just as many individuals are apparently uninhibited about copying software (see Chapter 3), they are also uninhibited about copying digital music even when it is protected by a copyright. For the music industry Napster was a villain for making this copying so easy, but for many college students Napster emerged as the "Robin Hood" of the Web, making available reams of music that they could not otherwise afford to purchase. While Napster was defeated in the courts, some contend that this company's intermediary status should have protected it from allegations of copyright infringement. Was Napster's defense of fair use a legitimate one from either a moral or legal perspective? How can digital music be protected in the future in a way that respects fair use? What is the future of copyright in cyberspace?

The second case in this chapter is about a small company called Ditto.com. This company operates a visual engine that enables users to search for images that have been assembled from different Web sites. Some copyright holders, however, objected to this practice. Is this company simply exploiting the weblike structure of the Internet in a positive way or has it violated any intellectual property rights?

The *Ticketmaster v. Microsoft* case is also about the general issue of interconnectivity. Microsoft's Seattle Sidewalk Web site linked directly to a subordinate Web page within the Ticketmaster site and therefore bypassed the home page with all its advertising. Has the company violated the protocol for linking? What is the responsible way to link from one Web site to another? Do restrictions on linking impede navigation in cyberspace?

In the hypothetical case called "Metatags and Search Engine Baiting" we consider the technology of metatags. A metatag is a piece of HTML code that describes the contents of a Web page. Because metatags are invisible to consumers, the potential for mischief is magnified. In this case, Kitchens&More uses a competitor's brand name in its keyword metatag in order to lure users to its site. Is this commercial fair play or does it constitute misappropriation of the competitor's trademark property?

At issue in this case about metatag use is the scope of trademark protection. A trademark is a word, phrase, or symbol that concisely identifies a product or service. Typical trademarks include the Nike "swoosh" symbol, names like Coca-Cola and UPS, and logos such as the famous bitten apple image crafted by Apple Computer. According to the terms of the Federal Trademark Act of 1946 (the Lanham Act), trademarks are generally violated in one of three ways: infringement, unfair competition, and dilution. Infringement, which is the issue in this case, occurs when a registered trademark is used by someone else in connection with the sale of its goods or services.

The final case study of the chapter, "Spiders at the Auction," is about eBay's efforts to restrict its popular Web site from "bots" or spiders that crawl through the site to collect auction data. Does this action amount to trespass as eBay has alleged? If such action is regarded as a form of trespass, what would be the broader implications for the Internet?

Case 4.1 The Napster Case

I'm fighting for freedom
Trade Laws? We don't need 'em
Especially when living
In the Information Age

—Lyrics to Napster's theme song

When Shawn Fanning dropped out of Northeastern University in January 1999 to write the Napster software program, he could not have anticipated the controversy this program would soon engender. Shawn was bored at Northeastern, but he became fascinated by searching for music files in cyberspace. This was a difficult process, so Shawn decided to develop software with better search functionality. Napster is a protocol that allows users to locate and share music files over the Internet. Thanks to the Napster program users who want to obtain a "containerless" music file in MP3 format[2] can search for that file and then download it onto their hard drive once it has been located. When Napster first appeared, it was lionized as "the most important application since the Web browser."[3] But in the summer of 2001 the flow of music came to an abrupt halt as a result of lawsuits by the Recording Industry Association of America (RIAA) and the rock group Metallica. This case chronicles Napster's business strategy along with its protracted legal battles, and it also considers the ethical issues raised by the Web-based distribution of digital music.

THE MUSIC INDUSTRY

Thanks to the Internet, the $40 billion commercial music industry is facing an unprecedented set of challenges. The industry has been an oligopoly, dominated by the five majors: Sony, Warner Brothers, Universal, EMI, and BMG. They control about 85 percent of the market for recorded music in the United States. Their general expertise has been in marketing—discovering a talent and working through different channels to make that talent a star. The labels have created many "pop stars" including Britney Spears and the Backstreet Boys.

The basic economics of the music business parallels those of other industries in the business of making intellectual products where the cost of reproduction is relatively low. It costs about 50 cents to produce a music CD, and most CDs now sell for about $16 to $18. But in addition to production expenses, that retail price must also cover the cost of marketing and distribution along with royalties to the artist and a markup for both the record producer and the retailer. Royalties to the performers typically average about $1.30 per CD (before various deductions for their share of production expenses, etc.).

The Internet threatens this model as it creates opportunities for artists who are not fortunate enough to sign record contracts with companies like Sony. The Internet is a catalyst for change because it enables disintermediation, that is, artists can sell their wares directly to the consumer without intermediates like the major recording companies. Any young music group or artist can record their music and sell it over their own Web site. Once a legitimate purchase has been made, the CD can easily be downloaded to the consumer's hard drive. This new paradigm for selling music could eliminate the need for mass production of CDs. It also implies that retailers would no longer need to carry big inventories of recordings. Selling and distributing music over the Web eliminate the expense and inefficiencies associated with the physical sale and distribution of music. The Internet can therefore easily replace the extensive physical infrastructure of the music industry.

The record companies themselves have been slow to adapt to this model for on-line distribution of digital music, but that is beginning to change. According to Mann, within a few years "listeners will rarely if ever drive to Tower Records for their music. Instead they will tap into a vast cloud of music on the Net."[4] Companies like Napster, however, have been far ahead of this trend as they seek to capitalize on the potential of this new technology.

COMPANY HISTORY

Once Shawn Fanning finished writing the software program, Napster began its fledgling operations on June 1, 1999 in San Mateo, California. The company initially received seed funding from John Fanning, Shawn's uncle, and several other investors. It then hired Eileen Richardson, a Boston venture capitalist, as its first CEO. A second round of money from "angel" investors residing in Silicon Valley was secured to keep the company afloat as it sought to build its user base.

The Napster service permitted users to obtain free MP3 files of popular music. Napster did not charge a subscription fee. The company aspired to transform its popular Web service into a source of revenue, but there did not appear to be a clear conception of a viable revenue model. Napster considered several potential sources of income. These included generating revenues through advertising and through the information which it could collect about the music tastes of its customers. Napster also reviewed the possibility of charging for sponsorships. Finally, it considered charging a monthly subscription fee for its service. One complaint of venture capitalists, who were approached about funding, was Napster's focus on its technology and its growing audience, but not on how it planned to generate a profit.

It did not take long for Napster to become an Internet phenomenon. Within days of going on-line Napster software was downloaded by several thousand people. By July 2000, it had over 21 million registered users; the company claimed that on any given evening at least 500,000 people were using their service. In the month of February 2001, the estimated number of songs downloaded from Napster peaked at over 2.5 billion. Napster became especially popular on college campuses where students quickly seized upon the opportunity to download their favorite songs. Hit songs like "U Remind Me" by rhythm and blues artist Usher could probably be located and downloaded in about five minutes.

Although the business side of the house got off to a shaky start, by late 1999 Napster seemed to be getting things in order. It had an experienced CEO, adequate funding, and a rapidly expanding user base. It was distracted, however, by lawsuits claiming that this music-sharing Web site facilitated copyright infringement on a massive scale. Napster executives had tried to anticipate the legal problems on its immediate horizon as it tried to get this company off the ground. According to *Business Week,* John Fanning, Napster's chief business strategist, claimed that he had read the U.S. Court of Appeals for the Ninth Circuit's rulings on copyright law. On the basis of his study of these rulings he concluded that copyright law was on the side of Napster. According to Fanning, "there is only a 10% chance that Napster could lose a court case."[5]

In the fall of 1999, Napster executives had met with representatives from the major record companies to discuss how they could cooperate in the distribution of digital music. The talks went poorly, however, thanks in part to Richardson's "abrasive style."[6] As a result, any chance of reaching a compromise with the music industry appeared to be lost. In December 1999 the Recording Industry Association of America (RIAA) filed suit for copyright infringement, demanding that Napster pay damages of $100,000 each time a song was copied. In April 2000 the rock band Metallica also sued Napster for contributory copyright infringement and racketeering. Mettalica was enraged that its music was being moved around the Net and downloaded without its permission, so the group filed suit according to its drummer Lars Ulrich "to put Napster out of business."[7]

Napster executives began to worry as expenses mounted and its funding ran low. But in May 2000 it received $15 million from Hummer Winblad, a Silicon Valley venture capitalist. Around the same time Richardson resigned and Hank Barry, a partner at Hummer Winblad, was brought in as the new CEO. Barry made strong efforts to build up Napster's management team, hiring former A&M Records executive Milton Olin as its chief operating officer. The company's legal problems, however, began to engulf its operations and interfere with Barry's plans for the future. By July 2000 all eyes at corporate headquarters were on a California district court where a key decision was imminent in the RIAA's suit.

THE NAPSTER ARCHITECTURE

Peer-to-peer technology differs from the traditional client-server model where content is provided by a centralized system (server) to the user (client). Peer-to-peer is a more decentralized approach to computing that allows for direct interactions and information sharing among personal computers. Napster is considered to be a modified peer-to-peer service since its users engage in direct file sharing with one another. But unlike other peer-to-peer programs, a Napster server functions as an intermediary with a centralized directory of downloadable music.

In order to copy MP3 files through the Napster system, the user must first download the MusicShare software from the Napster Web site, http://www.napster.com. Once the user has downloaded that free software, he or she is ready to make full use of Napster as long as they register with a username and a password.

If users want to make their music available to other Napster users, they must create a "user library" or directory on their hard drives. The user can then load the MP3 files into this directory. Finally, the names of these MP3 files, which are determined by the individual users, are uploaded to the main Napster server, while the content of those files remains on the user's hard drive. Registered Napster users can locate music files on the hard drives of other users through Napster's sophisticated search functionality. The Napster server contains a voluminous search index with a listing of the music titles stored on the systems of its disparate users. The search process is simple: After logging into the MusicShare software, the user enters the name of a song or a music artist; this search request is processed by the Napster server which returns a list of all MP3 files that meet the search criteria. The user can then designate that he or she wants a certain MP3 file on this list. At this point the Napster server determines the Internet address of the user requesting the file and the address of the "host user," that is, the user who has the available MP3 file. The Napster server communicates the host user's address to the user requesting the MP3 file, a connection is established with the host user, and a copy of the host user's MP3 file is downloaded to the requesting user's system. The music can be played on the requesting user's system through Napster's software or through other available software programs.

THE RIAA LAWSUIT

From its inception Napster had been regarded as a formidable threat to the recording industry. The five major recording labels looked upon the Napster service as "large scale piracy and a serious threat to album sales."[8] The Napster program was characterized as one element in a "rogue computer network determined to bring down the entertainment industry."[9]

Accordingly, the recording industry set out to prevent the "Napster model" from growing and spreading. Several lawsuits were quickly filed against Napster but the most prominent one was submitted by the RIAA on behalf of the major recording companies: *A&M Records, Inc. et al. v. Napster Inc.* The RIAA petitioned the court for a preliminary injunction to prevent Napster from operating. On July 26, 2000 Judge Marilyn Patel of the federal district court in California granted the plaintiff's motion for a preliminary injunction. But several days later in a surprising turn of events, the United States Court of Appeals for the Ninth Circuit issued a temporary stay of that injunction pending an appeal. Oral arguments were heard before the Ninth Circuit Appeals Court in October 2000. Both sides presented convincing cases.

The plaintiffs argued that a majority of Napster users were downloading and uploading copyrighted music. They estimated that almost 90 percent of the music downloaded by Napster users was copyrighted by one of the recording labels that were a party to this lawsuit. These actions constituted direct infringement of the musical recordings owned by the plaintiffs. According to Section 106 of the copyright law, the copyright holder has exclusive rights of reproduction and distribution, and both these rights were clearly being violated by Napster users. Since Napster users were culpable of direct copyright infringement, Napster itself was liable for *contributory copyright infringement*. According to one legal precedent, "one who, with knowledge of the infringing activity, induces, causes, or materially contributes to the infringing conduct of another, may be held liable as a 'contributory' infringer."[10] Napster was also accused of *vicarious copyright infringement* because it had the ability to control the direct infringer's actions and enjoyed financial benefits from those actions.

The music industry was particularly concerned about the precedent that had been established by this proliferation of unauthorized music with an underlying assumption that music should be free. In its main brief the RIAA summed up the problem quite clearly: "If the perception of music as a free good becomes pervasive, it may be difficult to reverse."[11]

In its defense, Napster's legal team led by David Boies presented several key arguments. It invoked the protection of the 1998 Digital Millenium Copyright Act (DMCA) which provides a "safe harbor" against liability for copyright infringement for intermediaries or "information location tools" (i.e., search engines). Napster contended that it was merely a search engine and therefore deserved to be protected by the DMCA. Napster also argued that a significant percentage of the system's use involved legally acceptable copying of music files. According to Napster, many songs were not copyrighted and others were being shared among users in a way that constituted fair use. According to trial documents, "Napster identifies three specific alleged fair uses: sampling, where users make temporary copies of a work before purchasing; space-shifting, where users access a sound recording through the Napster system that they already own in audio CD format; and permissive distribution of recordings by new and established artists."[12] There are four factors that help a court determine fair use: (1) the purpose and character of the use (for example, commercial use weighs against the claim of fair use); (2) the nature of the copyrighted work (for example, creative works receive more protection than factual ones); (3) the "amount and substantiality of the portion used" in relation to the work as a whole; (4) the effects of the use on the market for the work ("fair use, when properly applied, is limited to copying by others which does not materially impair the marketability of the work which is copied.")[13] All these factors are weighed together and decisions are made on a case by case basis.

Among the modes of fair use cited by Napster, "sampling" and "space shifting" deserve further comment. Napster argued that its users often downloaded MP3 files to sample their contents before making a decision about whether or not to make a purchase. Hence Napster's service helped promote sales of audio CDs. Space shifting occurs when a Napster user downloads MP3 files in order to listen to music they already own on an audio CD. Napster argued that its groundbreaking technology was analogous to the VCR. In the case of *Sony v. Universal,* the U.S. Supreme Court had held that VCRs did not infringe copyright since viewers were engaged in time shifting, that is, recording a television show for viewing at a later time. According to Stephanie Greene, "Relying on the Sony decision, Napster attempted to establish that its service has substantial noninfringing uses and that Napster users who download copyrighted music, like VCR users who record copyrighted television programming, are entitled to a fair use defense."[14]

Defenders and boosters of Napster also argued that industry sales did not seem to be suffering at all during the Napster years. Sales actually increased in 2000 and 2001, though others observed that this increase was a function of demographics: There had been a spike in the teenage population and this accounted for the larger volume of popular music being sold. Also there was additional evidence that Napster might be eating into CD sales. In May 2000 a company called Reciprocal released a study "showing that CD sales at stores near colleges—thought to be hotbeds of Napster users—had slipped slightly, whereas overall CD sales had risen."[15]

On February 12, 2001, the court of appeals handed down its ruling. The court essentially agreed with Judge Patel, claiming that Napster could be held liable for vicarious copyright infringement. According to the appeals court, "the district court correctly determined that Napster had the right and ability to police its system and failed to exercise that right to prevent the exchange of copyright material."[16] Napster had the capability to locate infringing material on its search indices and to block its users' access to that material.

The appeals court rejected Napster's fair use claims along with its argument that the DMCA offered it a "safe harbor," since subsection

512 (d) does not appear to protect contributory infringers. It found that sampling and space shifting are "commercial activities" that adversely affect the market for the record industry's products. According to the appeals court, "having digital downloads available for free on the Napster system necessarily harms the copyright holder's attempt to charge for the same downloads."[17]

As a consequence, the appeals court upheld Judge Patel's injunction with one modification regarding the scope of the injunction. Judge Patel had to impose some burden of proof on the five major record labels which were to identify copyrighted music and inform Napster that such music was being exchanged on their system. In summary, the court placed "the burden on plaintiffs to provide notice to Napster of copyrighted works and files containing such works available on the Napster system before Napster has the duty to disable access to the offending content."[18]

In March 2001 Napster agreed to implement a filtering system which would prevent copyrighted music from being exchanged on its system. In response, Judge Patel allowed Napster to continue operations as she ordered the recording companies to help Napster identify infringing material. As Napster began eliminating copyrighted MP3 files, its users departed in droves, and the number of songs downloaded fell to 360 million by May.

In the meantime Napster settled the suit with Mettalica. Although Mettalica was disconcerted by Napster's flouting of copyright law, some artists, such as American rock musician Courtney Love, were more sympathetic to Napster's objectives. According to Ms. Love, "Record companies stand between artists and their fans. We sign terrible deals with them because they control our access to the public. But in a world of total connectivity, record companies lose that control. . . . Artists can sell CDs directly to fans. We can make direct deals with thousands of other Websites and promote our music to millions of people that old record companies never touch."[19]

In July 2001 Napster discontinued its service so it could install new software that filters copyrighted files that were not authorized to be exchanged by its users. Judge Patel ordered that the system remain shut down until Napster could demonstrate that it was blocking all copyrighted material designated by the recording companies. The company promised to convert itself into a subscription service when it returned, assuming that it could work out a satisfactory arrangement with record labels and music publishers. While Napster's fate is still uncertain, some predict that it can never recover from these devastating setbacks.

APPENDIX TO CASE 4.1

Excerpts from Judge Marilyn Patel's ruling granting a preliminary injunction against Napster (July 26, 2000).

B. Proof of Direct Infringement

1. To prevail on a contributory or vicarious copyright infringement claim, a plaintiff must show direct infringement by a third party. See *Sony Corp. v. Universal City Studios, Inc.*, 464 U. S. 417, 434 (1984). As a threshold matter, plaintiffs in this action must demonstrate that Napster users are engaged in direct infringement.
2. Plaintiffs have established a prima facie case of direct copyright infringement. As discussed above, virtually all Napster users engage in the unauthorized downloading or uploading of copyrighted music; as much as eighty-seven percent of the files available on Napster may be copyrighted, and more than seventy percent may be owned or administered by plaintiffs.

C. Affirmative Defense of Fair Use and Substantial Non-Infringing Use

1. Defendant asserts the affirmative defenses of fair use and substantial non-infringing use. The latter defense is also known as the staple article of commerce doctrine. See *Sony*, 464 U. S. at 442. *Sony* stands for the rule that a manufacturer is not liable for selling a "staple article of commerce" that is "capable of commercially significant noninfringing uses." The Supreme Court also declared in *Sony*, "Any individual may reproduce a copyrighted work for a 'fair use'; the copyright holder does not possess the exclusive right to such a use." Defendant bears the burden of proving these affirmative defenses.
2. For the reasons set forth below, the court finds that any potential non-infringing use of the Napster service is minimal or connected to the infringing activity, or both. The substantial or commercially significant use of the service was, and continues to be, the unauthorized downloading and uploading of popular music, most of which is copyrighted.
3. Section 107 of the Copyright Act provides a non-exhaustive list of fair use factors. These factors include:
   (1) the purpose and character of the use, including whether such use is of a commercial nature or is for nonprofit educational purposes;
   (2) the nature of the copyrighted work;
   (3) the amount and substantiality of the portion used in relation to the copyrighted work as a whole; and

(4) the effect of the use upon the potential market for or value of the copyrighted work. [17 U. S. C. § 107.]

4. In the instant action, the purpose and character of the use militates against a finding of fair use. Ascertaining whether the new work transforms the copyrighted material satisfies the main goal of the first factor. See *Campbell v. Acuff-Rose Music, Inc.*, 510 U. S. 569, 579 (1994). Plaintiff persuasively argues that downloading MP3 files does not transform the copyrighted music. See *UMG Recordings, Inc. v. MP3.com, Inc.*, 92 F. Supp. 2d 349, 351 (S.D. N. Y. 2000) (concluding that repackaging copyrighted recordings in MP3 format suitable for downloading "adds no 'new aesthetics, new insights and understandings' to the original").
5. Under the first factor, the court must also determine whether the use is commercial. In *Acuff-Rose*, the Supreme Court clarified that a finding of commercial use weighs against, but does not preclude, a determination of fairness.
6. If a use is non-commercial, the plaintiff bears the burden of showing a meaningful likelihood that it would adversely affect the potential market for the copyrighted work if it became widespread.
7. Although downloading and uploading MP3 music files is not paradigmatic commercial activity, it is also not personal use in the traditional sense. Plaintiffs have not shown that the majority of Napster users download music to sell—that is, for profit. However, given the vast scale of Napster use among anonymous individuals, the court finds that downloading and uploading MP3 music files with the assistance of Napster are not private uses. At the very least, a host user sending a file cannot be said to engage in a personal use when distributing that file to an anonymous requester. Moreover, the fact that Napster users get for free something they would ordinarily have to buy suggests that they reap economic advantages from Napster use.
8. The court finds that the copyrighted musical compositions and sound recordings are creative in nature; they constitute entertainment, which cuts against a finding of fair use under the second factor.
9. With regard to the third factor, it is undisputed that downloading or uploading MP3 music files involves copying the entirety of the copyrighted work. The Ninth Circuit held prior to *Sony* that "wholesale copying of copyrighted material precludes application of the fair use doctrine." *Marcus v. Rowley*, 695 F. 2d 1171, 1176 (9th Cir. 1983).
10. The fourth factor, the effect on the potential market for the copyrighted work, also weighs against a finding of fair use. Plaintiffs have produced evidence that Napster use harms the market for their copyrighted musical compositions and sound recordings in at least two ways. First, it reduces CD sales among college students. Second, it raises barriers to plaintiffs' entry into the market for the digital downloading of music.
11. Defendant asserts several potential fair uses of the Napster service—including sampling, space-shifting, and the authorized distribution of new

artists' work. Sampling on Napster is not a personal use in the traditional sense that courts have recognized—copying which occurs within the household and does not confer any financial benefit on the user. See *Sony*, 464 U. S. at 423. Instead, sampling on Napster amounts to obtaining permanent copies of songs that users would otherwise have to purchase; it also carries the potential for viral distribution to millions of people. Defendant ignores critical differences between sampling songs on Napster and VCR usage in *Sony*. First, while "time-shifting [TV broadcasts] merely enables a viewer to see . . . a work which he ha[s] been invited to witness in its entirety free of charge," plaintiffs in this action almost always charge for their music—even if it is downloaded song-by-song. They only make promotional downloads available on a highly restricted basis. Second, the majority of VCR purchasers in *Sony* did not distribute taped television broadcasts, but merely enjoyed them at home. In contrast, a Napster user who downloads a copy of a song to her hard drive may make that song available to millions of other individuals, even if she eventually chooses to purchase the CD. So-called sampling on Napster may quickly facilitate unauthorized distribution at an exponential rate.

Defendant's argument that using Napster to sample music is akin to visiting a free listening station in a record store, or listening to song samples on a retail website, fails to convince the court because Napster users can keep the music they download. Whether or not they decide to buy the CD, they still obtain a permanent copy of the song. The global scale of Napster usage and the fact that users avoid paying for songs that otherwise would not be free militates against a determination the sampling by Napster users constitutes personal or home use in the traditional sense.

12. Even if the type of sampling supposedly done on Napster were a non-commercial use, plaintiffs have demonstrated a substantial likelihood that it would adversely affect the potential market for their copyrighted works if it became widespread. Plaintiffs claim three general types of harm: a decrease in retail sales, especially among college students; an obstacle to the record company plaintiffs' future entry into the digital downloading market; and a social devaluing of music stemming from its free distribution.
13. Any potential enhancement of plaintiffs' sales due to sampling would not tip the fair use analysis conclusively in favor of defendant. Indeed, courts have rejected the suggestion that a positive impact on sales negates the copyright holder's entitlement to licensing fees or access to derivative markets.

The court concludes that, even assuming the sampling alleged in this case is a non-commercial use, the record company plaintiffs have demonstrated a meaningful likelihood that it would adversely affect their entry into the online market if it became widespread. Moreover, it deprives the music publisher plaintiffs of royalties for individual songs. The unauthorized downloading of plaintiffs' music to sample songs would not constitute a fair use, even if it enhanced CD sales.

14. The court is also unconvinced that *Sony* applies to space-shifting. Defendant erroneously relies on the Ninth Circuit's assertion, in a case involving an inapplicable statute, that space-shifting constitutes non-commercial personal use. Defendant also implies that space-shifting music is sufficiently analogous to time-shifting television broadcasts to merit the protection of *Sony*. According to the gravely flawed Fader Report, space-shifting—like time-shifting—leaves the value of the copyrights unscathed because it does not displace sales. Defendant again cites Fader for the statistic that seventy percent of Napster users at least sometimes engage in space-shifting. In contrast, Jay opined that approximately forty-nine percent of her college-student survey respondents previously owned less than ten percent of the songs they downloaded, and about sixty-nine percent owned less than a quarter. See Jay Report. at 4, 21 & Tbl. 7. The court has already held that the Jay Report bears greater indicia of reliability than the Fader Report. Moreover, under either analysis, the instant matter is distinguishable from *Sony* because the Supreme Court determined in *Sony* that time-shifting represented the principal, rather than an occasional use of VCRs.
15. Defendant argues that, if space-shifting is deemed a fair use, the staple article of commerce doctrine precludes liability for contributory or vicarious infringement. Defendant fails to show that space-shifting constitutes a commercially significant use of Napster. Indeed, the most credible explanation for the exponential growth of traffic to the website is the vast array of free MP3 files offered by other users—not the ability of each individual to space-shift music she already owns. Thus, even if space-shifting is a fair use, it is not substantial enough to preclude liability under the staple article of commerce doctrine.
16. This court also declines to apply the staple article of commerce doctrine because, as paragraphs (D)(6) and (E)(2) of the legal conclusions explain, Napster exercises ongoing control over its service. In *Sony*, the defendant's participation did not extend past manufacturing and selling the VCRs: "[t] he only contact between Sony and the users of the Betamax occurred at the moment of sale" (*Sony*, 464 U. S. at 438). Here, in contrast, Napster, Inc. maintains and supervises an integrated system that users must access to upload or download files.
17. Nor do other potential non-infringing uses of Napster preclude contributory or vicarious liability. Defendant claims that it engages in the authorized promotion of independent artists, ninety-eight percent of whom are not represented by the record company plaintiffs. However, the New Artist Program may not represent a substantial or commercially significant aspect of Napster. The evidence suggests that defendant initially promoted the availability of songs by major stars, as opposed to "page after page of unknown artists." See 1 Frackman Dec., Exh. C (Parker Dep.) at 104: 16-105: 10, Exh. 235. Its purported mission of distributing music by artists unable to obtain record-label representation appears to have been

developed later. Other facts point to the conclusion that the New Artists Program was an afterthought, not a major aspect of the Napster business plan. Former CEO Eileen Richardson claimed in her deposition that she told the press Napster is not about known artists like Madonna. But, tellingly, discovery related to downloads by Napster executives reveals that Richardson's own computer contained about five Madonna files obtained using Napster. [See 1 Frackman Dec., Exh. A (Richardson Dep.) at 238: 2-240: 25.] Defendant did not launch the website aspect of its New Artist Program until after plaintiffs filed suit, and as recently as July 2000, bona fide new artists constituted a very small percentage of music available on Napster. In any event, Napster's primary role of facilitating the unauthorized copying and distribution established artists' songs renders *Sony* inapplicable.

18. Plaintiffs do not object to all of the supposedly non-infringing uses of Napster. They do not seek an injunction covering chat rooms or message boards, the New Artist Program or any distribution authorized by rights holders. Nor do they seek to enjoin applications unrelated to the music recording industry. Because plaintiffs do not ask the court to shut down such satellite activities, the fact that these activities may be non-infringing does not lessen plaintiffs' likelihood of success. The court therefore finds that plaintiffs have established a reasonable probability of proving third-party infringement.

D. Contributory Copyright Infringement

1. Once they have shown direct infringement by Napster users, plaintiffs must demonstrate a likelihood of success on their contributory infringement claim. A contributory infringer is "one who, with knowledge of the infringing activity, induces, causes, or materially contributes to the infringing conduct of another" [*Gershwin Publ'g Corp. v. Columbia Artists Management, Inc.*, 44 F. 2d 1159, 1162 (2d Cir. 1971)]. Courts do not require actual knowledge; rather, a defendant incurs contributory copyright liability if he has reason to know of the third party's direct infringement.
2. Plaintiffs present convincing evidence that Napster executives actually knew about and sought to protect use of the service to transfer illegal MP3 files. For example, a document authored by co-founder Sean Parker mentions the need to remain ignorant of users' real names and IP addresses "since they are exchanging pirated music." These admissions suggest that facilitating the unauthorized exchange of copyrighted music was a central part of Napster, Inc.'s business strategy from the inception. Plaintiffs also demonstrate that defendant had actual notice of direct infringement because the RIAA informed it of more than 12,000 infringing files.
3. The law does not require actual knowledge of specific acts of infringement. Accordingly, the court rejects defendant's argument that titles in the

Napster directory cannot be used to distinguish infringing from non-infringing files and thus that defendant cannot know about infringement by any particular user of any particular musical recording or composition.

4. Defendant's reliance on *Religious Technology Center v. Netcom Online Communication Services, Inc.*, 907 F. Supp. 1361 (N. D. Cal. 1995), does not alter the court's conclusion that plaintiffs have a reasonable likelihood of proving contributory liability. The cited passage from *Religious Technology Center* states: "Where a BBS [bulletin board service] operator cannot reasonably verify a claim of infringement, either because of a possible fair use defense, the lack of copyright notices on the copies, or the copyright holder's failure to provide the necessary documentation to show that there is likely infringement, the operator's lack of knowledge will be found reasonable and there will be no liability for contributory infringement for allowing the continued distribution of the works on its system."

   Napster is not an Internet Service Provider that acts as a mere conduit for the transfer of files. Rather, it offers search and directory functions specifically designed to allow users to locate music, the majority of which is copyrighted.
5. At the very least, defendant had constructive knowledge of its users' illegal conduct. Some Napster executives boast recording industry experience, [see 1Frackman Dec. (Richardson Dep.), Exh. 129 at ER00138], and defendant docs not dispute that it possessed enough sophistication about intellectual property laws to sue a rock band that copied its logo.
6. Plaintiffs have also shown that defendant materially contributed to the infringing activity. In *Fonovisa*, the owners of copyrights for musical recordings stated a contributory infringement claim against the operators of a swap meet at which independent vendors sold counterfeit recordings. The Ninth Circuit held the copyright owners' allegations were "sufficient to show material contribution" because "it would have been difficult for the infringing activity to take place in the massive quantities alleged without the support services provided by the swap meet." According to plaintiffs in the instant action, "Napster is essentially an Internet swap meet—more technologically sophisticated but in many ways indistinguishable from the [defendant] in *Fonovisa*." (Pl.'s Brief). The court largely agrees with this characterization. Unlike the swap meet vendors, Napster users offer their infringing music for free. However, defendant's material contribution is still analogous to that of the swap meet in *Fonovisa*. The swap meet provided support services like parking, booth space, advertising, and clientele. Here, Napster, Inc. supplies the proprietary software, search engine, servers, and means of establishing a connection between users' computers. Without the support services defendant provides, Napster users could not find and download the music they want with the ease of which defendant boasts.
7. Because they have made a convincing showing with regard to both the knowledge and material contribution elements, plaintiffs have established

a reasonable likelihood of success on their contributory infringement claims.

E. Vicarious Copyright Infringement

1. Even in the absence of an employment relationship, a defendant incurs liability for vicarious copyright infringement if he "has the right and ability to supervise the infringing activity and also has a direct financial interest in such activities." *Fonovisa*, 76 F. 3d at 262 (quoting *Gershwin*, 443 F. 2d at 1162).
2. In *Fonovisa*, the swap meet operator satisfied the first element of vicarious liability because it had the right to terminate vendors at will; it also controlled customers' access and promoted its services. Although Napster, Inc. argues that it is technologically difficult, and perhaps infeasible, to distinguish legal and illegal conduct, plaintiffs have shown that defendant supervises Napster use. Indeed, Napster, Inc. itself takes pains to inform the court of its improved methods of blocking users about whom rights holders complain. This is tantamount to an admission that defendant can, and sometimes does, police its service. Moreover, a defendant need not exercise its supervisory powers to be deemed capable of doing so. The court therefore finds that Napster, Inc. has the right and ability to supervise its users' infringing conduct.
3. Plaintiffs have shown a reasonable likelihood that Napster, Inc. has a direct financial interest in the infringing activity. Citing several non-governing cases from other districts, they contend that direct financial benefit does not require earned revenue, so long as the defendant has economic incentives for tolerating unlawful behavior. Although Napster, Inc. currently generates no revenue, its internal documents state that it "will drive [sic] revenues directly from increases in user base." The Napster service attracts more and more users by offering an increasing amount of quality music for free. It hopes to "monetize" its user base through one of several generation revenue models noted in the factual findings. This is similar to the type of direct financial interest the Ninth Circuit found sufficient for vicarious liability in *Fonovisa*, where the swap meet's revenues flowed directly from customers drawn by the availability of music at bargain basement prices. The ability to download myriad popular music files without payment seems to constitute the glittering object that attracts Napster's financially valuable user base.
4. Plaintiffs have shown a reasonable likelihood of success on their vicarious infringement claims.

F. Defendant's First Amendment Challenge

1. According to Napster, Inc., the requested injunction would impose a prior restraint on its free speech, as well as that of its users and the unsigned

artists that depend upon its service. This First Amendment argument centers on the fact that defendant offers an electronic directory, which does not itself contain copyrighted material.

2. Although an overbroad injunction might implicate the First Amendment, free speech concerns "are protected by and coextensive with the fair use doctrine" [*Nihon Keizai Shimbun, Inc. v. Comline Bus. Data, Inc.*, 166 F. 3d 65, 74 (2d Cir. 1999)]. This court has already determined that plaintiffs do not seek to enjoin any fair uses of the Napster service that are not completely contrived or peripheral to its existence.
3. The parties dispute the extent to which infringing and non-infringing aspects of the service are separable. Napster, Inc.'s interim CEO Hank Barry and Vice President of Engineering Edward Kessler both opine that the requested injunction would have the practical effect of compelling defendant to exclude all songs from its system, including those which plaintiffs do not own. In contrast, plaintiffs contend that Napster's New Artist Program, message boards, chat rooms, and file-sharing applications for business and scientific research would remain viable if the court granted the requested relief. Even if it is technologically impossible for Napster, Inc. to offer such functions as its directory without facilitating infringement, the court still must take action to protect plaintiffs' copyrights.

J. Irreparable Harm

1. Because plaintiffs have shown a reasonable likelihood of success on the merits of their contributory and vicarious copyright infringement claims, they are entitled to a presumption of irreparable harm.
2. The court rejects defendant's contention that it has rebutted this presumption by demonstrating that any harm is *de minimis*.

III. CONCLUSION

For the foregoing reasons, the court GRANTS plaintiffs' motion for a preliminary injunction against Napster, Inc. Defendant is hereby preliminarily ENJOINED from engaging in, or facilitating others in copying, downloading, uploading, transmitting, or distributing plaintiffs' copyrighted musical compositions and sound recordings, protected by either federal or state law without express permission of the rights owner. This injunction applies to all such works that plaintiffs own.

IT IS SO ORDERED.

Dated: July 26, 2000, MARILYN HALL PATEL Chief Judge, United States District Court

This excerpt has been take from *A&M Records, Inc. v. Napster, Inc.*, 114 F. Supp 2d 896 (N.D. Cal, [2000]).

Case 4.2 Ditto.Com

Ditto.com, a small company formerly known as Arriba Software, operates a popular visual search engine at the Web site www.ditto.com. In response to queries from users, Ditto.com will retrieve images instead of text. It produces a list of "thumbnail" pictures that are relevant to the user's query. While this functionality provides a valuable service to consumers, it has generated considerable controversy about the scope of intellectual property protection for on-line photographs and images.

Ditto.com's Web site includes a massive search index with over six million entries. Each entry is a thumbnail image that has been acquired through the use of Ditto's spider[20] which crawls its way through media Web sites that collect and store photographs or other images. According to the company's Web site, once the crawler does its work, "we then select, rank, weight, filter, and rate pictures, illustrations, clipart, photographs, drawings and other image-related material; next we index the images from the Web site."[21] All of this is done without the permission of the artist or photographer who created the image. When a user initiates a query, he or she receives the list of reduced thumbnail pictures ranked and in order of relevance. When the user clicks on one of these retrieved thumbnail images, two windows appear on the user's screen: The first is a stand-alone copy of a full-size image and the second contains the complete originating Web page where that image appeared.

The Ditto.com program presents two sets of problems for some artists and photographers. Some object to the fact that their works were indexed by Ditto.com without their knowledge or permission. They argue that when search engines like ditto.com display images without their permission and out of context, there is copyright infringement. There are also objections to Ditto's "deep linking" to the originating Web page for the image; this deep linking bypasses the home page which often includes advertisements and other promotional messages.

And there has been at least one lawsuit filed against Ditto.com. Leslie Kelly is a photographer from Huntington California who operates a Web site called www.goldrush1849.com. This site provides users with a virtual photographic tour of Sacramento and the California gold rush country. According to court documents, 35 of Kelly's photographs have been indexed in the Ditto.com image database with thumbnail versions made available to Ditto's users. Kelly filed suit for copyright infringement, arguing that Ditto.com had no right to copy and distribute his copyrighted photos without his explicit permission. In late 1999 a federal judge ruled in Ditto.com's favor, but the case has been appealed to the United States Court of Appeals for the Ninth Circuit.

At issue is whether the reduced size of the images (i.e., thumbnail versions) exempts them from copyright infringement. Specifically, is ditto.com's use of these images tantamount to "fair use"? In copyright law fair use is a limitation on the copyright owner's exclusive right "to reproduce the copyrighted work in copies."[22] There are four factors to be considered in a fair use decision:

1. Purpose and character of the use. (Is the use commercial or for nonprofit or educational purposes?; in general, there is a bias against commercial use.)
2. Nature of the copyrighted work. (Creative works tend to receive more protection than factual ones.)
3. Amount and "substantiality of the portion used in relation to the copyrighted work as a whole."
4. Effects on the potential market for the copyrighted work.[23]

In this controversial case, the judge concluded that search engine's activities amounted to "fair use" of the copyrighted images for several reasons. Judge Taylor concluded that while the use was commercial, "it was also of a somewhat more incidental and less exploitative nature than more traditional types of commercial use."[24] The judge also found that ditto.com's use was significantly transformative, that is, it adds something new or alters the original with a new expression. This is a highly significant factor given the Supreme Court's ruling in *Campbell v. Acuff-Rose*: "The more transformative the new work, the less will be the significance of other factors, like commercialism, that may weigh against a finding of fair use."[25] According to Judge Taylor, Ditto.com's use is notably different from the use for which the images were created: "Plaintiff's photographs are artistic works used for illustrative purposes. Defendant's visual search engine is designed to catalog and improve access to images on the Internet."[26] Judge Taylor also found that there would most likely not be a negative commercial impact since Ditto.com's activities would actually bring more users to the Web sites where the images are located. While factors (2) and (3) did weigh against the fair use defense, Judge Taylor felt that on the whole this case passed the fair use test especially because the "defendant's purposes were and are inherently transformative."[27]

Despite Judge Taylor's ruling, this case raises some nagging moral and legal questions. Is Ditto.com's functionality similar to Napster's as some have alleged? Does it allow users to steal on-line art since they can view and download images without even visiting the originating Web site? Does it support wholesale visual plagiarism? Does the reduced size of the image represent a real transformation of the original as Judge Taylor has maintained? If not, is the fair use defense really tenable here? Is the deep linking to the originating Web site morally acceptable in this case?

Case 4.3 *Ticketmaster v. Microsoft*

In 1997 Ticketmaster Group Inc. filed suit against Microsoft for federal trademark infringement and unfair competition. Ticketmaster is the largest ticket distributor in the world with revenues of nearly $2 billion. Shortly before this lawsuit, it set up a Web site, www.ticketmaster.com, to sell and market tickets to on-line consumers. Microsoft operates a Web site called Seattle Sidewalk which contains brief descriptions and reviews of cultural events in the Seattle area. This site also functions as a guide to recreational and cultural activities around Seattle. Seattle Sidewalk provides abundant links to related Web sites including several links to the Ticketmaster site. In this case, however, those links bypassed the Ticketmaster home page and went directly to the respective pages for purchases to events listed in the Seattle Sidewalk page. For instance, a listing on the Seattle Sidewalk page for the Seattle Symphony would include a direct link to a Ticketmaster subpage that would allow users to purchase their symphony tickets for a specific concert.

This is a prime example of deep linking, and Ticketmaster raised a number of objections to this practice. Deep linking occurs when the linking Web site does not link to the target Web site's home page but to a subordinate page within the Web site. According to Ticketmaster, by bypassing its home page Seattle Sidewalk users were not being exposed to the extensive advertising and promotional announcements that were posted there. This diminished the value of that advertising and ultimately the rates that could be charged to future advertisers.

Ticketmaster also claimed that links to the listed events on the Ticketmaster Web site without a contract were illicit. According to the company, "Microsoft was feathering its own nest at Ticketmaster's expense. It was, in effect, committing electronic piracy."[28]

Another problem with this mode of linking concerned Ticketmaster's relationship with MasterCard, which had been promised to receive greater prominence than other payment methods. But unless Ticketmaster could control how users navigated this site, it could not keep its commitment to MasterCard. Ticketmaster also complained that Microsoft was able to generate advertising revenues on the basis of this link because Microsoft posted a banner advertisement on the same page on which it displayed the Ticketmaster name and link. And, according to Wagner, Ticketmaster alleged that the links were done in such a way that they "presented information incorrectly and out of context."[29]

Microsoft replied by arguing that linking without a contract was not illicit. The publication of a site on the World Wide Web invites such links unless explicit steps are taken to prevent them. According to Joshua Masur, "From Microsoft's perspective, Ticketmaster's failure to avail itself of available technical measures by which linking can be limited implies intent to permit and even solicit inbound links."[30] Microsoft further argued that it was merely directing users to the appropriate Web pages on the vast Ticketmaster site without any intention of "feathering its own nest."

This case certainly raised the fundamental problem with deep linking which circumvents advertising and other identifying or promotional features on the home page. Deep linking not only reduces the value of the target site's advertising, but it also deprives that Web site of its proper exposure and recognition. On the other hand, it could be argued that Ticketmaster had no real quarrel here. Its Web site information is at least quasi-public. Ticketmaster therefore should not interfere with the Web's free flow of information. In its legal defense Microsoft argued that Ticketmaster violated an unwritten Internet code which gives any Web site operator the right to link to another site. Microsoft also argued that it had a First Amendment right to publish this public information. This implies that linking and deep linking are forms of expression protected by the First Amendment.

There was an out of court settlement to this lawsuit in February 1999. Although the terms of that settlement were not disclosed, Microsoft did agree to link to Ticketmaster's home page instead of to its subpages. The settlement was actually a disappointment for those searching for a firm legal precedent about controversial linking activities. As a result, at least in the United States there are currently no clear legal guidelines on the widespread practice of deep linking.

Case 4.4 Metatags and Search Engine Baiting[31]

Michael Warner had every reason to be proud of his young dot.com company. After only a short year of operations, they were in the black. He stared at the FY 2002 financial statements which showed profits of $963,000 on sales of just over $11 million. Things were also looking promising for the new fiscal year. The Web site was getting many hits and advertisers and commercial partners were more interested than ever. Warner was the creator of a Web site called kitchens&more. It sold high-quality kitchen equipment and supplies such as pans, small appliances, glassware, dishes, tableware, and linens at highly competitive prices.

But as he prepared for the company's weekly strategic planning session, Warner could not help but be worried about the progress of his biggest on-line competitor, George Somona & Co. This billion dollar California company was the leading purveyor of kitchen supplies in the United States. It had 85 stores dispersed across the country along with a robust and well-established catalogue business. Since its founding in the early 1950s George Somona had built up a powerful reputation for the highest quality products and customer service. The Somona brand was one of the company's major strengths. Its Web site had gone on-line only within the last few months, and early reports revealed a steady flow of customers. Would Warner's company, which did not have George Somona's physical infrastructure, be able to prevail in the face of such strong "bricks and clicks" competition?

From the beginning Warner's strategy was simple: use every tactic to build the customer base and attract Web surfers. This company was not a well-known brand and it needed to build up brand identity on the Web. The company invested in advertising and worked with portals like Yahoo and Lycos to disseminate its name through cyberspace. But some of its strategies for attracting consumers might appear to some to be rather unorthodox.

When the www.georgesomona Web page went on-line, Warner, a skilled programmer, gave instructions to his programmers to change the contents of the kitchens&more metatag. A metatag is a piece of HTML code that provides summary information about a Web page. These metatags, which are hidden from Web surfers but visible to search engines, can play an important role in helping consumers locate information. Some search engines rely heavily on metatags to index the contents of their databases. The "keyword" metatag is a list of key words or terms which can be used to describe a particular Web site or Web page within that site. If a user enters one of these terms such as "kitchens&more" into a search engine (like Google or Alta Vista), the search engine will provide the users with a list of all Web sites that satisfy this term. Warner asked his programmers to insert George Somona into the kitchens&more keyword metatag. The metatag would now look something like this: <meta name = "keywords" content = "kitchens& more, georgesomona, kitchen supplies, kitchen products">. Thus, if a user entered "George Somona" as a search term, the search engine would return the kitchens&more Web site as well as the George Somona site. Warner hoped that at least some curious Web surfers would check out his Web site instead of going to the Somona site.

There was some debate about the legality of this tactic—did this unauthorized use infringe on the George Somona trademark? After talking with several attorneys, Warner discovered that there was some ambiguity about whether or not this practice constituted trademark infringement. The legal issue centered around the "initial interest confusion" generated by this use of a metatag: Was this "confusion" sufficient to constitute real damage to the trademark? Others at the company who were involved in this debate questioned the ethical propriety of this use of metatag code. Wasn't this search engine baiting? Shouldn't kitchens&more respect the trademarks of its competitors? Warner was convinced that this was a trivial issue. He wasn't attempting to compel anyone to visit his site. Rather, he was proffering an invitation to Web surfers: "Those of you looking for George Somona, come and take a look at our Web site too!" What could be wrong with that?

Case 4.5 Spiders at the Auction

eBay, Inc. is one of the largest and most successful commercial sites on the entire World Wide Web. Founded in 1995, eBay introduced consumers to an innovative business model that brings buyers and sellers together in an engaging auction format in order to buy and sell many different items such as coins, consumer electronics, antiques, appliances, and so forth. Products sold on the Web site can range from a $1 baseball card to a $578,000 Shoeless Joe Jackson's baseball bat. With 38 million customers, sales for 2002 were projected to be $1 billion returning a net income of $150 million. eBay carries no inventory so it can keep costs low. But the biggest reason for success derives from the fact that eBay is "a master at harnessing the awesome power of the Net—not just to let customers sound off directly in the ears of the big brass, but to track their every movement so new products and services are tailored to just what customers want."[32]

eBay has had several disputes with auction aggregator services which accumulate data from different auction sites so that a consumer can see what is available at all these different sites. The advantage for the buyer is the ability to see if a product available on eBay might be available at a lower asking price on a different site. One such dispute occurred in 1999 with an aggregator service known as AuctionWatch. The AuctionWatch site offers a "Universal Search Function" which allows users to access the price, product, description, and bidding history from popular auction sites such as eBay, Yahoo, and amazon.com. For example, if a user were interested in Boston Red Sox baseball memorabilia, that individual could check the AuctionWatch site to ascertain all of the Red Sox memorabilia available for auction across multiple sites.

AuctionWatch relied on spider technology to locate this data at these different auction sites. A spider is a robotic search engine that can crawl through sites many times a day to extract shopping data. According to Karen Solomon, "The benefits of bots for consumers are indisputable, but some merchants are less than thrilled about the technology's parasitic presence."[33]

eBay officials were certainly "less than thrilled" with AuctionWatch's constant forays into its computer system. They asked the company to stop, but it refused to contain its auction bot activities. eBay claimed that its auction data was proprietary, though that data was not eligible for any copyright protection. eBay also argued that the auction bots burdened its servers and perhaps impeded performance for its regular customers.

Given AuctionWatch's categorical refusal to curtail its intrusive activities, eBay executives met with their lawyers to discuss the next step. Should they simply allow the auction bot to continue? Should they pursue legal action? One possible legal angle to deter AuctionWatch was to accuse it of "trespass to chattels." Trespass to chattels represents a tort action for the unauthorized theft, use, or interference with another's tangible property.[34] But was this bot really "trespassing" on eBay's property, including its servers? Hasn't eBay made its Web site available to the public on this public network?

NOTES

1. D. Burk, "The Trouble with Trespass", 4 *Journal of Small and Emerging Business Law* 27 (1999).
2. MP3 is a compressed digital music file; the compression allows for near-CD-quality files that are as much as 20 times smaller than standard music CD files. MP3 files are created through a technique known as "ripping" whereby a standard music CD is inserted into the computer, and, with the help of an MP3 encoding program, the CD's contents are compressed and copied to the computer's hard drive.
3. S. Clay, "Where Napster Is Taking the Publishing World," *Harvard Business Review* (February 2001), p. 144.
4. C. Mann, "The Heavenly Jukebox," *Atlantic Monthly,* (September 2000).
5. S. Ante "Inside Napster," *Business Week,* 14 (August 2000), p. 114.
6. Ibid.
7. Mann, "Heavenly Jukebox."
8. H. Lee, "Spawn of Napster," *Industry Standard* (May 8, 2000), p. 110.
9. F. Vogelstein, "Is It Stealing or Sharing," *U.S. News and World Report*, 12 June 2000, p. 38.
10. *Gershwin Publishing Corp. v. Columbia Artist Mgmt., Inc.*, 443 F.2d 1159, 2d Cir. (1971).
11. Plaintiff's Brief, *A&M Records et al. v. Napster,* No. C99-5183-MHP, N.D. Cal. (2000).
12. United States Court of Appeals for the Ninth Circuit, *A&M Records et al. v. Napster,* 239 F.3d 1004 (2001).
13. *Harper & Row Publishers, Inc. v. Nation Enters.*, 471 U.S., 539, 85 L. Ed. 2d 588 (1985).
14. S. Greene, "Reconciling Napster with the Sony Decision and Recent Amendments to Copyright Law" 39 *American Business Law Journal* 57 (2001) .
15. Mann, "Heavenly Jukebox."
16. *A&M Records Inc. v. Napster,* 239 F.3d, 9th Cir. (2001).
17. Ibid.
18. Ibid.
19. Quoted in "Big Music Fights Back," *Economist* (16 June 2001), p. 61.
20. A spider is an automated program that "crawls" through Web sites looking for certain information.
21. Available: www.ditto.com/about_us.asp.
22. 17 U.S.C. §106 (1).
23. 17 U.S.C. §107.
24. *Leslie A. Kelly et al. v. Arriba Soft Corp.*, 77 F. Supp. 2d 1116; U.S. Dist. (1999).
25. *Campbell v. Acuff-Rose*, 510 U.S. 569 (1994).
26. *Kelly v. Arriba.*
27. Ibid.
28. First Am. Complaint, *Ticketmaster Corp. v. Microsoft Corp.*, 97 Civ. 3055 C.D.Cal. (1997).

29. M. Wagner. "Suits Attack Web Fundamentals," *Computerworld* (May 5, 1997), p. 125.
30. J. Masur, "Links, Liability and the Law: The Strange Case of *Ticketmaster v. Microsoft*," 23 *Columbia VLA Journal of Law & the Arts* 419 (Spring 2000).
31. This is a hypothetical case study.
32. R. Hof, "The People's Company," *Business Week e.biz* (3 December 2001), p. 15.
33. K. Solomon, "Revenge of the Bots," *Industry Standard* (29 November 1999), p. 263.
34. Restatement (Second) of Torts, Sections 217–218 (1965).

5

Privacy and Information Access

INTRODUCTION

This chapter considers the pivotal question of accessibility to information and personal privacy. Organizations collect enormous amounts of data about their customers and they are able to build detailed and nuanced customer profiles. Some companies share this data with third parties without getting a customer's permission. This problem has been exacerbated by Internet architectures such as cookies and Web bugs which facilitate the surreptitious collection of such information. The issue of covert surveillance has also emerged in the workplace as well, where more and more workers are monitored by their employers.

Clearly, a key consideration in resolving these matters is respect for privacy rights. Almost everyone recognizes the importance of the right to privacy, but there is less consensus on its scope and meaning in the information age. There is also disagreement on the proper level of government intervention to protect these rights. In Europe, "data protection" is taken quite seriously by regulators, but the regulatory environment in the United States is less stringent. There is more reliance on the constraints imposed by the marketplace and social norms.

In the United States, an individual's right to privacy is protected to some extent by the Constitution, specifically by the First, Fourth, Ninth, and Fourteenth Amendments. But only the Fourteenth Amendment provides some basis for protecting an individual's "informational privacy." There are also numerous laws to protect privacy such as the Fair Credit Reporting Act (FCRA) of 1971. The FCRA sets standards for the legitimate use of credit reports and specifies a consumer's rights in challenging those reports. In more recent years, Congress has passed the Driver's Privacy Protection Act (1994) which requires the Department of Motor Vehicles to provide a means for drivers to "opt out" of the sale of their personal data to third parties, and the Children's Online Privacy Protection Act (1998) which requires parental consent before Web sites can collect data from children who are under the age of 13.

According to some philosophers, these legal rights are grounded in a *moral right* to privacy. Jim Moor, for example, argues that while privacy is not a core human value, it is the expression of a core value, that is, the value of security. According to Moor, while every culture needs security or protection from harm (along with other core values such as life, happiness, freedom, knowledge, ability, and resources), not every culture needs privacy. But in a "highly computerized culture in which lots of information is 'greased,' it is almost inevitable that privacy will emerge as an expression of the core value, security."[1] We can conclude, therefore, that because of its role in making us secure, privacy is a "plausible candidate" to be considered as an intrinsic human good within the context of such cultures.

Finally, it should be remarked that the issue of privacy is broader than consumer data protection. There are significant privacy and confidentiality needs on networks which are usually implemented by encryption technologies. But these technologies, which protect the information infrastructure, pose challenges for law enforcement authorities.

This chapter begins with several cases on consumer privacy. The first of these cases is the now classic "Lotus Marketplace: Households," which considers whether or not a marketing database, the joint effort of Lotus and Equifax, could potentially infringe on privacy rights.

One key issue that has emerged in the debates over data access concerns the ownership status of the data that has been collected. Do the collectors always have property rights to this data? If retail stores collect data about their shoppers' buying habits, do they "own" this information and can they dispose of it as they see fit? The Toysmart case brings these issues to the surface. During its bankruptcy proceedings this company tried to treat its consumer data as an asset, but the Federal Trade Commission had other ideas. The final case in this segment concerns the use of Web bugs to collect certain consumer data—is the Web bug a benign architecture or does it infringe on the consumer's privacy rights?

In the second section of this chapter we look at workplace privacy issues. The Johnson and Dresser case addresses the problem of e-mail privacy. The next case, "The Topper Travel Agency," looks at the broader issue of electronic monitoring in the workplace and the use of technology to collect and to measure various employee data. Does the use of this technology violate an employee's right to privacy or create an oppressive environment as some labor unions have alleged? How can the right to privacy and a decent working environment be properly balanced against a corporation's obligation to maximize profits for its shareholders?

This chapter on privacy cases concludes with a consideration of the precarious balance between public safety and personal privacy. Since September 11, 2001, Americans have been especially sensitive to this matter. The case on the FBI's carnivore technology looks at whether or not this form of government surveillance crosses the line by violating a citizen's Fourth Amendment rights. And the final case on encryption examines the government's efforts to deal with the national security threats implied by the use of strong encryption without violating individual privacy rights.

Case 5.1 The Lotus Marketplace: Households Product Controversy[2]

INTRODUCTION

When the details of the Lotus Marketplace product were made public in April 1990, no one at the well-known Cambridge computer company expected any vehement protests. But consumers and computer users besieged the company with letters and electronic mail messages, claiming that Marketplace: Households would be an irresponsible intrusion into their lives and a violation of their personal privacy.

Lotus was working in conjunction with Equifax Inc., one of the three major credit bureau companies in the United States. The proposed software package would enable small businesses and other organizations with limited resources to purchase targeted mailing lists. These lists could be used to solicit new customers through direct-mail marketing campaigns. But in the face of the controversy and firestorm of protest generated by this announcement, both companies had to decide whether there was a future for this innovative product.

LOTUS DEVELOPMENT CORP.

Lotus Development Corp. was founded in 1981 by computer wizard and entrepreneur Mitch Kapor. Its objective was to produce business productivity software for personal computers. In 1983, the company introduced its most popular and successful product, Lotus 1-2-3, a spreadsheet software package. Despite many competitive products such as Microsoft's Excel, Lotus 1-2-3 had dominated spreadsheet products since its first appearance in the PC software market. In 1991 its share of the PC spreadsheet market was still 60 percent. Lotus also marketed business graphics and database products. It combined its three major application packages, graphics, database, and spreadsheet, in another popular product known as Symphony. The company's other major businesses included CD-ROM products, financial information products for personal computers, electronic mail packages for local area networks, and later on, groupware products such as Notes.

Lotus was one of the fastest growing PC software companies during the decade of the 1980s. Its five-year (1986–1990) compound average growth rate in revenues was 28.8 percent. In 1991 Lotus reported healthy net earnings of $43.1 million. Its revenues for the same year were $828.9 million, a 19.7 percent increase over 1990.[3] But despite its financial success in 1991, Lotus stumbled in its introduction of Lotus 1-2-3 for Windows, Microsoft's popular new operating system for the IBM PC and compatible systems. In addition, as the market for spreadsheets became increasingly saturated, Lotus aggressively sought to market new products such as Marketplace: Households in an effort to sustain its high growth rate and propel it into the next generation of software products.

Lotus' role in this collaborative effort was to provide its considerable technical acumen in software development along with its expertise in the marketing of consumer software products.

EQUIFAX

Equifax, a billion dollar credit bureau, was founded in 1899 in Atlanta, Georgia. It was first known as the Retail Credit Company. Equifax grew quickly in the 1980s thanks in large part to the acquisition of many smaller, regional credit bureaus. Equifax was one of the "big three" credit bureaus which dominated this industry along with TRW and Trans Union. During the 1980s its annual return to investors had averaged an impressive 31 percent.[4] In 1990 Equifax reported profits of $63.9 million on total revenue of $1.08 billion. (This was up sharply from net income of $35.6 million on revenues of $840 million in 1989.)

Equifax collected data on consumers from a variety of sources including a consumer's credit history acquired from banks, employment history, and payment records from credit grantors. It received data from the U.S. Census Bureau and periodically purchased drivers' license data from the department of motor vehicles in most states. It also purchased data from other direct-mail companies on automobile and appliance purchases along with data about those making mail-order purchases. The company tracked this information on approximately 150 million individuals. The information was stored in the Equifax Consumer Marketing Data Base. Some of this information was compiled into a credit report that was sold to banks, retail stores, or other organizations that grant credit. The sale of such credit reports was the main source of revenue for Equifax and the other players in this mature industry. The more marketing-oriented data was used for other purposes such as its mailing list business.

A controversial practice of Equifax, TRW, and Trans Union was their participation in the mailing list business. At one time all three of these companies sold names, addresses, and limited financial data to direct-mail organizations or directly to companies initiating targeted direct-mail campaigns. In 1990 the mailing list business for Equifax totaled about $11 million. This practice had been heavily criticized as a violation of personal privacy. The direct-mail business fell under a gray area of the Fair Credit Reporting Act. According to this law, credit data can be sold only for "legitimate" business purposes. But the word "legitimate" is obviously ambiguous, and according to the credit bureau industry, should not have precluded the sale of this data to junk-mailers. Thanks to considerable public pressure all three credit bureaus have abandoned this business.

Equifax would obviously play a critical role in the development of this joint product with Lotus, since its Consumer Marketing Data Base was the primary source of information for the data to be made available through this product.

THE PRODUCT

In April 1990 Lotus and Equifax announced that its new Lotus Marketplace product would be available at the beginning of 1991. This CD-ROM (compact disk—read-only memory) database product was supposed to have two main components: Marketplace: Households and Marketplace: Business (for marketing to businesses). The Marketplace: Households product contained the following data fields: names, address, gender, age range, marital status, dwelling type, shopping habits for over 100 products (including luxury cars, vacations, gourmet foods), and estimated income level. The original product design also included a data field for classification of households according to 50 psychographic or lifestyle categories ranging from "accumulated wealth" to "inner-city singles." Both companies, however, had reservations about using these lifestyle categories, and so it is unclear whether this data field was to be included in the final product specification. Thanks to the Equifax Consumer Marketing Data Base, Marketplace could draw on information from 80 million U.S. households.

Marketplace was targeted at small and mid-size businesses interested in inexpensive, direct-mail marketing. Nonprofit organizations could also use this product for targeted mailings in fund-raising campaigns. If used correctly, this product would help these organizations identify prospective customers (or donors) in a cost-effective and efficient manner. Lotus sought to take advantage of CD-ROM's substantial storage capability and thereby bring the direct-mail marketing industry to the world of personal computers and desktops. The product also offered flexibility and convenience since it could be used for multiple purposes.

The minimum list size was 5,000 names. Although most of the data fields enumerated above could be used as parameters to generate the list, that list itself would contain only names and addresses. For example, a small vendor such as a luxury car dealer might want to do a localized targeted mailing to consumers with incomes greater than $100,000. The dealer might utilize the following criteria to generate the list: all the individuals in Fairfield County (Connecticut) who are over 40 years, who have an income in excess of $100,000, and who have a propensity to purchase expensive cars and other luxury items. Using these criteria, a list of names and addresses would be generated. The initial list appeared on the dealer's computer screen and would include only a partial address. Once the dealer agreed to buy the list, he or she would be given full access to the encrypted data on the disk after paying for an access code. This list in CD-ROM format would then become the permanent property of the dealer, who would have unlimited use of these names. This differs from other consumer database mailing list products which were rented to vendors for one-time use. The price of MarketPlace: Households was set at $695 for the CD-ROM software and the first 5,000 names, and $400 for each additional 5,000 names.

PRIVACY CONCERNS

Both Lotus and Equifax steadfastly maintained that they had addressed consumers' concerns about privacy. Hence they did not include telephone numbers or personal financial data on the disks available to vendors. They also made it impossible to query an individual name. One could not type in "Peter Brown" and expect to get his age, income level, and purchasing habits. Of course, if Brown were part of the targeted group selected according to broader criteria, then one would have this information. Lotus also promised that the product would not fall into the wrong hands, since it would be sold only to legitimate businesses. Businesses intending to purchase the product would be carefully screened in order to ensure that only respectable companies had access to this product. As a result, companies selling speculative investments or peddling pornography would not be allowed to subscribe to Marketplace: Households. Also, the product would not be sold to individuals, only to businesses. Furthermore, a carefully worded contract would limit the product's use by the purchaser and prohibit that company from reselling the names to another vendor. Finally, consumers would be given an opportunity to have their names excluded from this database by informing either company or the Direct Marketing Association (DMA). Both companies felt confident that these safeguards would protect confidential information about a consumer and hence not violate his or her privacy.

Critics of Marketplace, however, were not satisfied by the announcement of these safeguards. If the product were widely disseminated, how could Lotus *really* control how it was used? Could the company monitor and enforce the contract prohibiting the resale of the data? There were also concerns that consumers would not be able to delete their names from the database or make corrections in a timely manner. After all, by the time such corrections or deletions were implemented, inaccurate versions of the database would already be on the market. Could Lotus ensure the accuracy of this product?

As concerns over the product intensified, thousands of individuals wrote strong letters of protest to Lotus' corporate headquarters in Cambridge. Some of the letters were transmitted electronically and copied on hundreds of networks; this further fueled the controversy and provoked others to join in the protest.

In response to these protests Lotus agreed to delete immediately the names of anyone who contacted the company. In a short period of time it received over 30,000 such requests. However, this did not silence Lotus' critics who seemed to be growing more militant as the controversy intensified. In addition, organizations such as Computer Professionals for Social Responsibility added their voice to the chorus of protests; they were especially concerned that there would be no way to guarantee that everyone in the database had freely consented to have their information used in this way.

Privacy experts like Mark Rotenberg argued that the Marketplace was a "privacy disaster." According to Rotenberg, the information contained in this product "is the most easily accessible collection of personal data on American consumers that has ever been available in this country."[5]

Finally, Lotus and Equifax capitulated to these criticisms and on January 23, 1991, they reluctantly agreed to cancel the product. It was reported that Equifax and Lotus made this decision in the interests of consumer privacy and economics; both companies feared that a consumer backlash would affect their core businesses. According to the press release issued at the time of the cancellation, Marketplace: Households was terminated due to "public concerns and misunderstandings of the product, and the substantial, unexpected costs required to fully address consumer privacy issues."[6]

POSTSCRIPT

Despite the abrupt cancellation of Marketplace: Households, some of the product's supporters were surprised and confused by the criticism and hostility that it generated. They pointed out that the product could be a significant benefit to small and mid-size businesses which need to use targeted direct-mail campaigns to find new customers and increase revenues. It should be noted that the same information is purchased by large companies for higher fees for the purpose of DBM (Data Base Marketing) campaigns. Marketplace made the process of purchasing data less expensive for small businesses and hence gave them an opportunity to do their own DBM campaigns. Further, the product's supporters argued, Lotus and Equifax took great pains to address the privacy concerns of consumers. Thus, while the product had been canceled for political reasons, both companies still felt that this was a valuable product, which had incorporated reasonably adequate protections to safeguard consumer privacy.

Case 5.2 Toysmart.com and the Fate of Its Customer List

When Toysmart.com was incorporated in November 1998, it had high aspirations. Toysmart, located in Waltham, Massachusetts, operated an on-line toy retail store at www.toysmart.com, and it specialized in the sale of educational and developmental toys. Disney was a major investor in this company through one of its subsidiaries, Buena Vista Internet Group.

The prospects for the sale of toys on-line initially looked promising, and Toysmart's status as an early mover should have given it an edge against the competition. But it faced tough and well-capitalized rivals, such as eToys and the retail giant Toys 'R' Us, which had recently initiated its toysrus.com Web site. Also the on-line toy market grew more slowly than anticipated with only about $300 million in sales in 1999, far less than most projections.

Despite its best efforts the company was never able to gain momentum and generate a profit. As a result, in May 2000 it ceased operations and declared bankruptcy. In accordance with bankruptcy procedures, the company began soliciting bids for its assets in order to raise funds to pay off its creditors. This included physical assets such as unsold inventory, equipment, real estate, and so forth. But it also included intangible assets such as the domain name and trademarks along with the data Toysmart had collected about its customers. The transfer of that data to a third party, however, provoked a sense of unease. It also provoked some questions. What was included in this data and why should it be treated like the rest of Toysmart's assets?

During the course of its transactions with customers, Toysmart had the opportunity to collect considerable personal data such as consumers' names, addresses, billing information, purchases, shopping preferences, and family profile data. The Toysmart database also included children's names, birth dates, and a toy wish list. In September 1999 Toysmart received the TRUSTe seal or trustmark, indicating that TRUSTe, an organization that certifies on-line privacy policies, found those policies adequate. The TRUSTe seal meant that Toysmart had developed a viable and conscientious privacy policy. That privacy policy, posted on the Toysmart Web site, stipulated the following:

> (1) Personal information voluntarily submitted by visitors to our site, such as name, address, billing information and shopping preferences, is never shared with a third party. All information obtained by toysmart.com is used only to personalize your experience online.
> (2) When you register with toysmart.com, you can rest assured that your information will never be shared with a third party.

Toysmart was constrained not only by its privacy policy but also by the Children's Online Privacy Protection Act (COPPA) which had recently become law in 1998. According to COPPA, a company must get parental consent before collecting and sharing children's personal information.

Yet, despite its privacy policy and the restrictions of COPPA, Toysmart put its customer list up for bid along with the rest of its assets. The company did not seek out parental consent for the sale of information that pertained to children. It first solicited buyers for this data in a *Wall Street Journal* ad. However, because Toysmart had promised confidentiality for the data in their on-line privacy policy, the company was promptly sued by the Federal Trade Commission (FTC). The FTC pursued the case because it believed that Toysmart should adhere to its promise. According to Robert Pitosfky, the FTC chairman at the time, "Even failing dot.coms must abide by their promise to protect the privacy rights of their customers . . . [and] the FTC seeks to ensure these promises are kept."[7] The FTC also accused Toysmart of violating COPPA.

The company, on the other hand, was thinking about its creditors and the need to balance the creditors' interest with the privacy concerns of their customers. Hence they regarded this sale as a justified exception to their self-imposed and stringent privacy policy. One of the most valuable assets they had to sell was this customer data. In the off-line world of bricks and mortar the sale of such data would probably have been routine.

In addition, U.S. bankruptcy code served to effect an equitable distribution of *all* the debtor's property so that creditors could be paid. There was no precedent for handling the conflict between bankruptcy code and new laws like COPPA.

The Toysmart controversy ramified throughout the on-line business-to-consumer marketplace. In the summer of 2000 Amazon.com, the Internet's leading bookseller, informed its customers by e-mail that it was changing its privacy policy. According to that policy, Amazon now reserves the right to sell any of the consumer data it has collected. The revised policy states the following: "As we continue to develop our business, we might sell or buy stores or assets. In such transactions, customer information generally is one of the transferred business assets."[8] The bottom line is that Amazon does not want to make the same mistake as Toysmart, so it is putting its 23 million customers on notice that their personal data, including their shopping histories, is being regarded as a business asset.

Case 5.3 Privacy Pressures: The Use of Web Bugs at HomeConnection[9]

As Matthew Scott, president of HomeConnection, sat in his office waiting for several members of his executive team to arrive, he grew more worrisome about a story featuring his company in the morning paper. His impulse was to fight back and go on the defensive, but Scott knew that he had to be careful. However, he did not accept the article's implicit conclusion that HomeConnection had no regard for the privacy rights of its customers, and he was anxious to hear what his colleagues had to say about the matter.

HomeConnection was an Internet Service Provider (ISP) with several million customers, primarily clustered in the mid-West. An ISP links people and businesses to the Internet, usually for a monthly fee. HomeConnection was much smaller than the industry leader, America OnLine (AOL), but it was still seen as a formidable player in this industry. Thanks to Scott's management, the company had recorded increasing profits for the past three years, 1999 through 2002. One feature that attracted customers was the opportunity to create their own personal Web page. HomeConnection made this process easy and convenient.

In the past year HomeConnection had devised an innovative promotion to help increase its subscriber base. The company encouraged its users with their own personal Web pages to carry an ad for HomeConnection. The ad would offer new subscribers a heavily discounted rate for the first year of membership. In addition, as an incentive to display the ad on their personal Web pages, the company agreed to pay its users $25 for any new members who signed up for a subscription by clicking on the ad. The response to the promotion was stronger than expected, and HomeConnection's membership had risen by over 6.5 percent since the program's inception eight months ago. Scott was quite enthused about the results, and he did not anticipate that one aspect of the program would attract some negative attention.

In consultation with his marketing manager, Scott had authorized the use of Web bugs so that when users placed the ad on their Web pages they would also get a Web bug. A Web bug is embedded as a miniscule and invisible picture on the screen and it can track everything one does on a particular Web site. Web bugs, also called "Web beacons," are usually deployed to count visitors to a Web site or to gather cumulative data about visitors to those sites without tracking any personal details. In this case the Web bug transmitted information to a major on-line ad agency,

DoubleDealer. DoubleDealer would collect data about those who visited these Web pages, which ads they clicked on, and so forth.

The newspaper report cited HomeConnection as well as other ISPs and e-commerce sites for using this protocol without the permission of their customers. They quoted a well-known privacy expert: "It's extremely disturbing that these companies are using technology to gather information in such a clandestine manner; I don't see how it can be morally justified." The article had clearly resonated with some of HomeConnecton's users, and the switchboard had been busy most of the afternoon with calls from irate customers. Some wanted to cancel their subscription.

Scott felt that the company had done nothing wrong but was a victim of a pervasive paranoia about privacy. HomeConnection was not using these bugs for any untoward purposes—its purpose was to track the results of the advertising promotion, that is, how many people were clicking on these ads. Also, Scott himself had modified the company's privacy policy to indicate that Web bugs might be used sometimes. (However, there was no indication that Web bugs would be placed on the personal Web pages of its user base.)

As several of his managers made their way into the conference room adjoining his office, Scott made one last check with customer service. By now it was late in the day and the volume of calls and e-mails was dying down. It was now up to Scott to determine a response—did the company face a serious problem or was this just a tempest in a teapot?

Case 5.4 E-Mail Privacy at Johnson and Dresser[10]

Jason Perry left the executive office suite of Johnson and Dresser shortly after 3:30 P.M. and returned to his own office on the floor below. He had made a rare visit to the company's chief operating officer in order to discuss the company's questionable e-mail policies. The meeting had gone reasonably well and Perry was wondering about his next steps. As he checked over his notes and waited for his next appointment, he reviewed the events leading up to this meeting.

Perry had joined Johnson and Dresser, a moderate-sized retail brokerage firm, about seven years ago. He was hired as a senior systems analyst, but within two years he was promoted to the position of Information Systems (IS) director. He was relatively well known in the industry and aspired to work for one of the major brokerage houses on Wall Street.

A year or two after Perry's promotion, he oversaw the purchase and installation of an advanced electronic mail system that would be used throughout the company. Although many were slow to make the transition to an on-line communication system, within a short time almost the entire organization became dependent on e-mail.

The new product had been introduced at several training sessions where electronic mail was frequently compared to regular postal mail and where the confidentiality of one's communications was certainly intimated. Users were not told that all of the company's e-mail messages were archived and available for future inspection at any time. Moreover, users were strongly encouraged to use e-mail for communicating with their fellow employees. The firm clearly saw this form of electronic communication as preferable to the use of phone calls or quick office visits.

Perry did not expect that Johnson and Dresser would make much use of the archived messages, but when an insider trading scandal broke at the firm it was decided to check the e-mail of several brokers who had been implicated. All the brokers involved resigned quietly and nothing further came of the matter. The brokerage house had a strong reputation on Wall Street for integrity and always acted quickly when there were problems of this nature. The company was keenly aware of the importance of an unimpeachable reputation in order to maintain its current clients and attract new business.

In the aftermath of this potential scandal senior managers at the firm decided to inspect employee e-mail routinely. This was to make sure that no one else was involved in the insider trading scandal and to ferret out any other compliance problems or suspicious behavior. As a result some managers regularly asked for a compilation of e-mail messages before an employee's annual review. In the vast majority of cases they found nothing incriminating or damaging in these messages and the individuals never knew that anyone had been checking their electronic mail messages.

But there were some exceptions to this. One incident that bothered Perry a great deal involved a young analyst named Lisa Curry. She was a 10-year veteran at the company responsible for following the utility industry. She worked closely with brokers providing reports and advice on various utility stocks. Like others at Johnson and Dresser, she was a little wary at first of using the e-mail system. Soon, however, she came to rely heavily on electronic mail for a large portion of her communications with her fellow employees. Indeed over time she felt much less inhibited when she composed e-mail messages. Thus, although she was usually pretty diffident around the company, she found herself engaging in some intense e-mail discussions with Margaret Leonard, one of the few women brokers at the firm. She often sent Leonard messages that complained about sexist corporate policies or messages that conveyed the latest company gossip. None of these messages were especially incendiary or provocative, but they were fairly critical of Johnson and Dresser. Also, on occasion she criticized her boss for his lack of sensitivity on certain issues; she was perturbed, for example, at his condescending attitude toward some of the other women analysts.

Curry never dreamed that anyone would ever see these messages. Leonard assured her that she promptly erased the messages right after she read them. Curry let her know that she did the same with Leonard's messages. Both of them assumed that when they hit the delete key the messages would permanently be erased from the system. When Curry was due for her annual review, her manager decided to check her e-mail communications and found the messages she had sent to Leonard. He was furious that she was so critical of Johnson and Dresser and also chastised her for wasting so much time sending "trivial, gossipy" e-mail messages. He told her that she did not seem to be a real team player and that maybe she should look around for a company that had a philosophy closer to her own. The end result was that despite her excellent track record as an analyst, Curry received a small salary increment and a mixed performance review.

Curry was completely shocked by this. She could not believe that her messages were not considered completely confidential. She expected such confidentiality especially since she was not told anything to the contrary. Indeed, in her view she had been led to believe by the IS department that her privacy would be protected.

Among those she called in the company to complain about her treatment was Perry. She told him that his department's training sessions had duped people into believing that their e-mail messages would be confidential. She also pointed out that users should be told that messages would be archived and might be available for future scrutiny. Finally she stressed that she would be loath to continue using e-mail if everything she wrote would one day be scrutinized by her manager and "God knows who else at this paranoid company!"

Perry was sympathetic. He had received a few other complaints and was beginning to question the company's fairness. He told Curry he would look into the matter and try to craft a more open and responsible policy. He could make no promises since he knew that others in the company would need to be involved in any such policy emendations. Perry felt sorry for what had happened to Curry, and he did not want to see other employees get blindsided in the same way that she had.

Consequently, Perry decided to ask for a meeting with the chief operating officer in order to broach the issue of a revised e-mail policy that would better protect the privacy of Johnson and Dresser employees. During this session Perry argued that the company should probably at least take steps to inform employees that their messages were being stored and might be intercepted. However, while the COO did not disagree, he was worried about the ramifications of announcing to everyone that e-mail was being monitored. For one thing users might be less inclined to use e-mail, and the productivity gains realized by adopting this technology would be lost.

When asked about the legal implications of all this, Perry noted that according to current law the company was well within its rights to read an employee's e-mail. He wondered, however, if the company was living up to its high moral ideals by inspecting these messages. Isn't it a violation of confidentiality to read someone's postal letters? Why should electronic mail be any different? Should the company be proactive and declare electronic mail off limits except under unusual circumstances? Should it even continue to collect and store the large volume of e-mail messages generated by its many employees?

The COO was ambivalent about these suggestions, and he pointed out to Perry how the policy of archiving and inspecting e-mail had helped the firm uncover the insider trading scandal and take swift action. Maybe it needed to compromise employee privacy sometimes in order to protect the company against such abuses in the future. The more sources it could tap, the better it could discover problems and ensure that everyone at Johnson and Dresser was complying with the regulations of the Securities and Exchange Commission (SEC).

As the meeting came to a conclusion Perry was told to propose and defend a tenable and responsible e-mail policy that could be presented to the executive committee. He now began to think about what that policy should be. Clearly, there were many complex issues to untangle and key decisions to make.

Case 5.5 The Topper Travel Agency[11]

> Too many employers practice a credo of "In God we trust, others we monitor."[12]

Katherine Davis arrived early for work on a bright, sunny Friday morning to read over a long report and a petition from disgruntled workers documenting her company's alleged violations of their right to privacy. As she pulled into the empty parking lot of the corporate headquarters of the Topper Travel Agency, Davis realized that the situation was quite volatile and must be handled with extreme care. She had only recently taken the job as Topper's human resources director and this was her first major crisis. The company's president, Robert Donaldson, wanted her recommendations on the matter by the close of the work day. She had already discussed the situation at some length with the company's attorneys, but they were not very helpful. After that conversation yesterday afternoon Davis realized that the key issues in this dispute were not legal ones; rather, they were difficult and nettling ethical questions that defied easy answers.

THE COMPANY

The Topper Travel Agency was founded in 1972 by Gerald H. Topper and his brother William. The company began in a small suburban office with only four travel agents and a secretary for Gerald Topper. But within a few years the agency had already added three new offices to handle its growing business. Because of its reputation for superior service, the Topper Travel Agency continued to attract new business, especially from corporate clients. As a result, the company expanded quite vigorously in the 1980s and 1990s and by 2000 its revenues had grown to almost $800 million.

Topper's corporate headquarters was located in a large Midwestern city. The company continued to specialize in providing fast, reliable, efficient service to many of this area's largest and most distinguished corporations. The agency's growing revenues were matched by high profits as well. Indeed, the company had shown a profit every year since its inception. But recently due to the recession in 2001 and other forces, there were pressures on its profit margins. During the past year Topper's profit margin declined from 6.7 percent to 5.5 percent. The company was forecasting little growth in revenues or profits for 2002 due to the slow economy and more competitive pressures in the Midwest market.

A MONITORING SYSTEM

In response to these revenue and profit projections company president Robert Donaldson decided to focus on improving efficiency and reducing costs in order to prevent any further erosion in profit margins. The company wanted to be certain that its travel agents were working at maximum efficiency so it decided to install a sophisticated monitoring system produced by Rockwell International. In selling its monitoring system to Topper, Rockwell salespeople emphasized the productivity gains that could be achieved by faithful use of this system. They pointed out that one second shaved off 1,000 agents' calls each year could save the company $1,000,000 in labor costs.

The Rockwell monitoring system would be used primarily with the travel agents serving Topper's large corporate clients. The system measured the duration of each agent's phone conversation with a client. The company's standard for completing a simple airline reservation and processing the tickets was 108 seconds. Sometimes, of course, a client would make airline and hotel reservations along with arrangements to rent a car. In these cases Topper used a different time standard, but the same procedure for calculating variances. Variances were duly noted and summarized in a monthly report which was sent to supervisors and the human resources department. If an employee had a record of consistent negative variances, he or she received a reprimand from the department supervisor. A meeting was also scheduled with the employee in order to uncover an explanation of the problem and work out a tenable solution. A representative from human resources might be asked by the department to attend a follow-up meeting if the problems persisted. At that time the employee would be given a warning that he or she would be dismissed if the problem was not corrected within three months. So far only one employee had received a warning, whereupon she resigned from the company.

The monitoring system had other features besides its capacity for measuring the duration of phone conversations. The system could also detect when employees left their desks to go to the restroom, take a break, and so forth. The duration of these "interruptions" was also measured, thereby allowing a supervisor to monitor whether the employee was spending too much time going to the restroom (a 3 minute standard was set), or exceeding the time limits for a break (15 minutes) or lunch (45 minutes). The travel agent could not leave his or her desk for any other reason. Finally, the system enabled supervisors to listen in on employee phone calls. This would permit them to determine if employees were following the company's rigid instructions for booking reservations by phone. Once again, if an employee failed to follow the correct protocol or received and made personal phone calls during company time, they could receive a reprimand and eventually a termination warning.

EMPLOYEE REACTION

Electronic monitoring was not well received by most employees at the travel agency. Most of them regarded this computer system as an unwarranted and odious intrusion of their privacy. Employees felt that it was especially unfair for the company to listen in on phone calls. Sometimes incoming or outgoing personal calls were a necessity particularly in cases of an emergency or family crisis. And since the company monitored *all* phone conversations, managers were often privy to private, intimate details about an employee's personal life. Travel agents also complained bitterly that incessant monitoring of their phone calls was causing considerable stress and anxiety. According to one agent,

> This monitoring system is nothing more than an electronic whip to make us work faster. It produces incredible stress and I'm afraid sometimes that I'm going to crack under the strain.

One other longtime employee of Topper made the following observations:

> This new technology is terrible! It invades my privacy—this company knows everything I do even how long I spend in the bathroom. Also, if the clients knew that they were being listened to, they wouldn't like it one bit. And they wouldn't be happy that we are under constant pressure to get the call over with and move on to the next customer. It makes it real difficult sometimes to be courteous and thorough with each of our clients.

Despite these complaints, Topper's management steadfastly defended its right to monitor its employees in order to ensure that they were performing up to company standards. Indeed, as Chairman William Topper observed at the most recent board of directors meeting, since installing this system, productivity for the corporate travel agents had increased by almost 15 percent. If these productivity gains could be sustained, it would enable Topper to eliminate several positions by attrition and thereby cut costs and improve its profit margins. When Katherine Davis pointed out the high level of employee dissatisfaction with the new system, Topper's response was quite peremptory and defensive:

> This company has a right and an obligation to shareholders to manage this workplace with the most effective tools available. No company can succeed unless it changes with new technology, and this means that the employees must learn to adapt. We need this technology to stay competitive,

> to maximize profits, and to deliver quality service to our customers with greater efficiency.

Others observed that Topper was "way behind" in implementing this technology. Major airlines and travel agencies had begun monitoring a long time ago as a means of cutting costs.

DAVIS' DILEMMA

Shortly after this meeting, Davis received the petition from the travel agents outlining their complaints and requesting that the monitoring system be removed. About 75 percent of the agents had signed the petition. Since Davis was seen as a manager with some humane empathy and had been sympathetic to agents who had complained in the past, many saw her as their only ally among upper-level management. Thus, Davis had a difficult decision to make. Should she become an advocate for the employees and press the issue with Donaldson or defend management's right to monitor its employees and measure productivity?

Before deciding on a course of action she had to carefully weigh some "philosophical" and practical questions. For example, does the employee's right to privacy take precedence over the employer's right to monitor its employees, to check up on them, and see how they're doing? Were the company's practices really unfair or did employees simply resist the pressures to become more productive? Furthermore, was there a way to strike a better balance between these competing interests? Also, was the monitoring too intense? Should it be modified in some way to lessen the anxiety of the travel agents?

Regardless of how these questions were answered, something would have to be done. Davis was apprehensive that the decline in morale would soon lead to other problems such as increased turnover or higher health insurance costs due to the enhanced stress level. These negative effects might in the long run offset the productivity gains achieved by the monitoring system.

As Davis arrived at her office on the fifth floor of the Topper building she began to prepare her report and recommendations to Donaldson, the company's president. She recalled the words that concluded the agents' petition:

> We used to enjoy working at this agency and helping its customers. Now we find this workplace to be an uncomfortable and hostile environment. We don't object to management checking on us, but we do object to this

electronic straitjacket that has brought so much stress and anxiety into our lives.

Thus, Davis had to sort through many conflicting feelings and different perspectives in preparing her final recommendations to Donaldson.

Case 5.6 The FBI's Carnivore Technology

After much public ridicule, the FBI has changed the name of its controversial e-mail surveillance program from "Carnivore" to the "DCS-1000." But this name change is unlikely to stick and it will probably not help Carnivore's woeful reputation among civil libertarian groups. Nor will it temper their criticisms of this surveillance technology. Critics of Carnivore maintain that it violates civil rights, especially the right to privacy; supporters argue that such programs are essential to help maintain public safety, especially in the aftermath of September 11. But while America's travails with terrorism have sensitized citizens to the security side of the equation, there can be no doubt that technologies like Carnivore are at the center of the debate about finding the proper balance between the government's capabilities for conducting surveillance and a citizen's privacy rights.

WHAT IS CARNIVORE?

In the simplest terms, Carnivore represents the equivalent of an Internet wiretapping system. The "tap," however, is placed not on an individual's direct connection, but on an e-mail server that could belong to an organization with which the individual is affiliated. It is also quite easy to hook Carnivore into an Internet Service Provider's (ISP) network (used by the surveillance target), and this is the FBI's preferred way of operating. The program falls under the category of a "packet sniffer," and it is designed to record the header information in an e-mail, that is, the origin, destination, and subject matter, rather than the actual content of the message.

Thus, the Carnivore program provides the Internet version of the phone-tapping mechanism that records the numbers dialed by a suspect along with the numbers of incoming calls. This is known as "pen register" information. While federal authorities need a warrant for this type of data, those warrants are much easier to obtain than warrants for a full-fledged wiretap that listens to actual conversations. Investigators need only to demonstrate that the information has relevance for their investigation. Carnivore reads the headers of all the e-mails that pass through this tap and then selects the ones that are the targets of its surveillance.

PRIVACY CONCERNS

The most ardent opponents of Carnivore argue that it tramples on the Fourth Amendment:

> The right of the people to be secure in their persons, houses, papers, and effects, against unreasonable searches and seizures, shall not be violated. . . .

In their view, Carnivore constitutes an unreasonable search in cyberspace. They argue that the historic constraints against unreasonable searches such as subpoenas and wiretap orders should be fully respected, but that's not the case with this surveillance technology.

The American Civil Liberties Union (ACLU), for example, contends that when Carnivore reads the headers of anyone who is not the target of the investigation, those people's rights are violated. The ACLU also contends that Carnivore casts too wide a net since it collects too much innocent data. Also, can the FBI be trusted to filter out the data that it doesn't need? What's to stop them from being overzealous in their collection of header information?

Another civil liberties group, the Electronic Frontier Foundation (EFF), objects to Carnivore because it captures more information than the use of those pen registers and trap and trace devices used for traditional telephone wiretapping. In Internet communications the contents of messages and sender/recipient header data are not separate. According to the EFF, even though Carnivore filters out unwanted e-mail and other communications information, "the Carnivore system appears to exacerbate the over collection of personal information by collecting more information than it is legally entitled to collect under traditional pen register and trap and trace laws."[13] Even if the FBI were ignoring the content, header information includes more than just e-mail addresses of the sender and recipient—it also includes the size of the message, how it has reached its destination, and time of transmission. This data goes beyond the scope of a warrant for trap and trace data (i.e. phone numbers of incoming calls).

While the U.S. judicial system has not yet been called upon to render a legal judgment about Carnivore, the Supreme Court has been particularly sensitive to how new technologies might interfere with this

Fourth Amendment right. In *Kyllo v. the United States* (2001), the Court prohibited law enforcement's use of thermal imaging cameras to look inside a suspect's house without a search warrant. According to Justice Antonin Scalia, who wrote the majority opinion, the Court is grappling with a fundamental question about the Fourth Amendment: "what limits there are upon this power of technology to shrink the realm of guaranteed privacy."

Carnivore technology has posed a particular problem for some ISPs. They are worried that the FBI will accidentally (or perhaps even deliberately) collect the e-mail headers from other customers who are not the subject the warrant. For this reason Excite@Home has so far not allowed the FBI to install a Carnivore box on any of its servers since it might compromise the privacy rights of its customers. The president of a smaller ISP, Iconn LLC in Connecticut, goes even further. He says, "I will go to jail before I allow the FBI to install Carnivore on my system."[14]

Defenders of Carnivore point to the unique problems associated with trying to tap e-mail. Unlike a traditional phone tap, it's not possible to tap one individual line used by a criminal suspect. Thanks to the Internet's packet switching technology, packets of information on the Internet can take multiple routes in order to reach their destination. This leaves the FBI little choice but to scan messages at a certain central point such as an ISP server. The alternative is to abandon efforts to scan the e-mail messages of suspected criminals or terrorists.

Those inclined to support technologies such as Carnivore also contend that it's getting more and more difficult for intelligence agencies to engage in on-line surveillance. There are so many digital messages traveling over so many communication conduits that interception becomes a more formidable challenge than tracking a phone call. The use of strong encryption compounds the problem. Law enforcement authorities argue that if the United States is serious about the war on terrorism, it must rely more heavily on technologies like Carnivore to help in this fight.

Case 5.7 Crypto Wars

One way to ensure privacy and the confidentiality of Internet communications is the use of encryption. Encryption makes data transmissions much more secure. It also provides safety for the exchange of credit card numbers with e-commerce vendors. The problem with this technology is that it can be abused to conceal communications between criminals or terrorists and thereby thwart the best intelligence efforts of law enforcement agencies. As a result, encryption technology has always made government officials uneasy, since it can fall into the wrong hands. Consequently, for many years there have been export controls on encryption products, which prohibited the export of encryption technology beyond a certain strength.

In February 1994 the Clinton administration announced the controversial Clipper chip as a government standard for cryptography. Under this standard the government would hold in escrow a digital key that could be used to decipher any encrypted message in case of an urgent intelligence requirement or for other situations approved by the courts. In the face of widespread opposition President Clinton withdrew this proposed standard, but many are apprehensive that the unpalatable idea of a government agency holding the key to all electronic communications will be resurrected in the future. For some, the Clipper chip became a symbol of a fast-approaching Big Brother environment, a potent threat to personal privacy and basic civil liberties. To others, however, it set the stage for a better key escrow plan that could play a role in safeguarding national security. Obviously this issue has even greater salience after the events of September 11, 2001.

CRYPTOGRAPHY

The term "cryptography" generally refers to data encryption, which is currently used to safeguard confidential electronic communications. Data encryption is nothing more than a secret code. These codes have been used by the military, including generals such as Julius Caesar, for over 2,000 years. Others who have worked extensively with cryptography include Francis Bacon, who several centuries ago developed certain cryptographic algorithms that are still in use today.

Essentially cryptography works by taking a message such as "we will invade tomorrow" and translating it into some sort of unintelligible gibberish. The only way this gibberish can be translated into something intelligible is by means of a key. For example, the key used by Caesar was the replacement of a letter by the letter that was three places ahead of it in the alphabet (thus the letter "d" would be replaced by the letter "g"). With the aid of this key, presumably known only by one's troops or allies, messages can easily be decrypted and rendered meaningful.

Computer cryptography or encryption has been in widespread use since the 1960s and is recommended "when sensitive data, such as business financial or personnel information, are stored on line, archived to off-line media, or transported across a network. . . ."[15] It can be coded in either hardware or software. Although numerous encryption algorithms have been developed, the most popular commercial one is the DES, or Data Encryption Standard, which the government has utilized as its standard since 1977. The DES was originally created in the 1960s by IBM researchers, but it was modified by the National Security Administration (NSA) before being adopted as a standard. In addition, there is the RSA, or Rivest-Shamir-Adelman algorithm, that was created by these three individuals at MIT. The DES is currently used in many e-mail and networking packages and was recertified by the government in 1993.

The DES is a symmetric private key cryptography system; this simply means that the same secret binary key is utilized for both encryption and decryption. In order for this to work properly, both parties, the sender and receiver of the data, must have access to this key. The key itself then must be communicated in a secure fashion or it could be intercepted by a third party and otherwise fall into the wrong hands. This is a serious disadvantage of the private key scheme.

The other popular encryption technique, RSA, is based on a public key cryptography. Public key cryptography, based on asymmetric algorithms, works as follows: Each party has access to a pair of keys, one public and one private; the public key is used to encrypt a message while a secretive private key is used to decrypt the message. If Mark wants to send a message to Jill, he uses her public key to send the message, but only Jill can decrypt that message with her private key. The obvious advantage of public key cryptography is that the sender and receiver of the message do not have to exchange a secret private key before they begin to communicate.

DES keys are 56 bits long, so there are 2^{56} keys. In 1998 the Electronic Frontier Foundation demonstrated that it could break a DES key in about two days using a $200,000 computer system. Hence, to ensure full, ironclad confidentiality users need to rely on strong encryption, that is, a 128-bit algorithm which is virtually unbreakable.

THE CLIPPER CHIP SCHEME

The task of protecting sensitive military or government communications in the United States falls to the NSA, the National Security Agency. The NSA is charged with the difficult challenge of implementing the Computer Security Act of 1987 which calls for a national standard for computer encryption. As John Markoff points out, "The goal of a national voice- and data-security standard is intended to provide privacy for

Government, civilian and corporate users of telephone and computer communications, while also assuring that law enforcement agencies can continue to eavesdrop on or wiretap voice and data conversations after obtaining warrants."[16]

The standard proposed by the Clinton administration in conjunction with the NSA was the MYK-78 or as it was most commonly called, the Clipper chip. The Clipper chip was a specialized computer chip with an encoded algorithm known as Skipjack, which would give law enforcement authorities (with a warrant) access to all encrypted data communications. All new computers (and telephones) would eventually be required to include this encryption chip, whose key, held by the U.S. government, could be deployed to override any encryption software.

According to the NSA's elaborate plan, the government would maintain in escrow the master key to each Clipper chip. These unique numeric keys would be divided between two government agencies which would effectively act as custodial agents. In other words, one agency would hold one-half of a key and the other agency would hold the other half. Whenever the FBI was granted a legal warrant to wiretap, it could then extract the serial number from the Clipper chip in usage and request the two portions of the unique key from the respective government agencies holding them in escrow. Once the two portions of the key were combined, the FBI would be able to use this key in order to decode the data transmission.

When the Clipper chip technology was introduced, it was met by fierce protests from many quarters. Civil libertarians, politicians, Information Technology (IT) managers, and many others voiced strident opposition to this project. Indeed opponents can be found at both ends of the political spectrum, from groups such as the ACLU concerned with infringement on free speech to hard-core conservatives who are suspicious of the government's meddling in the lives of its citizens. The Clipper chip's primary supporters seemed to be defensive government officials and law enforcement authorities. Most corporate leaders and managers were indifferent, but few backed this plan.

One of the arguments advanced by opponents of the Clipper chip was the excessive secrecy underlying this whole endeavor. The Clipper chip's algorithm was considered a classified secret, and therefore it was not subject to any external review or testing by independent experts. But what if the NSA had incorporated some sort of "trapdoor" that would enable the government to engage in covert surveillance *without* the need to retrieve a key? Moreover, computer experts in academia and business expressed their uneasiness with the secrecy enshrouding Clipper. How could they test the internal functionality of this technology in order to feel assured that the encryption system was secure enough to overcome the efforts of hackers anxious try to break the code?

The most basic arguments against the Clipper chip, however, were not technical but philosophical. Opponents vigorously contended that this technology was a serious threat to civil liberties, especially the right to privacy, and that it would give the government too much control over the lives of ordinary citizens. They claimed that this approach violated the Fourth Amendment which does allow law enforcement agencies to conduct "reasonable searches" (including wiretaps and electronic surveillance) whenever necessary. But it appeared unreasonable to have the keys to every data transmission burrowed away in the files of two federal bureaucracies. Should the government hold the key to all encrypted communications, including those of innocent and law-abiding citizens, even if that key would be used on rare occasions to thwart the schemes of criminals? For many libertarians, the answer was a resounding no. They saw the Clipper chip as the beginning of a cyberspace police state, a way for government to increase its hegemony over Internet technologies.

Finally, one must consider the potential for abuse and the possibility that the keys would fall into the wrong hands through negligence or sheer malevolence. After all, could those custodians guarding these keys be completely trusted? What if corrupt officials leaked those keys for a fee or there was some other sort of security breach?

But there were some cogent arguments on the other side of this debate. Those who supported Clipper chip technology contended that it was vital in order to undermine the plans of terrorists who might be using encrypted communication to plan their attack. According to one account, "if the crypto revolution crippled NSA's ability to listen in on the world, the agency might miss out on something vital—for instance, portents of a major terrorist attack."[17] Clearly the risks of not being able to decipher encoded information could be disproportionate to the costs and disadvantages of implementing the Clipper chip scheme. According to Steven Levy, government officials were hoping that the "public will realize that allowing Government to hold the keys is a relatively safe price to pay for safety and national security."[18]

Law enforcement authorities were especially insistent about the need for this technology. In 1995, during the height of the controversy, FBI Director Louis Freeh offered these remarks to a congressional committee:

> Unless the issue of encryption is resolved soon, criminal conversations over the telephone and other communications devices will become indecipherable by law enforcement. This, as much as any issue, jeopardizes the

> public safety and national security of this country. Drug cartels, terrorists, and kidnappers will use telephones and other communications media with impunity knowing that their conversations are immune from our most valued investigative technique.[19]

Supporters of the Clipper chip also pointed out that there were safeguards to minimize the possibility of abuse or security breaches. The plan required two people at each escrow agent to open the safe where the key was kept; in addition, one individual from each of the custodial agencies would be involved in assembling the key. This would make it quite difficult for anyone to extract the key without the proper authorization.

Also, as Dorothy Denning observed, protection against abuse would be buttressed by an extensive auditing of the system: "By examining detailed audit records, it will be possible to determine if keys are used only as authorized and to decrypt only communications intercepted during authorized surveillance."[20] Some proponents of this technology, such as Professor Denning, believed that there would be sufficient checks and balances to counter the potential for abuses or fraudulent behavior.

These arguments, however persuasive, fell on deaf ears. Eventually, the Clinton administration succumbed to the concerted opposition to Clipper by civil libertarians and certain commercial interests, and it abandoned this plan.

A KEY RECOVERY PLAN

Law enforcement authorities were still convinced that they needed some sort of backdoor access to encryption programs without which they could not loosen up export controls. After the demise of the Clipper chip proposal the U.S. government swiftly issued a new encryption plan in 1996 called Key Management Infrastructure (KMI). Critics dubbed the proposal Clipper 3.1.1. As part of the KMI plan, the regulatory oversight of encryption products was transferred from the State Department to the Department of Commerce. This effectively put an end to the NSA's involvement in the process of crypto exports. Encryption technology was no longer officially regarded as a weapon, but as a tool of commerce. The government also began referring to key "escrow" as key "recovery." The basic elements of the KMI plan were explained in a NSA White Paper: "The solution is an encryption chip that provides extra privacy protection . . . but one that can be read by U.S. government officials when authorized by law. . . . The key escrow system would protect U.S.

citizens and companies from invasion of their privacy by hackers, competitors and foreign governments. At the same time, it would allow law enforcement to conduct wiretaps in precisely the same circumstances as are currently permitted under the law."[21]

KMI authorized a government infrastructure with key recovery services. Encryption products of any strength could be exported as long as the keys were escrowed with government approved "escrow agents." The government or a specially authorized neutral organization would hold the private keys for decryption and provide them to law enforcement authorities on demand. All escrow agents would need certification by the U.S. government. If this plan was acceptable the government promised that companies could immediately export 56-bit keys (up from 40 bits) provided they complied with this plan for handling keys that exceeded 56 bits and filed a plan within two years for installing key recovery in new 56-bit products. Companies who did export strong encryption products (56-bit key and beyond) were required to submit semiannual reports to the Commerce Department. As Weitzner indicated, the government's new approach was simple: "no escrow, no export."[22]

Like the Clipper scheme, this key recovery plan met with the same recalcitrant opposition from privacy advocates, Internet activists, and commercial interests. They remained troubled because the U.S. government would not abandon the requirement of key recovery. Privacy experts warned that the involvement of an independent third party, the central administrator holding the escrowed keys, had the potential to make sensitive communications more vulnerable. The government's plan left many unanswered questions: How costly would it be to have this massive key escrow system? Would such a system be scalable? And how could circumvention and abuse of the key escrow system be prevented? How could the government guarantee security for a repository of escrowed keys?

POLICY REVERSAL

In January 2000 the Clinton administration finally reversed its stand on tight export controls. It issued a set of new encryption regulations that represented a fundamental change in U.S. policy. In the U.S. government's view, these revised principles would help achieve balanced competing interests between the competing interests of e-commerce privacy protection, and national security. The specific policy changes included the following: Any encryption commodity or software of any key length can now be exported to any nongovernment end user in any country (except the seven countries that support terrorism); it must first undergo an initial technical review; a new product category for the most widely available products has been established called "retail encryption commodities and software"; these retail encryption products of any key length can be exported to any end user (except in the seven states supporting terrorism); finally, postexport reporting is required for exports of products with keys above 64 bits (unless they are finance specific).[23]

Some civil liberties groups such as the ACLU still voiced some discontent with the new Clinton encryption policy. There was concern that "while the new regulations appear to permit free postings of encryption source code to Internet discussion lists, these postings may be illegal if the author has 'reason to know' that they will be read by a person in one of the countries that are banned from receiving such material."[24]

The new policy was widely supported and enthusiastically promoted by Vice President Al Gore and many members of Congress. However, some were caught off guard. For several years, a pro-export bill known as Security and Freedom through Encryption (SAFE) was opposed by the administration and loyal Democrats. According to Steve Levy, Curt Weldon, a Pennsylvania congressman who led the charge against SAFE, expressed his frustration: "How can you be implementing this policy? For years, you have been telling us that exports of strong crypto will compromise security and empower criminals. And now you're telling us you've changed your minds."[25]

At the time, President Clinton's policy reversal appeared to close the debate on encryption export controls. But the terrorist attack on September 11, 2001 changed all that. There is no evidence that encryption played any role in the events leading up to September 11, but there is evidence that Osama bin Laden and the al Qaeda terrorist group "have in the past used encryption to protect their phone conversations and E-mail communications."[26] As a result, legislators are once again calling for laws "that would make such conversations and messages less private by creating a 'back door' in encryption products."[27]

Thus, in the aftermath of September 11, the debate on encryption has been reopened once again. And the question at the heart of that debate remains the same: How can the United States protect itself and gather intelligence if terrorists use strong encryption products for which there is no backdoor access?

NOTES

1. J. Moor, "Toward a Theory of Privacy for the Information Age," in *Readings in Cyberethics*, ed. R. Spinello and H. Tavani (Sudbury, MA: Jones & Bartlett, 2001), pp. 349–359.

2. This is a revised and updated version of a case which originally appeared in R. Spinello, *Ethical Aspects of Information Technology* (Upper Saddle River, NJ: Prentice Hall, 1995).
3. "The Datamation 100," *Datamation* (15 June 1992), p. 96.
4. L. Kretchmar, "How to Shine in a Sullied Industry," *Fortune*, (24 February 1992).
5. M. Rotenberg, "Data Protection, Computers, and Changing Information Practices," testimony before the Government Information, Justice, and Agriculture Subcommittee of the Committee on Government Operations of the House of Representatives, May 16, 1990.
6. Quoted in L. Gurak, *Persuasion and Privacy in Cyberspace* (New Haven, CT: Yale University Press, 1997), p. 19.
7. Quoted in Cheryl Rosen, "The Politics of Privacy Protection," *Information Week* (17 July 2000), p. 112.
8. See the Amazon Web site: www.amazon.com.
9. This is a hypothetical case, but it is based on a real situation.
10. This is a hypothetical case study.
11. This is an updated version of a case which originally appeared in R. Spinello, *Ethical Aspects of Information Technology* (Upper Saddle River, NJ: Prentice Hall, 1995). The case is based on an actual situation but most names, dates, and places have been altered.
12. Marlene Piturro, "Electronic Monitoring," *Information Center* (July 1990), p. 31.
13. Electronic Frontier Foundation (EFF). "The Fourth Amendment and Carnivore," testimony before the House Judiciary Committee on the Constitution, July 28, 2000.
14. L. Kahaner, "Hungry for your E-Mail," *Information Week* (23 April 2001), pp. 59–64.
15. C. L. Symes, "Cryptography and Computer Systems Security," *IBM Systems Journal* 30 no. 2 (1991), p. 133.
16. John Markoff, "U.S. as Big Brother of Computer Age," *New York Times*, 6 May 1993, p. D7.
17. Steven Levy, "Battle of the Clipper Chip," *New York Times Magazine*, (12 June 1994), p. 39.
18. Ibid., p. 40.
19. Louis Freeh, testimony before the House Judiciary Committee's Hearing on Encryption Technologies, March 30, 1995.
20. Dorothy E. Denning, "Clipper Controversy: Key Escrow Scheme Protects Personal, National Security," *Computerworld* (25 July 1994), p. 106.
21. National Security Administration, "Encryption, Law Enforcement, and National Security," White Paper (Washington, D.C.: NSA Office), 1995.
22. D. Weitzner, "Feds versus Freedom," *Wired* (December 1996), p. 94.
23. Fact Sheet: Administration Implements Updated Encryption Export Policy, Center for Democracy and Technology (2000), available on-line at http://-www.cdt.org/crypto/admin.

24. A. Harrison, "Civil Liberties Groups Slam Encryption Export Rules," *Computerworld* (17 January 2000), p. 10
25. S. Levy, *Crypto* (New York: Viking Press, 2001), p. 306.
26. J. Rendleman, "Mixed Messages," *InformationWeek* (1 October 2001), pp. 18–19.
27. Ibid.

6

Security and Cybercrime

Computer security problems have a long and complex history—the disruption of operations through viruses, worms, and logic bombs along with unauthorized access have plagued computer users for many years. These problems are not trivial and can cause serious economic harm. The infamous "ILoveYou" virus unleashed across the Web in 2000 is estimated to have cost about $11 billion. Denial of Service (DoS) attacks are one of the newer weapons deployed against commercial Web sites. These attacks overwhelm Web servers with fake requests from hijacked personal computers all over the world. As a result, real customers cannot access these sites and business is lost. Particular concerns have recently arisen about the growing threat of cyberterrorism. Digital assaults on the Internet infrastructure could have potentially devastating consequences.

There is also evidence that hacker attacks are on the rise. The Software Engineering Institute's CERT Coordination Center reported that attacks have grown from 6 in 1988 to 52,658 in 2001. The number of incidents reported to CERT in 2001 has almost doubled from what was reported in 2000 and increased steadily in the last five years.[1] While some of this may be due to greater public awareness of security breaches, the trend is still quite alarming.

Most companies recognize that for purely pragmatic reasons their business demands careful attention to security issues. But it should not be overlooked that there is also a moral responsibility to ensure that systems are secure and that data is adequately protected. This responsibility stems from the fact that careless or shoddy security procedures could allow sensitive data to fall into the wrong hands and thereby cause considerable injury for the data subjects. For instance, if careless security allows intruders access to financial records or credit card numbers, innocent people could easily be victimized.

Yet despite persistent security breaches, security remains all too lax. A security study conducted by Cisco found vulnerabilities in each of the 33 sites examined by Cisco. The study further found that these vulnerabilities "could be traced to outdated software or lax system administration maintenance, not to inherent flaws in the systems."[2] Businesses are slowly learning that they must devote more resources to protecting their Web sites and networks.

Many security breaches are caused by hackers, and some hackers have insisted that most of their intrusive activities do no real harm and do not constitute a serious ethical transgression.[3] But is there any merit to this claim? Also, how do we measure the damage caused by such intruders? If no files or data have been stolen or corrupted, does this mean that the intrusion should be dismissed as insignificant?

The cases in this chapter will take into account all of these issues. They will explicitly consider the moral challenge of ensuring a secure environment along with questions about the gravity of unauthorized access and the appropriate penalties for those who are culpable of violating another's property rights.

Most experts agree that the biggest threat to information technology security is still from within the organization. Many troubling questions come to the surface in the first case of the chapter called "The Disgruntled Consultant." After an employee is terminated, he corrupts a system scheduled for immediate delivery to a major client. What is the company's responsibility for the actions of this rogue employee and is there some obligation to compensate the injured party?

In the next case, "Security Breach at IKON," a company must decide what to do when customer data is inadvertently exposed. Among other issues, this case raises the question of what constitutes "adequate" security for a commercial Web site.

The other four cases in this section shift away from this corporate focus and deal with the hacker phenomenon. In the hypothetical case entitled "A Harmless Prank" university officials must determine a fitting punishment for a clever but penitent student hacker. Electronic trespassing is a serious offense and it's important to send a strong signal, but extenuating circumstances make it difficult to arrive at a just and fair decision.

Similar questions arise in a case called "Interview with a Hacker," which presents a view of this subculture through the eyes of one of its former members. He articulates the so-called "hacker ethic" that one can look around on the Internet but not destroy someone else's data. Other opinions are expressed in the interview about this culture and its norms of behavior.

The case about Craig Niedorf, a young man arrested for propagating a secret text file on the Internet, deals with the government's apparent overreaction to the misappropriation of sensitive information. How much power should the government have to curtail activities and set limits on the mysterious new frontiers of cyberspace? This case bears some similarity to "Piracy on the Internet" in Chapter 3, since it too deals with some key civil liberties issues.

Finally, "Hacktivism" considers whether hacking can be morally justified as a form of civil disobedience. In this case a political activist faces criminal charges for defacing the Web site of a power company but argues that he acted to protest this company's questionable environmental policies.

Case 6.1 The Disgruntled Consultant

Donald Chase had just celebrated his tenth anniversary at TTI Consulting when he received the bad news. Due to declining revenues and a shrinking customer base he was one of seven consultants who was being dismissed. His boss, Dr. Phillip Bluestein, informed Chase at 11:00 A.M. on Tuesday that his services were no longer needed. Dr. Bluestein had usually been rather abrupt in his dealings with subordinates, and unfortunately this situation was no different. Chase was told to pack his things and clear out of the building by noon.

Crestfallen, Chase returned to his small office on the third floor of the TTI building. He struggled to suppress his anger and resentment. He had given his heart and soul to this company during the last 10 years and felt betrayed by this sudden dismissal. These feelings were perhaps accentuated because he had just recently completed a major project for one of TTI's established clients, the Northwest Commerce Bank. He had worked long hours and weekends to finish its complex cash management application on schedule. Chase had completed this sophisticated program only several days ago, and during a brief internal demo he had received considerable praise from upper management including Dr. Bluestein. Managers at Northwest were eagerly awaiting delivery since they estimated that this new system would save the bank about $60,000 a month thanks to more efficient cash management.

However, at the time of Chase's dismissal the application had not yet been delivered to the client. It remained on Chase's IBM PC which was linked to the company's extensive client/server network. Chase kept the only backup copy of this system in his brief case; this had enabled him to work on the application at home at his convenience.

As Chase began packing his belongings, Dr. Bluestein appeared at the doorway. They briefly discussed the Commerce Bank application, and Chase pointed out to Bluestein how the application could be accessed on his PC. This discussion was followed by a cursory overview of the programs that comprised this system. It appeared to Chase that Bluestein wanted to make sure that everything was in tact for the system's imminent delivery to Commerce Bank. Bluestein remained with Chase as he finished packing a few boxes of books and other materials. Chase then put only a few additional items in his brief case and left his office followed by Bluestein He did not return the backup copy of the Commerce Bank system. After saying goodbye to a few friends, Chase left the building and drove home.

Upon his return home Chase decided to seek revenge on his ungrateful employer. He used his PC to connect to the company computer system, entered his user ID and password, and accessed the only copy of the Commerce Bank application. He proceeded swiftly to disable several key programs by inserting some code that subverted the display of menu screens and corrupted data. Chase also had the presence of mind to cover his tracks by erasing the audit file that accompanied the program; thus there was no record of this unauthorized access to this application.

Executives at TTI were not aware of what had happened until two days later when an associate of Chase proceeded to do one final quality assurance test before final delivery of the program to the bank. When she logged in to the application, she quickly realized that it had been tampered with and called Dr. Bluestein who strongly suspected sabotage. He immediately and repeatedly called Chase's residence but there was no answer; also Chase's large severance check had already been cashed.

As Commerce Bank waited patiently for its cash management system, the company quickly launched an internal investigation. It was apparent that the layoffs represented a chaotic situation within TTI; as a result, there was inadequate communication between certain departments. For example, the company's security manager had not been informed about the layoffs until the day after they had occurred. At that point user IDs and passwords for the discharged employees were revoked. However, this was much too late to save the Commerce Bank application from this deliberate act of sabotage. When asked by the executive vice president about this communication failure, the human resources manager informed her that his department had never coordinated layoffs and dismissals with the security manager. "We've never had the sense in this company that we should lock the gates and put up barricades when people leave," he said; "Our employees are trusted colleagues even after they've been let go."

As the investigation continued, Dr. Bluestein faced a difficult decision about how he would deal with his contact at the Commerce Bank who was eagerly awaiting the cash management program that was now overdue. Chase was an especially clever and adept programmer and consequently Bluestein estimated that it would take at least several weeks to unearth the bugs and fix the system properly. Also, all of the other consultants were assigned to high-priority projects, so there might be some delay in getting started on this work.

Bluestein wondered what he should tell the people at Commerce. Should he be candid about the company's untimely security lapse? Commerce was one of TTI's most security-conscious customers, and hence this revelation might jeopardize lucrative future contracts. But Commerce had been told last week that the project was finished and that they would receive it right on time. How, then, could he explain what could have gone wrong to delay delivery by several weeks and maybe longer? Also, Bluestein wondered about the corporation's legal and moral responsibility for what had happened. Chase was clearly the main culprit here, but to what extent was the corporation also liable for his transgression? And if the company were liable, should it make some restitution to its customer whose business was adversely affected because of this mishap? Bluestein began sorting through all these questions as he stared at the pink phone messages in front of him.

Case 6.2 Security Breach at IKON[4]

Chester Davis was not looking forward to an emergency meeting of the Information Technology (IT) staff. It was just about 9:00 A.M. when he entered the third-floor conference room and the meeting was just about to get underway. He poured some coffee and took one of the few remaining seats around the walnut conference table. He gazed at the putty-colored walls and pulled out his notes relating to today's topic: a gaping security hole at the company's Web site.

Davis worked in the IT department of a specialty clothing store called IKON. It was founded in 1988 and enjoyed an excellent reputation among young, upscale consumers. IKON had 227 stores located throughout the east and southeast with projected 2002 sales of $650 million. But despite IKON's success and profitability, the company lagged behind in the area of electronic commerce.

IKON had waited until 1999 before embarking on a project to build a B2C (business to consumer) Web site where customers could place orders or obtain product information and catalogs. Finally, in early 2000 the company's Web site was made available to much fanfare and even critical acclaim—the Web site team invested heavily in aesthetics and the site stood out among competitors' plainer looking sites. Unfortunately, less attention was paid to the Web site's security.

Brian Dobson, the associate VP for information technology, was the Web site development team's leader and Davis was in charge of security issues. Davis recalled a conversation with Dobson about the security planned for the Web site. At their initial planning meeting Dobson had laid out his views on security:

> Security should not be a big deal for a project like this. Just make sure that the application is restricted to authorized users and that the network is reasonably secure. Nothing too fancy, Chester, because we just don't have the time or the funding.

But Davis had been insistent that more needed to be done.

> I'm afraid that I can't agree with you, Brian. I have developed a comprehensive security plan with a good deal of emphasis on network security and detection measures. My plan calls for a managed firewall, intrusion detection,[5] authentication through passwords, and antivirus services. I also think that we should do vulnerability assessment, a periodic probing of the system to reveal any weaknesses. Also, my plan calls for ongoing security testing as new applications or servers are added to make sure that security holes have not opened up. Finally I think it would be prudent to subscribe to a security intelligence service that will notify us of potential threats or newly uncovered vulnerabilities in systems or hardware.

Dobson picked up the security specs and associated cost estimates from a pile of folders on his desk. He studied them for a few minutes and then said,

> I've just been looking over these specs, and I think that the level of security which you are proposing is unnecessary. It's overkill. Also, let me point out, that nobody higher up at IKON is pushing for this kind of security. It doesn't seem to be a big deal for them. We obviously need a firewall, authentication, and virus protection, but let's knock off the intrusion detection. This would require heavy IT resources to be able to differentiate between normal traffic and an intrusion. Also, we'll do a full security audit before we launch, but we do not have the resources to continue testing for security breaches. Finally, I am not going to authorize a subscription to some security intelligence service—it's too expensive.

Davis raised some further objections but to no avail, and Dobson's security scheme was adopted.

It was now a year and a half later as the IT team assembled to discuss a major security breach at the IKON Web site. Dobson revealed that thousands of customer files on the Web site had somehow become exposed. A customer, who reported the security breach, was requesting a catalog and received an error message. That message showed him the way to the IKON database where he was able to peruse the names, addresses, phone numbers, e-mail addresses, and in some cases the credit card numbers of IKON's on-line customers. That database included over 100,000 names. No one yet knew the exact cause of the breach, how long it had existed, or whether other customers had accessed this data. Dobson had called in an outside security consultant and her initial assessment was that a series of changes recently undertaken by IKON may have led to the problem. The Web site had recently gotten a new "look" and links to several new partners had been added; a new server was also added to the configuration for load balancing. A security patch was quickly developed to provide a temporary fix for the problem.

As the meeting came to an end, Dobson turned to his team for some advice. He had a meeting scheduled for that afternoon with the company's chief operating officer to review the damage. The company had to decide whether or not to tell its customers about the security breach, since their personal data may have been exposed to hackers. What would such a revelation do to IKON's credibility? How should customers be informed about this? What might IKON say to allay their concerns about the prospect of future problems? IT also needed to develop a plan so that the probability of this happening again in the future would be minimized. Someone suggested that outsourcing security might be the answer.

Davis was pretty silent during the meeting, but he was surprised at Dobson's final comment that this incident should not reflect on the work of the development team which had incorporated "adequate" security procedures into the Web site design. As Dobson saw it, this security breach was just an unavoidable fluke.

Case 6.3 A Harmless Prank

Steven Mackey was a junior and a computer science major at Riverview State College, a moderate-size four-year college located in the Midwest. He had worked with computers since childhood and he chose to attend Riverview because of its excellent computer science department. He consistently received good grades and he was highly regarded by the department and its faculty. During this second semester of his junior year he was learning two new computer languages, C++ and JAVA, and he was taking a difficult course on compilers.

Steven was also known among his friends and fellow computer science students as a typical "hacker." He enjoyed traversing through the Internet, especially at night, and he sometimes boasted about his ability to crack codes and break into computer systems that he had not been authorized to use. Some of the other students in the computer science department admired Steven's antics; in their eyes these transgressions merely confirmed his technical expertise. Steven's exploits were also well known around other circles of the campus, but since he had not tampered with any university systems he was never reprimanded by faculty or administrators.

One late evening in April just three weeks before Riverview's final exams, Steven and his girlfriend decided to see if they could tap into the administrative network at Riverview. This network included the files of the administrators at Chauncey Hall who were responsible for managing the financial affairs of the university. Many of these files contained confidential data about university finances or personnel matters. Steven was most interested in the payroll file which included the salaries of all Riverview employees, including the faculty. He was not interested so much in looking at those salaries but in demonstrating his exceptional ability by cracking the passwords to this file. His interest in doing this was stimulated by one of his professors who mentioned that he had helped design the security system for this file and that he considered it virtually impregnable. Steven construed this boasting as a challenge to the class, while others seemed to pay little attention to this remark.

But Steven was intrigued and excited about this challenge. He worked for four and a half hours to achieve this objective. It was relatively easy to tap into the university network since its security was rather weak. But the payroll file did prove to be another matter. Steven ran algorithms used to crack passwords, but they kept failing. Eventually, however, through sheer ingenuity and persistence he broke the code and gained access to the file. He was so elated that he didn't even bother to look at any of the salaries or the other information maintained there. By now he was so exhausted that he simply logged off the computer and went to sleep.

The next day the system administrator found evidence that there had been an unauthorized entry into the IBM mainframe's CICS system at 2:36 A.M. She also detected that the payroll file had been accessed, but that no individual records had been read. University officials and campus police were notified immediately, and they were quickly able to trace this intrusion to Stephen's computer. No one was surprised that Stephen was the culprit, given his penchant for this sort of activity.

Stephen was summoned before the dean of students, Dr. Lillian Green, who confronted him with the overwhelming evidence. In his defense Stephen sheepishly claimed that this was a harmless incident, "just a prank," which merely disproved his professor's contention that the payroll file was "virtually impregnable." He claimed that gaining entry to a supposedly secure system was both a hobby and a challenge. Indeed, Stephen argued, he had done the university a favor by exposing the vulnerability of this file which was hitherto thought to be so secure. Furthemore, he pointed out that he did not look at any of the payroll data, and finally, he gave to the dean some specific instructions on how to buttress security for the administrative network. He said he had been formulating these recommendations since the morning after his break-in.

Dean Green became less hostile as the meeting proceeded since she saw that Steven was not a mean or especially devious person. Moreover, she appreciated his candor and sincerity. Prior to the meeting with Stephen she had reviewed his academic record and ascertained that he had a 3.4 grade point average and that he had not been subject to any disciplinary actions during his enrollment at Riverview. Given this and Stephen's contriteness, she was inclined to be somewhat lenient with him.

Nevertheless, this unfortunate incident was not viewed so benignly by college administrators who were furious over the break-in. Also, whatever sanctions were imposed on Stephen would be construed as an important signal from the dean's office. There was some apprehension that others might try to mimic Stephen's exploits.

After Stephen completed this explanation of his actions, he apologized and promised not to try this again. Dean Green thanked him for his cooperation and honesty, but she also pointed out that this was a serious offense that the university could not take lightly. She told him that her assistant would call him tomorrow to set up a second appointment. At that time she would discuss the university's decision regarding an appropriate penalty for his actions.

Later that day in the faculty dining room she discussed the young man's plight with a small group of administrators and faculty members. Some of her colleagues felt that a stern lecture and a warning to Stephen were sufficient. But others felt that a more severe punishment was in order, perhaps even suspension for a semester. One person said that he would have no qualms expelling a student for doing this. Such a bold action would send a clear message to other "hackers" on campus that this sort of antisocial and deviant behavior would not be tolerated. The dean listened carefully to this advice as she tried to decide how the university should deal with "on-line offenders" such as Stephen.

Case 6.4 Interview with a Hacker

> hacker n. . . . [depracated] A malicious meddler who tries to discover sensitive information by poking around.[6]

In February 1995, the author interviewed Ed Jones (fictitious name), a professional computer programmer who also describes himself as a "hacker." Mr. Jones is a 28-year-old college graduate who was often described as a computer "genius" as far back as the eighth grade. During his high school and college days he worked with computers incessantly. In the following interview he is asked some pointed and specific questions about his experiences and his overall philosophy of computers, the Internet, and many other topics.

The interview has been edited and condensed by the author.

***Question*: Mr. Jones, how would you describe a hacker today?**

When most of us on the net use the term "hacker," we're simply referring to a person who enjoys programming, a person who enjoys solving computer problems and puzzles. Hackers love to focus intently on a problem—it's called being in hack mode and it's almost a mystical experience for some of us. For most hackers their lives revolve around a computer and their community is the electronic network.

Question: **But the term now has a negative connotation, doesn't it?**

Yes, it seems to. But this is the way the media has come to use the term. They have clearly distorted its original meaning. We like to refer to malicious hackers as "crackers." They're the ones with the outlaw sensibility who cause big problems by undermining security or stealing someone's files.

Question: **We hear a lot these days about the hacker ethic. Is there a simple definition of this?**

I've always liked the way that Steven Levy described this in his book about hackers. Some of the main tenets of this "ethic" are that access to computer systems should be unlimited and unrestricted. I think he called it the "Hands-On Imperative." Also all information should be freely accessible in order to help others learn and develop their skills. Most hackers deeply mistrust authority and bureaucracy which they see as impediments to learning and progress.[7]

Question: **In other words, the hacker credo is that access to information should be free and not monopolized by big corporations?**

Sure—that's exactly what we're saying.

Question: **Is this sort of activity common? Are there a lot of hackers or crackers around today who engage in devious behavior?**

I still have many friends that you would describe as "hackers," though I have outgrown it myself. Yes, I would have to say that it's still common.

For many computer cyberpunks and others, slogging around on the Internet and breaking into computer systems is really exciting and enticing because it's so challenging. There will always be hackers who deviate from the rules of society. It's also too tempting, especially since so many system administrators don't have a clue about security. And as systems become more open the threats posed by these individuals will continue to grow.

Question: **It seems that hackers are lionized by the press and that the hacker subculture is admired, particularly by impressionable young people.**

A lot of this hacker coverage is just hype, if you ask me. It doesn't mean very much. They're not big heroes, just a bunch of people fighting for freedom, you know, freedom of expression on the Internet and freedom to explore this new frontier.

Question: **Most of us think that if "freedom" manifests itself in exploiting security weaknesses and logging on to someone else's system, there's a problem. We regard such activity as a form of trespassing and a violation of property rights. Do you agree with this?**

I'm not sure what I think about that, but let me say that most hackers I know believe that this network is a public place and that anyone connected to the network is part of that public place. After all, companies, schools, and government agencies choose to get on there knowing full well the possible consequences. In our estimation, information on the Net is in the public domain and we have every right to access it if we can find a way to get at it.

Question: **But break-ins are a security manager's worst nightmare. Don't you think that they cause considerable damage and disruption?**

In some respects these break-ins can provide a helpful service to organizations by identifying security weaknesses and vulnerabilities. Otherwise these individuals would not pay any attention to these problems, and a real thief or someone into corporate espionage might cause bigger headaches. I think that our intrusions have actually led to many enhancements in system security. Hackers believe that they keep organizations on their toes and that otherwise they wouldn't pay any attention to security issues. In other words, we keep them one step ahead of the real bad guys.

Question: **In other words, hackers are performing a great service to their country by engaging in these activities?**

Well, that's a pretty sarcastic way to put it, but right! It sounds strange but there is something to be said for this point of view. Also, study after study shows that the big problem is not with hackers but with ex-employees and other insiders.

Question: **There's another issue that people bring up about this and that's the fact that hackers tie up computer resources through their unauthorized forays into different systems.**

I've heard this complaint a few times, but it's a real bogus argument. For one thing most hackers work during the late night or early morning hours when no one else is usually on the system. It's a perfect time to do some exploring and probing of some system. Hence, contrary to popular opinion, we are not wasting computer resources.

Question: **But let's be frank about this. Aren't you trespassing on someone's property?**

Ahh, yes and no. But either way, I really don't see the problem here. What's wrong with snooping around, especially if I do not alter any data or screw up some commands or programs? Also, we're not interested in copying anything; most of the stuff we see is really boring and it's of no interest. So where's the damage. It's the same as walking across Farmer Brown's field—as long as I leave the animals and the crops alone, what harm have I done? People do that all the time in this country and everyone leaves them alone.

Question: **What's your motivation for this? What's the big thrill? I have to admit that I don't get it.**

Yea, no offense, but people like you will never "get it." My friends and I grew up with computers and we love working with them. And doing this stuff on the Internet is like pushing forward into new frontiers. I suppose that we do it because it's a terrific challenge. It's a way of testing our computer acumen and ingenuity. It sharpens our skills and wits. And, I repeat, it doesn't do any real harm to anyone.

Question: **But can you do *anything* on the Internet? Is there a line that one shouldn't cross?**

The line, I think, is between snooping around and outright theft. For most respectable hackers it's OK to look around some corporate or government system, but you shouldn't steal data and try to profit from it.

Question: **What do you think of those people who get their kicks out of propagating a virus or worm through a web of computer systems? Isn't *this* going a bit too far? Does it cross the line that we're talking about?**

The prevailing wisdom is that viruses and worms are intellectual curiosities. However, I do admit that this is pushing it, especially if one unleashes a virus that destroys property and ends up costing somebody a lot of money.

But let me make a few remarks about those who do work with these viruses and other strange programs. Some of these guys get a little carried away, but creating a virus is a real learning experience; they just have to keep these things under control and not let them wreak havoc on some mission-critical application. Viruses that propagate themselves but allow programs to run normally are no big deal. They might include nice display hacks that are sort of fun. On the other hand, nasty viruses that nuke someone's data are definitely a problem.

Question: **Well, we've covered a lot of ground here. Thanks very much.**

Don't mention it.

Case 6.5 The Case of Craig Neidorf

A SUMMARY OF EVENTS

Craig Neidorf was a young pre-law student at the University of Missouri when he found himself at the center of an investigation by the U.S. Secret Service and Southwestern Bell. He was being accused of serious crimes including fraud and theft. The "crimes" were allegedly perpetrated while Neidorf was a young teenager.

Several years before entering the University of Missouri he had started an electronic newsletter known as *Phrack.* According to one account of this story, "*Phrack* provided information that could be useful for someone trying to gain access to a system for free use of telecommunications lines."[8] In other words, *Phrack* provided information that sometimes facilitated the illicit intrusion of certain computer systems. It liked to publish articles that revealed a system's vulnerabilities and its security holes. In this respect, according to Dorothy Denning, "it is not unlike some professional publications such as those issued by the ACM."[9] Of course, such publications did not encourage users to exploit those vulnerabilities, and sometimes *Phrack* would encourage such exploitation. Neidorf was the publisher of this journal and in that role he solicited and edited articles for publication.

In January 1990 Neidorf was confronted by Secret Service agents along with representatives of Southwestern Bell (also called Bell South). The subject of their inquiry was a document about the E911 or the Enhanced 911 that had been published in a recent issue of *Phrack.* These officials claimed that the E911 text file published in *Phrack* was a proprietary document that belonged exclusively to BellSouth. They estimated its worth at approximately $23,900. They further maintained that the document functioned as a guide to the workings of the 911 computer system and that in the hands of some clever hacker it could allow for the manipulation of that system. In short, the illegal publication of this document could be a serious hazard for public safety. Finally, it was alleged that the document had been pilfered by Robert Riggs "as part of a fraudulent scheme . . . to break into computer systems in order to obtain sensitive documents" that would be made available to the hacker community through the medium of *Phrack.*[10]

Shortly after the investigation was initiated, a federal grand jury in Chicago indicted Neidorf on 10 counts of wire fraud and interstate transportation of stolen property. The maximum penalty for these crimes was a 65-year prison term.

In his defense, Neidorf's attorney, Sheldon Zenner, argued that *Phrack* was not a subversive sort of publication, but simply one that allowed for the dissemination and free exchange of information. With the help of Dorothy Denning, a computer science professor at Georgetown University, he set out to prove that the E911 document published in *Phrack* did not contain any secrets. Professor Denning's investigative work attempted to prove that there was an abundance of other material in the public domain that also provided ample information about breaking into a system. Thus, it was unfair to single out this document and its publication in *Phrack.*

The case did go to trial, but half way through the trial the government decided to drop the charges. Neidorf was vindicated and the government was embarrased by its apparent overzealousness. It is important to note that during the trial Riggs gave testimony about his role in this incident. He described how he downloaded the file from a BellSouth computer system and sent it to Neidorf via e-mail for publication in *Phrack.* It was also revealed during the trial that pamplets made available by BellSouth contained just as much information about the E911 as did this document. Whatever was in this document, then, was already in the public domain. Presumably, as these revelations were made public at the trial, the government realized the superficiality of its case and so made the decision to drop the charges just four days after the trial had begun.

SOCIAL AND ETHICAL ISSUES

Aside from the issue of potential government harassment there are many other questions raised by the case of Craig Neidorf. The most obvious issue concerns First Amendment rights. Does the right of free expression extend to the publication of documents that delineate security flaws? According to Deborah Johnson, "What is at stake here is freedom of expression on-line and how much power the government, or anyone, should have to patrol and control on-line activities."[11] Perhaps a larger and more important question is whether or not our First Amendment rights extend to electronic communications without qualification? Should publications in on-line newsletters or pronouncements on Internet bulletin boards enjoy precisely the same level of protection as articles in newspapers or speeches given in the city common? In answering this question one must carefully consider the different *nature* of these communications which are capable of reaching tremendous volumes of people very quickly.

Another critical issue that emerges in this case concerns the liability of those who operate bulletin boards especially on public media such as the Internet. Should those organizations or individuals (such as Neidorf) who operate and monitor bulletin boards be held accountable for everything that is published on them? To do so would clearly encumber the exchange and dissemination of information. As some have pointed out, we do not hold the phone company accountable for what transpires over phone lines so why should we hold the operators of bulletin boards accountable for the information that is exchanged through this electronic format. Or is this a weak and inappropriate analogy?

The final point about this case that deserves some discussion is the apparent overreaction exhibited by the U.S. government and BellSouth. Were the actions of these constituencies warranted by the publication of the E911 text document or was this blown out of proportion? Was this another manifestation of "hacker hysteria" among law enforcement officials? Or were Neidorf and his colleagues culpable of a crime and hence a legitimate target of these officials? And, should the offense of publishing information about how to gain unauthorized access to a company's host computer system be considered as a felony?

Clearly, the Neidorf case generates many other questions, but these are certainly the most dominant and controversial ones. It is worth noting that although this incident happened in 1990, some of these complex matters have still not been resolved or even adequately addressed by computer professionals and law enforcement authorities.

Case 6.6 Hacktivism

Hacking web sites is one of the newest forms of cybercrime, but sometimes this is done to send a political message. The number of politically motivated Web site attacks has grown dramatically during the early

2000s. Such attacks are usually launched by a group or individual with a grudge against the target site. The phenomenon has become known as hacktivsim. Mannion and Goodrum define hacktivism as "the (sometimes) clandestine use of computer hacking to help advance political causes."[12] Sometimes the process of hacktivism is encouraged or abetted by legitimate political interest groups. In 2000 a pro-Israeli Web site "provided tools that visitors could use to attack Web sites affiliated with Hezbollah, an anti-Israel terrorist organization; the setup involved more than 8,500 servers in both Israel and the United States to flood Hezbollah Web sites with hundreds of thousands of hits a day."[13] One of the most common forms of hacktivism is the use of Denial of Service (DoS) attacks. With DoS attacks, hackers are able to download software from underground Web sites that enable them to hijack scores of computers in which they implant the downloaded program. They then instruct these machines to send requests for information to the targeted Web site. These constant messages clog the system, and the whole process eventually brings the Web server of the target site to its knees.

As a way of reflecting on the ethical implications of hacktivism consider the following hypothetical scenario:

> It is a blustery winter afternoon and Cynthia Wilson is on the phone working out the details of a plea agreement for her most recent case. Her assistant informs her that her next appointment has arrived, and she hastily wraps up the conversation. As she puts down the phone, a young man is escorted into her office. Cynthia works for a national law firm located in New York City. The firm specializes in the new legal field of cybercrimes, but this case will be a first if she decides to accept it. The man's name is Michael Johnson. He is one of the leaders of an environmental group known as "Green Justice"; among other activities, its members attack so-called "enemies of the environment." Johnson explains that he has been accused of violating the computer crime statute for the state of New York. That statute forbids "(1) unauthorized access to a computer with intent to do some further bad act and (2) damage to computer related property." She is familiar with the statute and she presses Johnson for more details. He admits to organizing a massive break-in to the Web site of New York Northern Electric (NYNE), an electric utility company designed to hack the company Web site. NYNE was planning to proceed with the construction of dams in a certain part of the state in order to generate hydroelectricity. Despite the need for more energy sources in New York, some environmentalists predicted ecological havoc if the dams were built. Certain plant and animal species would be devastated by the flooding. Migration patterns of several species of birds would be disrupted. Johnson decided as an act of civil disobedience to attack NYNE's computer system. He and his cohorts were able to deface the Web site and initiate denial of

service attacks that shut down NYNE's system for over 12 hours. The attack received widespread publicity and after a long investigation Johnson and several other members of Green Justice were apprehended for this crime.

Johnson admits committing this crime but believes that he was acting for a higher cause and that his actions are morally justified despite the fact that he has broken the law. Cynthia is impressed with this young man's candor and conviction, but now she must decide whether or not to take this case. Is this brand of hacktivism a legitimate form of civil disobedience or just an excuse to create mischief? Are there moral or political arguments that she might use to persuade a skeptical jury?

NOTES

1. Software Engineering Institute, "CERT Report on Internet Security," Pittsburgh, PA: Carnegie Mellon University, 2002.
2. J. Levitt and G. Smith, "Are You Vulnerable," *InformationWeek* (21 February 2000), p. 172.
3. See, for example, E. Spafford, "Are Computer Hacker Break-ins Ethical?" *Journal of Systems Software* (January 1992), pp. 41–47.
4. This is a hypothetical case study, but it is based on an actual situation.
5. Intrusion detection entails monitoring the system in order to determine when inappropriate access to the network has occurred.
6. E. Raymond, ed., *The New Hacker's Dictionary* (Cambridge, MA: MIT Press, 1991), pp. 191–192.
7. Cf. Steven Levy, *Hackers* (New York: Doubleday, 1984), pp. 26–36.
8. D. Denning, "The U.S. vs. Craig Neidorf," *Communications of the ACM* 34, no. 3 (March 1991), p. 25.
9. Ibid., p. 28.
10. Ibid., p. 26.
11. D. Johnson, *Computer Ethics,* 2d ed. (Upper Saddle River, NJ: Prentice Hall, 1994), p. 107.
12. M. Mannion and A. Goodrum, "The Hacktivist Ethic," in *Readings in Cyberethics,* ed. R. Spinello and H.Tavani (Sudbury, MA: Jones & Bartlett, 2001).
13. G. Hulme and B. Wallace, "Beware Cyberattacks," *InformationWeek* (13 November 2000), pp. 23–24.

7

Liability, Reliability, and Safety Issues

INTRODUCTION

As computer technology becomes more powerful and more widely used for mission-critical applications, the consequences of failure become more grave and potentially calamitous. Millions of individuals and organizations count on their computers to manage inventory, help fly airplanes, process sophisticated financial transactions, and so forth. Hardware reliability can sometimes become a problem thanks to faulty chips which can wreak havoc with these systems. Most complex software products such as computer operating systems have millions of lines of code where mistakes can lurk for many months or even years before they manifest themselves in some way and perhaps lead to a catastrophe. Thus software "bugs" or errors can be quite disruptive and costly. In extreme cases these bugs can undermine the safety of a critical product or system. Defects can create gaping security holes that can be easily exploited by hacking.

These inevitable problems with software programs generate numerous questions about the moral and legal liability for the vendors who produce and market these programs. Should these companies be held liable for *all* of the defects that lurk in their programs even if those programs were thoroughly and conscientiously tested? Or should there be liability only in those situations where there is carelessness or negligence? What if a bug lurking in millions of lines of code causes a plane crash or the loss of life on an operating table? What is the vendor's moral and legal liability for such catastrophes, especially when the problem is virtually unforeseeable? And what is the vendor's obligation to inform customers about a problem, however obscure, once it is uncovered?

One can arguably conclude that vendors which supply software and hardware products have a minimal obligation to ensure that their products are as reliable and as bug-free as possible so that they will function as intended. A company that rushes its product to market without adequate testing would certainly be negligent both from a legal and moral perspective.

In recent years the software industry has been plagued by vendors selling new products before they are ready for the marketplace. Others have engaged in the questionable practice of "preannouncing" new products or announcing unrealistic release dates. Some prominent companies have announced the availability of new products even though they are a long period of time away from the actual release date when it is difficult to estimate a completion time. Such mythical products have become known throughout the industry as "vaporware." We also include in this category of vaporware those products that are brought to the market prematurely, often without adequate testing or preparation.

Some have defended vaporware as inconsequential and even as a means of survival in the competitive software industry. But it can often have adverse consequences for a company's stakeholders. It has been alleged, for example, that Microsoft has used the tactic of vaporware to enhance its monopoly position in the software industry. If vaporware is deliberately used to exclude rivals from the marketplace, it could be construed as a violation of antitrust laws. Also, according to Richard Stern, "deliberately false vaporware announcements . . . harm the public and also discourage potential market entrants from creating new software."[1]

The concept of liability goes beyond accountability for flawed products and the first case in this chapter, "Prodigy Services Company and Bulletin Board Liability," raises some novel liability issues. Should on-line service providers or ISPs be held liable for the content of their subscribers' electronic messages or other communications? In this case Prodigy is held liable for libelous comments posted on its bulletin board. The reason is that Prodigy monitored communications in order to ensure that content was consistent with its family-friendly philosophy. In the eyes of the court, Prodigy was considered a publisher, fully responsible for its content. But was this ruling fair? To what extent should on-line service providers bear responsibility for preventing the defamatory statements made by its users?

The next case, "The Therac-25," dwells on a different aspect of liability. It considers the issue of product safety from the viewpoint of the users and the so-called software penumbra, that is, those affected by the software.[2] The case chronicles the lethal problems associated with this defective radiotherapy machine. The primary issues are the company's apparent failure to test this product adequately and its reactive response to the crisis which it precipitated.

We then turn to the more common, but not inconsequential, problem of software reliability, the theme of "NCR's Warehouse Manager" case. NCR unknowingly marketed a bug-ridden application that caused damage to the financial and inventory records of several companies, seriously disrupting their businesses. How should NCR respond and what is a fitting compensation for the victims of this faulty software?

A second case study on reliability is "Intel's Pentium Chip Product Controversy," dealing with the infamous, but commercially successful, Pentium chip. This case raises some interesting questions about true product reliability and consumer perception of reliability. What are the management and ethical lessons that high-tech companies can learn from this public relations debacle?

The last in this trio of cases on reliability concerns Sun Microsystems and a more muted product controversy than the Pentium chip. Major customers have been frustrated by server crashes thanks to a faulty SRAM chip. Did Sun act appropriately in its handling of this crisis? Did it learn anything from Intel's painful experience?

In the last two case studies we focus on the problem of vaporware. "The Product Manager" case provides an elaborate description of a company apparently promoting vaporware to its customer base. But there is some ambiguity about the release date and this creates a true quandary for the product manager. The second case on this topic is entitled "Chicago," the code name for Microsoft's new version of Windows 95, a product that has been subjected to many significant delays. Some discern a similarity between Microsoft's actions and IBM's strategy for its 360 mainframe computer which was also introduced to the market well behind schedule despite IBM's deliberate efforts to keep expectations high. Like its predecessor, this case considers the moral and social implications of vaporware.

Case 7.1 Prodigy Services Co. and Bulletin Board Liability

In May 1995 a New York state judge sent shock waves through the legal community and the on-line industry when he issued an opinion stating that Prodigy Services Co. was responsible for the content of its subscribers' electronic messages. The opinion was written as a response to a $200 million lawsuit filed by the investment banking firm Stratton Oakmont Inc., which claimed that Prodigy should be held liable for slanderous messages left on a popular Prodigy bulleting board. Those messages accused the firm of fraudulent behavior and criminal conduct. Prodigy responded by maintaining that it could not and should not be held responsible for what its subscribers posted on its bulletin boards.

Because of this and similar cases, the explosive issue of Internet Service Provider liability has emerged as a challenging and potentially expensive problem for on-line vendors. In the wake of this ruling, executives at Prodigy must reexamine the company's current policies and mechanisms for screening electronic messages. As the company's top executives reviewed the May decision and subsequent events, they knew that the road ahead would be filled with many pitfalls and perils.

COMPANY BACKGROUND

Prodigy Services Company was formed in 1988 as a joint venture of International Business Machines Corp. (IBM) and Sears, Roebuck & Company. The company operated an electronic information and communications service that could be accessed over telephone lines with a modem and a personal computer. This proprietary service was known simply as Prodigy. It made available to users a wide array of on-line activities from shopping to travel arrangements to stock trades.

Subscribers also had access to e-mail facilities which enabled them to transmit private messages to other members. In addition, they were provided access to Prodigy's public bulletin board service which enabled members to post electronic messages that could be read by other subscribers. The bulletin boards were divided into 114 broad topics and subdivided by subjects. Thus, bulletin boards might be devoted to various hobbies, political and social issues, health concerns, investment advice, and so forth.

Prodigy's subscriber base grew steadily and by 1993 it had signed on just over one million subscribers with revenues estimated at $250 million. Its market share was about 25 percent, second only to

CompuServe which led the industry with 35 percent of the market. By 1995 the number of subscribers had doubled to two million. The nascent ISP industry had solid growth prospects, but Prodigy had to contend with established competitors such as CompuServe, America Online, and GEnie. In more recent years it also had to contend with new entrants such as Microsoft Network. In contrast to these other online service providers Prodigy carried a wide range of advertising, and many of its advertisers also sold their products through the Prodigy home shopping network.

Prodigy stood out among its competitors as the most family-oriented service because of its user-friendliness and its publicized efforts to promote wholesome interactions on its bulletin boards. CompuServe, on the other hand, which was owned at this time by H&R Block Inc., was geared more toward computer hobbyists. It offered users on-line chat services with software companies and other "technies," and it enabled Internet connectivity.

SCREENING POLICY

In an effort to fulfill its family-friendly philosophy, Prodigy decided to screen messages posted to its bulletin boards. Prodigy provided its members with ample warning that their messages would be subjected to scrutiny and possible censorship. Users had to indicate their acceptance of the membership agreement before being allowed on to one of its bulletin boards. This agreement included the following terms:

> Members agree not to display any defamatory, inaccurate, abusive, obscene, profane, sexually explicit, threatening, ethnically offensive, or illegal material. . . . Prodigy reserves the right to review and edit any material submitted for display or placed on the Prodigy service, excluding private electronic messages, and may refuse to display or remove from the service material that it in its sole discretion believes violates this Agreement or is otherwise objectionable.

When the company first went on-line it developed a three-step process for reviewing bulletin board messages. In the first step, "all notes were screened by a computer program that searched for key words deemed obscene or indicating solicitations or blatant expressions of hate."[3] If notes were rejected for this reason, they were returned to the sender with a brief explanation. Prodigy had another set of key words that was used to flag messages that *might* be a problem; these messages were then subject to further review by Prodigy staff members. Finally, if other Prodigy subscribers called attention to problem messages, they would be scrutinized and removed if necessary. In general, then, the company's philosophy was to exercise limited editorial control in order to provide its users with a reasonable level of protection from offensive messages. Obviously this became increasingly difficult as the volume of messages continued to grow. In 1995 company officials estimated that about 60,000 messages were posted to its bulletin boards each day.

Prodigy continually reasserted its commitment to the ideal of free speech but recognized that some limits on free expression were necessary. It sought to provide a balance between respect for the right of free expression and the preservation of family and cultural values which mattered a great deal to the majority of its subscribers.

It is worth noting that CompuServe and others in the on-line industry had adopted a strict hands-off approach to the content of electronic messages, which were not monitored in any way. Prodigy itself had also begun moving closer to that model. For example, in late 1995 it began providing users the opportunity to set up their own Web pages, but there were no plans to screen the content of those pages.

FREE SPEECH CONTROVERSIES

From its inception the Prodigy bulletin board service triggered controversies about free speech and censorship. For example, in 1989 Prodigy closed a bulletin board that involved a debate between gays and fundamentalist Christians. The reason given was the low volume of interaction and a lack of interest among the user base, but users who did participate charged Prodigy with censoring their messages. In another case the company put a stop to an on-line protest about its rate increase, canceling the subscriptions of about a dozen members.

In 1991 the company became embroiled in a more serious controversy when it came under attack by the Anti-Defamation League (ADL) for failing to prevent the posting of anti-Semitic messages. The ADL complained that these notes were ethnically offensive and that they violated Prodigy's own policies. The notes contained remarks such as the following: "The holocaust is really an edifice . . . to the naive gullibility of the world in which even the most outrageous survivor's tales and the falsest testimonies are totally believed without the slightest doubt of criticism"; "Did it ever occur to you that Israel might be the cause of most of the trouble in the Middle East?"[4]

In the midst of a firestorm of protests over these and similar postings, Prodigy responded by announcing that it would revise its guidelines in an effort to thwart the posting of such offensive and insulting messages in the future. The offensive category would now include expressions of bigotry such as those manifested in the messages cited by the ADL. The ADL was criticized by both the *Washington Post* and the *New York Times* for its efforts to censor free speech on the network.

THE LIBEL LAWSUIT

Despite its vigilance, problems continued for Prodigy when it found itself the subject of $200 million lawsuit filed by Stratton Oakmont Inc., an investment banking firm on Long Island, New York. The company's president claimed that he had been libeled on Prodigy's most popular electronic bulletin board known as "Money Talk." The messages, which were anonymously posted in October 1994, said that the president and others at Stratton had committed criminal and fraudulent acts in connection with the public offering of stock for a company known as Solomon-Page Ltd. The messages said the offering "was a major criminal fraud," and that Stratton was a "cult of brokers who either lie for a living or get fired." Stratton had been investigated by the SEC for "boiler room brokerage activities" and in 1994 the company was fined $500,000 and asked to pay $2 million in restitution to its clients.

The New York superior court took up the Prodigy case in order to determine whether it was appropriate to sue an on-line subscriber service for libelous messages posted on a bulletin board by one of its subscribers. Prodigy maintained that it should not be held liable for the actions of its subscribers, but a New York state judge, Justice Stuart Ain, issued a contrary ruling stating that Prodigy *was* responsible for the content of its subscribers' electronic messages. Prodigy and others in the online industry had consistently claimed that they should be treated like bookstores or lending libraries. On-line service companies, they argued, are similar to these entities since they function as passive conduits of information with no control over content. The judge's ruling did not dispute this analogy, but it pointed out that Prodigy had marketed its online services by emphasizing its editorial control, and this put it into a different category from other on-line providers: "Prodigy's conscious choice to gain the benefits of editorial control has opened it up to a greater liability than CompuServe and other computer networks that make no such choice."[5] The judge cited the software screening program and its "content guidelines" as clear evidence of Prodigy's editorial control. Since Prodigy enforced these guidelines, it was subject to liability for its users' assertions based on the legal theory that "one who repeats or otherwise republishes a libel is subject to liability as if he had originally published it."[6]

The ruling was in sharp contrast to a decision in an earlier liability case, *Cubby, Inc. v. Compuserve, Inc.*[7] In this case Compuserve was not held liable for defamatory statements made about Cubby by one of its users. The reason was that it made no effort to monitor or control the content of its users. The *Cubby* and *Stratton Oakmont* cases, therefore, reveal an important legal principle: The more editorial control an on-line service provider exercises, the more liability they will have for the defamatory comments of their clients.

The lawsuit was eventually dropped by Stratton Oakmont, Inc. after Prodigy issued a formal apology for the libelous remarks. However, Prodigy's appeal to reargue the case was turned down, and hence Justice Ain's ruling still stood, thereby exposing Prodigy for libelous statements made in the future through its bulletin boards.

PRESSURES CONTINUE IN 1996

In the midst of these legal disputes, Prodigy executives contemplated their next steps. They realized that they were caught in an untenable and awkward position. Prodigy sought to occupy a middle ground between functioning as a publisher and adopting a laissez-faire, "anything goes" approach to content. If it chose to exercise editorial control over offensive messages, it would be held liable for whatever its users posted on bulletin boards according to the standard set forth by Justice Ain. Unfortunately, this included messages of libel or slander that could not easily be detected by means of key word searches looking for offensive language or other hot-button words. Thus, by exercising any discretionary, editorial control over the elements of content (such as offensive language) that it could control, it would be held liable for content that it in all likelihood it could *not* control.

Moreover, to further complicate matters, some respectable political groups were calling for on-line service providers to exercise even more editorial control. In January 1996 the Simon Wiesenthal Center sent a letter to Prodigy (as well as America Online, Compuserve, and Microsoft Network) requesting that the company block access to Web sites set up by white supremacists and neo-Nazis. The letter also called on these companies to enforce "ethical rules of engagement" for on-line communications. It urged Prodigy not to provide a platform for the destructive propaganda of hate groups such as the Aryan Nation.

As Prodigy executives reflected on this letter, Judge Ain's ruling was clearly on their mind. If they chose to continue and perhaps strengthen their policy of enforcing some ethical rules of engagement in cyberspace, they would also have to take responsibility for the content of all messages posted on their bulletin boards. They would be liable, therefore, for libelous or slanderous remarks and even for inaccuracies that might cause some damage to subscribers.

The top management of Prodigy had to determine how they could best deal with these conflicting demands and how they should respond to the Simon Wiesenthal Center. They also had to decide what actions, if any, to take next.

Case 7.2 The Therac-25

As software products become more powerful and pervasive, the risk that they will cause a great calamity increases significantly. One such calamity happened in the late 1980s when a product known as Therac-25, a radiotherapy machine, was allegedly responsible for several deaths due to a flaw in the machine's software. How could this happen and who is to blame? Moreover, how can similar tragedies be prevented in the future? There are no easy answers to these and other questions raised by this troubling case.

COMPANY AND PRODUCT BACKGROUND

The Therac-25 was manufactured by Atomic Energy of Canada, Ltd. (AECL) located in Ottawa, Canada. AECL was not a private corporation but a "crown corporation" of the Canadian government. It entered the field of medical linear accelerators or radiation therapy machinery during the early 1970s when it joined forces with a French company called CGR. These companies first produced the Therac-6 which was then followed by the Therac-20. Shortly before AECL introduced the Therac-25 this business relationship was terminated. The division of AECL involved in radiation machines has recently been privatized and separated from AECL. It is now called Theratronics International Limited.

The Therac product line of medical linear accelerators was highly regarded and included some of the most sophisticated radiation therapy machines available. The price of these products was typically in excess of $1 million. Medical linear accelerators are used to treat cancerous tumors or skin lesions with radiation. The machine is capable of providing two types of radiation therapy, X-ray and electron, depending upon the type of cancer that is being treated. When delivering X-ray therapy, a high intensity electron beam is deflected by a tungsten target interposed between the patient and the beam and then yields the proper level of therapeutic X-rays. When the machine functions in this fashion, it is operating in "X-ray mode." But in its so-called "electron mode" the Therac's built-in computer system, Digital Equipment Corp.'s (DEC) PDP-11 minicomputer, removes the tungsten target from the beam's path and reduces the intensity of the electron beam by a factor of 100. This electron mode was used to treat superficial skin lesions while the more powerful X-ray mode was used to treat malignant cancer tumors.

The Therac-25 was introduced to the marketplace in late 1982. This product was different from its predecessor, the Therac-20, in several important ways. Like the Therac-20, the Therac-25 was controlled by the DEC PDP-11, but unlike that machine the Therac-25 relied much more heavily on the system's software, especially for controlling safety. Whereas the Therac-20 included mechanical interlocking devices to prevent accidental overdoses, the Therac-25 contained no such interlocks. The elimination of these devices helped keep costs under control. The machine's safety precautions were completely controlled by the sophisticated software. Other advantages of this machine were its higher energy level along with its improved user friendliness.

A FLAWED PRODUCT

According to company records, a total of 11 Therac-25's were sold and installed prior to the product's recall for safety problems. Shortly after the machine's introduction there were several fatal accidents. Apparently in some circumstances, the Therac-25 malfunctioned by delivering a fatal dose of radiation to an unsuspecting patient. Moreover, there was no clear indication that this had happened, no warning or intelligible error message.

During the malfunction "the Therac scrambled the two modes, retracting the target as it should for electron mode but leaving the beam intensity set on high for X rays; the unobstructed high-intensity beam traveled through the accelerator guide destroying any human tissue in its path."[8] In other words, when the two modes were scrambled, the tungsten target would be removed but without any reduction in the beam power. The beam struck the patient with the same force as a bolt of lightening, and, although built-in error checking mechanisms abruptly stopped the dose, much of the damage had already been done. Of course, an overdose of radiation can be fatal.

THE VICTIMS

The first reported incident happened at the Kennestone Regional Oncology Center located in Marietta, Georgia. On June 3, 1985 a woman with malignant breast cancer was at the center to receive radiation therapy and accidentally received an overdose of radiation. The cause was not clear at the time, but it appears as if the modes were scrambled and the machine operated in the electron mode without deflecting the electron beam. AECL was immediately informed of the incident although they were not given specific information. They did not conduct a full investigation of the incident. The woman filed suit in November 1985. Although a severe radiation burn was verified, AECL denied that it was caused by their machine, and eventually the lawsuit was settled out of court.

One month later in a clinic in Ontario, Canada, another patient received an overdose. In this case AECL dispatched an engineer to investigate the incident. In addition, the Food and Drug Administration (FDA) and its Canadian counterpart, the Bureau of Radiation and Medical Devices, were informed that there might be a safety problem with the Therac-25. The patient died in November, but the cause of death was cancer and not the radiation overdose. AECL's investigation determined that there was probably a "transient failure in the microswitch used to determine the turntable position."[9] The company made some adjustments and declared that "the new solution indicates an improvement over the old system by at least five orders of magnitude."[10] It should be underscored, however, that at this point the company only suspected the cause of the accidents. It had not yet determined a definitive cause.

Meanwhile two far more serious incidents occurred at the East Texas Cancer Center in Galveston, Texas. On March 21, 1986 Voyne Cox received a lethal dose of radiation during a routine radiation therapy session at the center. Cox felt a shock go through his whole body when the first dose was administered, but there was no indication of an overdose on the machine's computer terminal. Instead it appeared that he had actually received an underdose, so the operator repeated the procedure and ended up giving Cox a second overdose. Cox tried to get help but was unable to communicate with the operator due to disconnected or broken audio and visual monitors that completely isolated the patient from the operator. The technicians instead observed a message that read "Malfunction 54"; this meant that there was some kind of discrepancy between the prescribed dose of radiation and the real dose, but it was not evident that the message was signaling an overdose. Within days, however, Cox became quite ill: He felt excruciating pain, vomited frequently, and eventually lapsed into a coma. In September 1986, just five months after receiving the fatal dose of radiation, he passed away in a Dallas hospital.[11]

Officials at the East Texas Cancer Center initially denied that there had been any radiation overdose, but the radiological physicist at the hospital contacted AECL about Cox's unusual reaction. The company instructed the hospital to conduct a series of diagnostic tests; they uncovered no problems so the hospital continued to use the machine. AECL did not inform the East Texas Center about the other incidents in Ontario and Georgia. One month later the same thing happened to Vernon Kidd, another patient at the cancer center. He too died shortly after the fatal treatment. Right after the lethal dose was administered to Kidd, the hospital discontinued using the machine.

At this point AECL finally began to suspect that there was a more serious problem with their machine and they initiated an investigation of these disturbing incidents. Their internal study uncovered the core problem: When operators erroneously selected the X-ray mode and then quickly corrected their mistake with a series of rapid keystrokes, the machine would get confused. For example, in the case of Cox the operator entered a full screen of prescription data and then keyed in "x" (X-ray mode) instead of "e" (electron mode). To fix this error she used a cursor to move up the screen and changed the "x" to an "e." But unbeknownst to the operator, this editing maneuver led the Therac-25 to scramble the two modes by removing the tungsten target while not reducing the high-powered electron beam. The esoteric "Malfunction 54" message was displayed, but there was no straight forward explanation of what this meant in the user manuals.

With the help of the resident physicist in East Texas, AECL was able to duplicate the problem and to verify its cause. According to one report, "They determined that data-entry speed during editing was the key factor in producing the error-condition: if the prescription data was edited at a fast pace . . . the overdose occurred."[12] AECL quickly developed a "fix" for this problem that forced the operators to start at the beginning and reenter all treatment data when a mistake had been made. They also disabled the "cursor up" key on the terminal keyboard. The same problem was found in the Therac-20, but it had never led to a fatality since this machine was equipped with an interlocking safety device that automatically prevents an accidental overdose.

POSTSCRIPT

The East Texas fatalities were obviously brought to the attention of the FDA which immediately required a CAP or Corrective Action Plan.

After two more incidents in Yakima, the FDA ordered a recall on February 10, 1987 and took the Therac-25 out of use. Despite the software fix implemented after the overdoses in East Texas, the FDA concluded that "software alone cannot be relied upon to assure safe operation of the machine."[13]

But after extensive negotiations with the FDA, an agreement was finally reached about an acceptable CAP. This included (among other things) interlocking devices to prevent an overdose in the case of a software malfunction along with many software adjustments including the elimination of the problematic editing keys.

There have been many post-mortems on how such a dangerous problem could go undetected. According to one perceptive report on the Therac-25 machine in *Forbes* magazine, the fundamental difficulty with this product was not software bugs but poor design and a "failure to model reality." Unfortunately, according to *Forbes*, "no one had thought to test the machine's reaction to quick resets; the automatic safety check should have been done *before* the dose was administered."[14] Moreover, despite AECL's claims to the contrary, the machine's level of user-friendliness was still a problem since it did not generate clear and unambiguous error messages. A more intelligible error message might have led the company to solve this fatal problem much sooner. Finally, in the opinion of software safety experts, the company's biggest problem was its lack of commitment to make "its safety protocols fail-safe."[15]

Lawyers for the two Texas victims, Cox and Kidd, filed lawsuits against the vendor, AECL, the East Texas Cancer Center, and even the radiation technicians at the hospital. The suit alleged that the product was seriously defective and that the hospital was negligent in its use of this product. A key issue in these cases was whether these fatalities could be attributed to a defective product *and* medical malpractice, as the lawsuits contended. The hospital vigorously disputed that they were at all to blame for what had happened. In their view, this was an open and shut case of product liability.

Case 7.3 NCR'S Warehouse Manager

In the relatively short history of software there have already been several notoriously flawed products that have fallen far short of the expectations of unsuspecting customers. One such product is undoubtedly the Warehouse Manager. This program was marketed by NCR Corp.

(now known as AT&T Global Information Solutions or AT&TGIS) in the late 1980s. It ran on the company's proprietary ITX operating system and cost approximately $180,000 (exclusive of installation, training, and setup expenses).

According to a report in the *Wall Street Journal,* one "victim" of this product was Hopper Specialty Co. located in New Mexico. Hopper was a profitable distributor of industrial hardware for oil and gas drillers. The company purchased the Warehouse Manager in 1988 in order to keep track of the quantity and prices of the many items in its vast inventory. The product also generated invoices and produced itemized monthly reports showing the revenues for each of Hopper's many products.

Hopper purchased this software program partly because of the convincing sales pitch of NCR. The company's sales staff claimed that the product had been effectively deployed at over 200 locations. They did not mention, however, that at those myriad sites Warehouse Manager was working on a different operating system that was made by Burroughs Corp. NCR had licensed this software from Burroughs and converted it to run on its own proprietary ITX hardware system. Thus, what was sold to Hopper was a product that had been substantially revamped and recoded.

It appears, however, that this version of the product was not adequately tested since it caused tremendous problems for its small customer base. Difficulties occurred with even the most standard computer operations. One problem was the system's response time—basic commands that should have taken no more than a second or two ended up taking minutes. Also, according to Michael Geyelin, "operators at different terminals would find that when they tried to get simultaneous access to the central computer, both their terminals would lock up; NCR engineers referred to this as the 'deadly embrace.'"[16] When this so-called "deadly embrace" occurred, users had to log off the computer and then log back on, and sometimes during this process data would be lost or destroyed. In other words, Warehouse Manager was not a genuine multi-user software system which would automatically prevent any such data integrated problems. These and other flaws made it manifest to NCR that there were compatibility problems of serious magnitude—Warehouse Manager simply did not function effectively in the ITX operating environment. This disappointing discovery prompted NCR to stop selling the product in the middle of January 1988, just about nine months after the product's official release.

Hopper did *purchase* the system well before this date, but NCR's salespersons had not been forthcoming about Warehouse's well-documented problems. Also, Hopper had not yet received the product when NCR announced its sales moratorium in January. Despite that announced moratorium, NCR began the installation process in February 1988, and Hopper began using the system in September of that same year. But the end result was sheer chaos for Hopper's business operations. The slow response times and terminal lockups often left frustrated Hopper customers waiting in long lines. The system allegedly mixed up the prices of various items, causing clerks to sell them to unsuspecting customers at the wrong price. Finally, "the most damaging problem stemmed from huge gaps between what the computer told Hopper Specialty was in stock and what was actually there. The Warehouse Manager might show 50 parts in stock, for instance, when in fact Hopper needed to order 50. Other times, it would show that items were on order then they were sitting on the shelf."[17]

Throughout this entire period of time Hopper was never informed that such problems had been documented at other sites and that Warehouse Manager sales had been suspended. Rather, customer support analysts at NCR consistently gave Hopper the impression that they were the only ones experiencing any sort of malfunctioning.

Obviously this bug-ridden software seriously disrupted Hopper's entire business structure. The company consistently lost revenues since it couldn't keep track of what it had in stock. Clients couldn't rely on Hopper to get parts or equipment in a hurry and this put Hopper at a tremendous disadvantage. Many loyal customers went to Hopper's competitors where they could get more reliable service.

Indeed, Hopper claimed that this system devastated the small company and cost it millions in lost revenues and profits. According to a report in *Computerworld*, "After purchasing the system in 1988, Hopper watched his then $4 million business dwindle to $1 million in annual sales today."[18] In addition, employees were laid off and benefits reduced for those employees still at the company. Hopper filed a lawsuit against NCR in which it sought $4.2 million in lost profits in addition to the total cost of the software which is about $300,000.[19] In its lawsuit Hopper accused NCR of fraud, negligence, and unfair trade practices.

Hopper, of course, was not the only customer to have experienced severe problems with Warehouse Manager. There were 30 other cases against AT&TGIS, and most of these have been settled. However, there has been some criticism about the nature of those settlements. According to published reports, AT&T relies on its standard Universal Agreement to settle all such software product liability cases. This agreement "limits payments to the original cost of the products and services acquired, minus depreciation for use of the equipment."[20] The company has been criticized for such modest compensation given the heavy losses that have been incurred by many of its clients because of this malfunctioning software.

AT&TGIS refused, however, to pay the $4.2 million in damages demanded in the Hopper lawsuit. Moreover, the NCR Universal Agreement signed by Hopper requires that all disputes be arbitrated instead of litigated in the courts and the courts have refused to hear the case. According to Geyelin, "in legal papers drafted in Hopper's case, NCR contends it 'had every reason to believe' that Taylor Management's software worked on NCR equipment, despite NCR's own internal communications to the contrary."[21]

AT&TGIS has completely discontinued the system and it has publicly acknowledged that the product was a failure. It has consistently claimed, however, that its liability should be limited to the purchase price of the software.

Case 7.4 Intel's Pentium Chip Product Controversy

This celebrated case began in the summer of 1994 when the Intel Corporation began marketing a new computer chip known as Pentium for personal computers. In an unusual strategy for a semiconductor company it heavily advertised this chip with the "Intel Inside" campaign. Problems began for Intel in October 1994 when a mathematician uncovered a division error. Intel admitted that it too had discovered the error over the summer but chose not to say anything because of the obscurity of this flaw. There was tremendous negative publicity, and while the press berated Intel for its insouciance and arrogance, IBM decided to halt sales of PCs with the Pentium chip. Eventually the beleaguered company agreed to replace the chip for anyone requesting such a replacement.

THE INTEL CORPORATION

The Intel Corporation was founded in 1968 by Robert Noyce, Gordon Moore, and a group of scientists including the present CEO, Andy Grove. Its initial objective was to replace magnetic-core computer memories with semiconductor memories. The company's first product was a bipolar Static Random Access Memory (SRAM). This was immediately followed by a Dynamic Random Access (DRAM) chip with more memory capacity than the SRAM; this product was known as the 1103 DRAM and it soon became an industry standard.

But Intel ran into heavy competition in the DRAM market, and it quickly moved on to other products. In 1974 Intel developed the 8080, the first commercially successful microprocessor, and it soon became the industry standard for 8-bit microprocessors. (A microprocessor acts as the central processing unit of a computer.) Although this product was quite successful, competitive products from Motorola and Zilog were challenging Intel's preeminent position in the microprocessor business. Intel's next offering was a 16-bit microprocessor known as the 8086 which was introduced in 1978. Sales volume for the 8086 started slowly and did not gain much momentum until 1980. This was the result of several factors including the success of Motorola's 16-bit microprocessor.

But Intel did not sit idly by in the face of this competitive threat. According to one analysis, "When Motorola's competitive 16-bit microprocessor began gaining momentum, Intel responded by initiating Operation Crush—an 'all out combat plan,' complete with war rooms and SWAT teams, to make the 8086 architecture the industry standard."[22] Intel succeeded in its efforts. In 1980 IBM adopted the 8086 chip for its personal computer, and other personal computer manufacturers followed suit.

Thanks to the success of the 8086 and Intel's other offerings, the company's sales increased to $885 million by 1980. The company expanded from 12 employees in 1968 to 15,000 in 1980. Thus, in a little over a decade Intel had established itself as a major player in the semiconductor industry.

Intel's rapid growth and profitability continued throughout the 1980s. Its most popular microprocessors introduced during that period were the 386 and 486 chips, both 32-bit chips. The 386 was one of the most widely used chips on the market, running PC computers made by vendors such as IBM, Compaq Computer, and Dell Computer Corporation. And thanks to astute planning Intel was the sole source of the 386 except for IBM. Its successor, the 486, was developed in 1989 and became known as the "mainframe on a chip" thanks to its superior processing power.

The Pentium chip, released in March 1993, was a much faster chip than the 486. Sales of the Pentium chip were beginning to accelerate in 1994, as manufacturing capabilities were ramped up. Prior to the controversy, analysts estimated that Intel would sell between five million and six million chips in the fourth quarter of 1994. Thanks to its performance advantages over competitive products, the Pentium chip was expected to be a highly successful and profitable product.

Intel's success and dominance of this industry at the time of this problem is indisputable. By 1991 Intel has become the largest U.S. semiconductor supplier. In 1993 the company earned a net profit of $2.3 billion on sales of $8.7 billion. Analysts estimated that about 55 percent of Intel's revenues came from the sale of microprocessors and related products while about 20 percent came from memory chips and embedded control semiconductors. The remaining portion of its revenues came from system sales such as LAN products based on its chips.

CORPORATE CULTURE AT INTEL

Intel began as a functional organization but over time a matrixlike management structure began to evolve. The company explicitly encouraged substantial interactions among its divisions. Matrix relationships were cultivated by team projects and other programs that transcended departmental boundaries. Many innovative ideas originated from these teams, and for the most part these ideas "rode on the backs of 'product champions,' middle managers within Intel who became fanatically wedded to these ideas."[23] Many of the successful product champions became cultural heroes. Further, this entire tradition seemed to enhance the company's identity as a technologically superior organization capable of extraordinary accomplishments. It is no surprise then that Intel valued its competencies in engineering and manufacturing over other functions in the organization.

To be sure, some of Intel's extraordinary success can be attributed to its aggressive behavior and an attitude of confidence bordering on righteousness. This aggressiveness was clearly manifest in the company's well-known Orange Crush campaign. Intel employees were generally known for being extremely intelligent but opinionated and somewhat arrogant. Company meetings were typified by heated debates and sharp confrontations.

In addition, the Intel culture became quite insular over time. Andy Grove fostered a corporate paranoia that kept Intel quite vigilant about its environment and protective of its turf. Thus, according to John Markoff, "Inward looking and wary of competitors, [Intel] developed a bunker mentality, a go-for-the-jugular attitude and a reputation for arrogance."[24] In the mid-1980s this reputation for arrogance dogged Intel which was perceived by customers as aloof and unresponsive.

One reason for Intel's belligerent and defensive management style was its experience with Japanese competitors in the early 1980s. Several of those companies nearly drove Intel from its computer memory chip business. The company survived this ordeal thanks to the generosity of

IBM, which invested $250 million in Intel at that critical time in exchange for 12 percent of the company. Thus, Intel's difficult experiences with the Japanese intensified its paranoia and helped shape the unique Intel culture. That closed and performance-oriented culture seems based on the core values of employee discipline, product quality, risk taking, and engineering excellence.

MARKETING THE PENTIUM CHIP

The Pentium chip, a worthy successor to the 386 and 486 line of chips, was the most powerful and fastest line of chips produced by Intel. This high-performance premium priced chip reached the market in March 1993 and was an immediate success. With its Pentium product Intel hoped to deter the progress of clones produced by companies such as AMD.

One of the reasons for Pentium's success can be attributed to "two ambitious leaps in marketing, both considered unprecedented in an industry where chips are considered to be of interest to manufacturers, not customers."[25] First, the company spent $150 million on an aggressive advertising campaign centered around a logo that read "Intel Inside" in order to promote its own name. Then it spent another $80 million to promote the Pentium chip itself. Most consumers are unaware of the chip contained within their PCs but thanks to the success of this campaign Intel became well known beyond the community of "techies" and computer professionals. Intel sought to create some brand recognition among consumers in order to counter the threat of clones.

The ads for the Pentium processor stressed that the powerful chip would increase the life span of a computer, "since it will still have plenty of horsepower when tomorrow's applications come along." These print ads saturated many popular publications such as *Business Week, Time,* and so forth. The end result was an unusually high profile for an engineering company that specialized in making computer chips.

But during October 1994 a mathematician disclosed a flaw with the Pentium chip that could lead to erroneous results in some mathematical calculations. This flaw in the chip's floating-point unit is obscure, but with certain numbers the Pentium cannot divide correctly. Consider, for example, the following calculation:

$$4{,}195{,}835 - ((4{,}195{,}835/3{,}145{,}727) \times 3{,}145{,}727)$$

The correct answer is quite obviously 0, but the flawed Pentium chip yielded a solution of 256! Apparently Intel failed to perform a basic test that would have detected the error before the product was shipped.

The *Electrical Engineering Times* published the first article on the flawed chip. The company quickly admitted that it had become aware of the problem during the summer of 1994 but chose not to say anything because it felt that this was an obscure flaw that would affect very few users. Intel corrected the problem but admits that it continued to sell the flawed chip to computer makers until its production changeover to the new chips was completed. The company offered to replace the flawed chips but only to those users who qualified because they were doing sophisticated calculations. On November 22, 1994, CNN broadcast a report about the Pentium chip, and two days later articles about the problem appeared in the *New York Times* and the *Boston Globe*.

Despite the increasing negative publicity, however, Intel maintained its defensive posture. The company was besieged with complaints and questions from concerned customers who had purchased a computer with a Pentium chip or were contemplating such a purchase. On the Internet, Intel was the subject of ridicule and fierce criticism for their lack of concern about the problem and especially for not having disclosed the problem when they had first encountered it over the summer.

Insiders at Intel admit that the company once again adopted a "bunker mentality" as it tried to cope with this growing crisis. A committee was formed to deal with the problem; it held two meetings a day, one in the morning and one in the evening. In the end these company officials concluded that they were on the right track in resolving the problem; at the center of their deliberations was a careful assessment of the very low probabilities of this problem's occurrence. In short, the company focused primarily on technical arguments and issues. Throughout the next several weeks, the company became convinced that its customers had accepted the explanation it had disseminated through the press: The Pentium's computational errors were so rare that ordinary users would never encounter them.

The company's CEO, Andrew Grove, felt that the situation was under control as some of the negative publicity began to subside. Many consumers, however, balked at the need to "explain" exactly why they needed a new chip. Customers who called the company's hot line were asked a sequence of questions about how they were using the machines. They were offered a replacement chip only if they "passed" this qualification process. During the interview Intel reps asked users about their occupations and their computer applications and software. Some users bristled at being forced to justify their need for an unflawed chip; some pointed out that even if they were not now doing sophisticated calculations, this did not mean they would not be doing these calculations in the future or using software packages that were doing such calculations.

Further, in an effort to placate its angry and bemused consumers Grove posted an apology on the Internet on November 27. In his apology Grove pointed out that "no chip is ever perfect." He also reiterated the company's replacement policy that restricted such replacements to those doing intensive mathematical calculations. Many of those who responded to this message, however, pointed out that Intel did not sound too contrite or sincere in its on-line apology.

A potentially serious fallout from the controversy was skepticism among the corporate user base. Consequently Intel embarked on a vigorous campaign to allay the concerns of its biggest users. This included sales calls and a promise to expedite the replacement of flawed chips. According to one report, "One reason for Intel's concern is the fact that several IS managers say they have delayed Pentium system purchases, waiting for a chip with the corrected floating point unit, despite Intel's assurances that most users will never run across the problem."[26]

Just as these positive pubic relations efforts were beginning to have some effect, IBM unexpectedly announced on December 12 that it would immediately cease shipping computers with the flawed chip. According to a report in the *New York Times,* "an IBM spokesman said the company had decided to halt shipments at the height of the busiest season for personal computer sales after determining that 'the risk of error may be significantly higher' for common calculations than Intel had indicated to its customers."[27] Intel had claimed that the flaw was so obscure that it might occur once every 27,000 years for the average consumer. But IBM said that its researchers had reached a far different conclusion: "The flaw could arise as frequently as once every 24 days for an average user."[28] For a corporate user with 1,000 machines this might mean one or two errors a day! Some analysts criticized IBM's bold move as self-serving, since IBM was developing the PowerPC chip in conjunction with Motorola that competes directly against the Pentium. Perhaps this was IBM's way of undermining sales of the celebrated Pentium chip?

Regardless of the purity of IBM's motives, its announcement caused major problems for Intel. The flawed Pentium chip was now back in the limelight and Intel found itself once again defending its actions to a skeptical public. Intel responded angrily to IBM's announcement, intimating that IBM had manipulated the test conditions in order to get these prejudicial results. But the damage had been done.

Most other vendors, however, offered their support to the embattled chip maker. According to Vijayan, ". . . almost all of the industry's top vendors, including Hewlett-Packard Co., Gateway 2000, Inc., AST Research Inc., Dell Computer Corp., Digital Equipment Corp., and Acer America, Inc., had allied themselves behind a battered Intel and declared the bug too inconsequential in most cases to merit withholding the chip."[29] Nonetheless IBM's announcement was a serious blow to Intel's efforts to suppress this controversy. Consumers felt more confused than ever as they wondered whom to believe, Intel or IBM. Indeed, the credibility of the entire industry seemed to be at stake.

RESOLUTION

Despite the IBM announcement Intel steadfastly refused to modify its much criticized replacement policy. To a certain extent, Intel's intransigence could be attributed to its cultural traits that emphasized a rational and calculated approach to the solution of problems. Thus, it continued to defend its policy of replacing chips only on an as-needed basis and only if the consumer would respond to questions on how they were using the product. Meanwhile reports kept appearing that described fresh, new encounters with the defective chip. A major New York City bank discovered serious errors in financial calculations, while scientists at Long Island's Brookhaven National Laboratory generated erroneous results as they tried to calculate the impact of colliding subatomic particles. Similar reports of problems with fairly routine calculations surfaced on the Internet and in various trade journals. Also, concern over Intel's handling of this crisis continued to effect adversely the company's stock. During the week of the IBM announcement Intel's stock was down $3.25 and closed at $59.50.

As Christmas approached Intel had had enough. On December 20 the company finally announced that it would reverse its policy and that it would now offer all customers a free replacement upon request with no questions asked. Also, the company agreed to cover the replacement expense for anyone who requested it. Unfortunately, the company also indicated that it would be several months before new chips would be available on a widespread basis. Intel also initiated an advertising campaign apologizing for the flawed chip *and* its inept management of this problem.

Analysts provided various estimates of what Intel would need to spend in order to replace the defective chip. By the end of December 1994, roughly five million chips had been shipped, but Intel projected that only 20 percent of those chips would need to be replaced. If this were true, the cost of the replacement would be at least a $100 million charge before taxes or approximately $63 million after taxes. This seemed to be a small price to pay for the positive publicity that accompanied the announcement of this decision. Implementing this decision, however, would be a formidable challenge for Intel. It took several months to ramp up its production of the corrected chip and the replacement process continued through the fall of 1995. But with this decision Intel's public relations debacle finally appeared to be at an end.

Case 7.5 Sun's Server Problems

Sun Microsystems is the leading supplier of UNIX servers with a market share of 43 percent of this $32 billion market. Other major competitors include IBM and Hewlett-Packard. But in 2001 quality control problems were causing dismay among its customers and threatening Sun's hegemony in this market.

Some of Sun's biggest clients, including America Online, eBay, and Verisign, experienced the persistent problem: sudden crashes of its high-end UNIX servers known as the UltraSPARC II. These servers are part of the company's Enterprise server line and they range in price from $50,000 to over $1 million. The problem was eventually traced to a SRAM memory chip which Sun had purchased from IBM. Under certain conditions the bug triggered a system failure with the need to reboot.

The chips involved are cache memory chips that store data for more immediate access; caching improves performance for frequently requested data. The problem arises when the chips are disrupted by stray radiation (such as cosmic rays); the tainted chips end up with failures at the bit level as a 1 becomes a 0 and vice versa.

Sun's behavior during this controversy has been called into question by its customers and by others in the information technology press. The problem was first detected and reported by several users in late 1998, but Sun did not issue a public statement about the problem or officially acknowledge this bug. Nor did the company disclose the bug to new buyers. No notice appeared on the company's Web site about the problem.

In November 1999, Verisign Global Registry Services, a major domain name registry on the Web, was out of commission for several hours after its Sun server crashed. According to *Forbes*, Verisign complained to Sun about the crash, but it received no explanation. Sun did not convey its knowledge of the bug to Verisign nor did it confirm that other customers had the same problem. Several months later Verisign executives came across a product bulletin from the consulting firm called the Gartner Group discussing the flaw and naming some companies with server crashes. One irate Verisign executive confronted Sun: "I said to Sun, 'My God, you knew about this problem, and you didn't tell me? That's unconscionable.'"[30] Verisign now relies more heavily on IBM's UNIX servers than it does on Sun's products.

Sun did agree to fix the bug for its aggrieved customers, but this process too was fraught with some controversy. Sun insisted that those companies seeking repair of its servers sign a nondisclosure agreement in which they promised to keep the repair a secret. Sun was criticized for this policy in the trade press including journals such as *Computerworld,* which alleged that the nondisclosure agreements were part of an orchestrated effort to cover up the problem and prevent other Sun customers or potential customers from becoming cognizant of the faulty chip. After some companies protested, Sun abandoned this policy. In an interview with *Computerworld,* Scott McNealy, Sun's CEO, denied the ulterior motivation attributed to Sun by the press. According to McNealy, "As part of the conversation of what we were going to do to fix a current quality problem, we were going to share with our customers a whole road map of our product strategy."[31]

Some of Sun's customers also felt that the company has tried to deflect responsibility for these flawed chips, especially by blaming IBM. According to the project manager of a European bank affected by the problem, "Sun is responsible for the problem. Their architecture was fundamentally flawed because there was no ECC checking on the cache memory."[32] This manager is referring to error checking and correcting memory that is usually performed on all processors including Intel's microprocessor chips for PCs. This testing is designed to detect cache errors and fix the affected bits. The company has admitted that this basic level of testing was not done for these chips, though the problem has been corrected in the UltraSparc III.

Some of Sun's customers and industry observers wonder why the company performed so poorly in managing this controversy, particularly in light of the mistakes made by the well-publicized problems associated with Intel's handling of the Pentium chip controversy. Despite this negative role model, Sun seemed to fall into the same pattern of behavior including defensiveness and diffidence. Sun has continued to fix its defective servers, hoping that its image will not be further tarnished.

Case 7.6 The Product Manager[33]

A MEETING IN BOSTON

It was late Friday afternoon and Richard Martin was rushing to Boston's Logan airport to catch the last flight back to San Francisco. As the cab traversed the busy, confusing streets of downtown Boston, Martin gazed at the surrounding urban landscape. He felt truly elated over the speech he had just given. He had come to Boston for Jupiter Software's East Coast user group meeting. Martin was the product manager for the company's popular relational database product, INFORM-2. In his speech he unequivocally announced that the long-awaited release of INFORM-3 would be available on May 1, 1990. In this speech and in private meetings with Jupiter's major clients he exhorted Jupiter's nervous customer base to wait for this timely new release and not to jump ship to more advanced competitive products. Thanks to the work of Jupiter's talented engineering staff, he was able to present a demo of this new product despite the fact that some pieces of the product were still not even coded or designed. But the "demo" was a great success and added significant credibility to Martin's confidence and insistence that the product would be ready for distribution by May 1.

But as Martin settled into his first class plane seat and peered at the changing scenery below, his mood began to change rather dramatically. His speech and visit to Boston were assuredly a great success on one level, but he began to wonder about the ethical propriety of announcing a release date in such unequivocal terms, especially when no one at the company was really confident about this date. Martin's confident and dogmatic style at the meeting masked feelings of insecurity and concern about the May 1 target that pervaded the entire company. Unfortunately this was the first of many such user group meetings and Martin was scheduled to make the same speech and exude the same level of confidence in several other cities across the United States, Canada, and Europe. But as the plane reached its cruising altitude, he wondered about his future at Jupiter and whether he was the right man to continue this tour of the company's user group meetings.

THE COMPANY

Jupiter Software was founded in the late 1970s by three California entrepreneurs. One of these individuals, Larry Connors, was an engineer with undergraduate and graduate degrees from Stanford. After completing his studies at Stanford, Connors went to work for the data processing department of one of California's largest banks. Shortly after his arrival Connors developed a sophisticated input screen to facilitate data entry for the bank's clerks. This input screen allowed clerks to enter data more quickly into the firm's hierarchical IBM database. This tool was quite successful and Connors was sure that he could sell it to other companies with similar data input requirements. So he promptly resigned from the bank and formed his own company, Jupiter Software. Connors needed additional capital to get this company off the ground so he invited two friends to invest $25,000 in return for a major stake in Jupiter. These individuals were "silent" partners who were not involved in the day-to-day operations of Jupiter. The company earned a small profit on first year revenues of around $100,000.

During this time much was being written about the potential and promise of relational database technology. Hierarchical and network databases prevailed among large commercial users, but they were often criticized for their complexity and inflexibility. The relational model showed great promise because of its simplicity and flexibility. According to this model, each record in the file is conceived as a row in a two-dimensional table and each field becomes a column in that table. The table could be augmented with new fields if necessary and tables could be joined to each other if they had an item in common through a simple "join" or "relate" command (see Exhibit 1). The Relational Database Management System (or RDBMS) was organized for maximum flexibility, ease of use, and quick retrieval of information.

Larry Connors astutely realized that the benefits of relational technology far outweighed its liabilities. Consequently, he hired a small group of engineers to expand his simple data input form into a full-scale

Exhibit 1

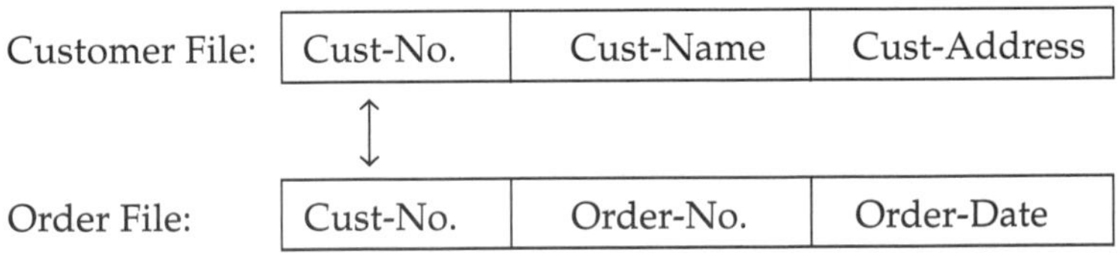

Customer File:	Cust-No.	Cust-Name	Cust-Address
	↕		
Order File:	Cust-No.	Order-No.	Order-Date

These files can be joined together on the common field, Cust-No.

relational database. By 1981 INFORM-1 was born. It was initially designed for the IBM mainframe, but as the product grew in popularity it was ported to DEC, Hewlett-Packard, and Data General minicomputers. Sales quickly took off on all of these platforms as relational technology found great favor with many companies looking for an alternative to the more primitive database technologies of the 1960s and 70s.

By 1985 revenues reached $12 million and the company was growing very rapidly. Connors moved the company from a small building in San Mateo and leased the second and third floors of a major office building in Burlingame, a city close to San Francisco and just on the periphery of the famous Silicon Valley. The engineering staff had expanded to 25 and new sales offices were opened in Boston, Washington, D.C., Atlanta, Dallas, and Toronto. The company also signed on distributors to sell INFORM throughout Europe. In 1986 Jupiter's sales almost doubled to $21 million as the company released a new version of the product, INFORM-2. This new release included more sophisticated functionality than the first release, such as a better report writer, additional security features, and an input screen or data entry form that provided more substantial validation of data as it was being entered into the database by end users.

Jupiter's niche in the database market place was the departmental DBMS which normally resided on a departmental processor such as a minicomputer. Departmental computing systems were considered a high-growth segment of the market. International Data Corporation, a leading consulting firm, estimated that shipments of departmental DBMS software would increase at a compound annual growth rate of 30 percent through at least 1995. Surveys of current customers and prospective buyers revealed the salient minimum requirements of an acceptable departmental DBMS:

- SQL compatibility (The Structured Query Language was the standard method of querying the database to retrieve the appropriate records.)
- Performance-oriented systems
- Distributed processing capability
- Multivendor interfaces (i.e., to IBM mainframes and various PC platforms)
- Transaction processing
- Easy-to-use end-user interface

As the RDBMS market evolved, commercial systems without these important features would be at a serious competitive disadvantage.

JUPITER'S MANAGEMENT TEAM

As the company continued to expand, Connors realized the need to make the sometimes difficult transition from an entrepreneurial environment to a management environment. Hence in the 1984–85 time frame he brought a skilled team of professional managers to Jupiter. Jeff Bennet became the vice president of marketing; he was lured away from a competitor with a hefty salary and stock options. During this time Richard Martin was promoted to a newly created job, associate product manager for INFORM. Martin had joined Jupiter in 1984 after receiving his M.B.A. degree from a prominent East Coast university. His good friend from college, Joe Casey, had joined Jupiter a year earlier as manager of the marketing services department. He persuaded Martin that this was an opportunity that he shouldn't pass up. Martin agreed. He moved to California after he was hired by Jupiter as a consultant and marketing support specialist. He provided training to INFORM's new customers in addition to consulting services on how to design and utilize this system efficiently. Martin was highly effective in this role as he quickly mastered the intricacies and nuances of this sophisticated and complex software. Thus, when Mary Hastings, INFORM's young product manager, sought an associate, Martin was her first choice for this position.

The product manager reported to the vice president of marketing and was responsible for shepherding new releases of the product through various stages from coding to beta testing. Hence this individual occupied a critical position in Jupiter's management hierarchy. He or she was the key interface person between Jupiter's marketing departments and its engineering staff. Perhaps more than anyone else the product manager had to make sure that a new product or release was what the market wanted, that is, what the customer valued and considered important. To be successful at this difficult job the product manager had to have both technical skills and marketing acumen. Both Hastings and Martin fit the bill and worked very well together for over a year.

The management team was rounded out by the sales manager, Dennis Johnson, and the vice president of product development, Jeffrey Coleman. Coleman had an engineering degree from Stanford and was responsible for managing Jupiter's engineering staff, the QA (Quality Assurance) teams, and the documentation workers. Finally, during these growth years the company was pressured to elevate its phone support for its rapidly expanding customer base. As a result, a separate customer support department was established and was initially headed by Louise Cassidy from the marketing services department. With this management team securely in place, Connors hoped to take Jupiter to new heights.

1987 TO 1989

Sales for Jupiter's INFORM-2 product peaked in 1987 at $28 million. By then there were sales offices all over the United States as well as in London, Paris, and Singapore. But as competition among relational database vendors intensified and the market began to mature, it became increasingly difficult for Jupiter's seasoned sales staff to close new business. Although revenues increased by about 33 percent in 1987, Jupiter had actually lost some of its market share during the previous year as other companies grew at an even faster rate. Thus, its overall market share fell from a high of 11.2 percent in 1985 to about 9.5 percent in 1987. As a result, despite the revenue growth and continued profitability there was cause for alarm and incipient concern among Jupiter's executives.

The reasons for Jupiter's emerging problems were manifold, but for the most part they could be attributed to its failure to keep up with technology. The latest release of the product, INFORM-2, was revised in the mid-1980s to include some minor enhancements to the data entry screens and the report writer along with some query optimizers to speed up the retrieval process. But INFORM-2 was being eclipsed by competitive products in both performance and functionality. For example, INFORM-2 did not provide for On-Line Transaction Processing (OLTP) which was becoming a required feature of relational database systems. OLTP allowed multiple users to work on the same data file by locking a record that was retrieved by a particular user until that user completed his or her update. In addition, INFORM-2 used a proprietary query language instead of SQL, the industry standard language. Finally, the product sorely lacked a robust report writer, and its performance deteriorated significantly when the number of records in the database exceeded 100,000 records.

Competitors such as Oracle and Ingress became highly adept at exploiting these vulnerabilities and consequently prevailed repeatedly in head-to-head competition with Jupiter. The word in the marketplace was that INFORM-2 was a fine tool for small to medium-size applications but was not well suited for large-scale departmental applications where 100,000+ records and transaction processing were the norm. For these applications, products like Oracle and Ingress were seen as far superior.

The company's managers worked hard to counter this negative image but to no avail. As a result, for the first time in Jupiter's history sales dropped precipitously in 1988 to about $19.5 million and the company posted its first loss of $2.1 million. To get its costs under control Connors quickly implemented a layoff of 10 percent of the staff at the Burlingame headquarters and closed three of the company's eight sales offices.

Of course, Connors knew all too well that the company's dim prospects could not be reversed unless INFORM-2 could be revised to include considerable new functionality such as support for SQL, transaction processing, a better report writer, and so on. A team of engineers had been working feverishly on this project throughout the previous year but had made little progress. Much of the blame for this lack of progress could be laid at the feet of Coleman, the VP of product development. Unfortunately, he was not an effective leader; for example, he had difficulty resolving disputes among his engineers regarding many design issues for the new product which was to be called INFORM-3. In early 1988, Connors, still perturbed by the company's first unprofitable year, met with his board to discuss the fate of Coleman. After a brief meeting, it was decided that Coleman had to go; no one had confidence in his ability to accelerate the progress of INFORM-3's development. On February 11, 1989 Coleman was asked to resign. Several days later Connors announced that Coleman's replacement would be Warren Clemens, a 33-year-old engineering graduate of MIT. Clemens had worked briefly for Coleman after he first moved to California, but the two men rarely saw eye to eye, so Clemens went to work for another database company in Silicon valley.

Shortly before Coleman and several loyalists among the engineering staff were fired, Connors arranged a clandestine meeting with Clemens to discuss his possible future at Jupiter. Connors wanted a virtual guarantee from Clemens that he would "get the new product out the door in a big hurry." As a result of this meeting and the prospect of a substantial bonus, Clemens publicly committed to getting this product to the marketplace within 14 months. This would mean that the new product would be ready for sale by May 1990.

On February 21, a company meeting was called in Burlingame. Connors enthusiastically announced the appointment of Clemens as the new director of engineering. With Clemens by his side, he also announced the release date of May 1, 1990 for the revitalized INFORM database. Connors exhorted *all* Jupiter employees to wholeheartedly support this effort, and he encouraged skeptics to seek employment elsewhere:

Jupiter will succeed in getting INFORM-3 to market by next May. Our whole future depends on this. But we need 110 percent effort from everyone in the company. If you're not committed to this or you think this is impossible, maybe you shouldn't be here!

Although most of Jupiter's employees were still skeptical, they decided that remaining at Jupiter was probably worth the risk. Many had substantial stock options so Jupiter's success could pay off handsomely for them. Also, shortly after the meeting, Connors distributed more stock options as an additional incentive for employees to remain with the company. But the task ahead was truly Herculean. Clemens believed that all of Coleman's work was virtually worthless so he decided to start from "ground zero." Also, because of the radical nature of the changes, it was necessary to design and code the product from scratch. According to Clemens, it would not be expedient to modify the "spaghetti-like code" written by some of his inept predecessors. Clemens hired six new engineers to complement the staff of those who remained after Coleman was fired. Thus, he had a total staff of 24 engineers. Most of them were quite competent and had experience with other companies in the Valley. Nonetheless, experts estimated that to construct a viable relational database product for the minicomputer environment it would require at least three years and 35 to 40 engineers. Could Jupiter beat these impossible odds and construct INFORM-3 in 15 months with only 24 engineers? Connors was convinced that this was possible and that this project would become legendary in the software industry.

As sales plummeted further in 1989, there was even greater urgency in getting this new product to market. Jupiter continued to lose sales to its competitors and to lose money because INFORM-2 didn't measure up to more sophisticated competitive products. Its main source of revenue at this point was from the existing customer base. In 1989 there were approximately 2,800 installations of INFORM-2. As is customary in the software industry, each site was required to pay an annual maintenance fee which entitled the customer to product upgrades, bug fixes, compatibility adjustments, and customer support. The fee ranged from $1,200 to $4,100 depending upon the size and memory capacity of the hardware. Since the average fee was about $2,600, maintenance fees generated about $7.3 million in revenues for Jupiter.

The customer base, however, was becoming increasingly disenchanted and disillusioned with Jupiter. Many clients had purchased the product in its infancy in the early 1980s but their needs had outgrown INFORM's limited capabilities. They had been promised a major upgrade for several years but nothing happened. The company and its managers were often ridiculed at user group meetings for failing to deliver. Some customers started to jump ship and purchased a new RDBMS. As one disgruntled user said: "I'm tired of Larry Connors' empty promises. I can't wait any longer for this mythical INFORM-3."

The summer of 1989 represented a crucial juncture in Jupiter's troubled history. There was tremendous discontent among the user base; many customers were quite skeptical that they would ever see INFORM-3 after Coleman's abrupt termination. The company was rife with rumors that many clients would not renew their maintenance agreement when the fall billing was issued (Jupiter billed its client base every fall for the maintenance renewals of all customers). The loss of this revenue would obviously be devastating to Jupiter. Hence to rescue his floundering company, Connors knew that decisive action was essential.

A NEW PRODUCT MANAGER

By the summer of 1989 the development effort for INFORM-3 was in high gear. Tensions began to mount in the company, however, especially over Clemen's dogmatic and uncooperative management style. As product manager it was Mary Hasting's responsibility to assure that INFORM-3 addressed the needs of the market. But Clemens often did not involve her in the design of key modules such as the input screen and the report writer. When she confronted him about this he would complain: "I just don't have the time to be consulting *you* about this stuff! You'll just have to trust my instincts."

A marketing team was assembled in June and met every week with the lead engineers. The purpose of these meetings was to provide key departments with knowledge of the new product so they could begin to prepare training manuals, brochures, and other promotional material. It was essential for these groups to work together to plan and develop a product that would balance market requirements with technical feasibility. But the meetings between the marketing and engineering personnel were usually volatile and unproductive. Clemens and Hastings argued vociferously at times. She continued to demand more involvement in the design of INFORM-3, but Clemens steadfastly resisted. Larry Connors tried to mediate this hostile dispute but usually ended up siding with Clemens. On one occasion he excoriated Hastings for not being a "team player." By mid-July Hastings was completely frustrated, and she handed in her resignation.

Richard Martin was the logical choice to succeed Hastings as product manager. He had performed admirably as associate product manager, and he was intimately involved in the development effort of INFORM-3. He was often more conciliatory to Clemens and frequently made valiant efforts to bridge the widening gap between the engineering and marketing groups. Hence on July 15, 1989 he was promoted to product manager. At the same time Connors put pressure on Clemens "to get Richard Martin more involved." Clemens responded by inviting Martin to the Monday morning meetings of the engineering and quality assurance staff under his control. At this meeting the lead engineers discussed their progress on the modules under their responsibility.

After attending several of these meetings and familiarizing himself with the work that had already been accomplished, it became increasingly clear to Martin that the May 1, 1990 release date was highly improbable. He estimated that the design and coding of a functional system could be completed by May 1, but only under extremely optimal conditions. This assumed that the individual engineers would keep to their demanding schedules and that there would be no resignations or long spells of absenteeism. But even under these conditions the product would most likely be ready for quality assurance testing sometime in late March or April. This would mean that there would be about one month available for the Quality Assurance (QA) process, and most would agree that this was not adequate time to thoroughly test the product and fix all its bugs. Also, there would be no time to ship the product to beta sites for testing by customers with real-life applications; this was normally done after the QA department had exhausted its search for the product's elusive bugs and flaws. Thus, beyond any doubt, May 1 was a *very* optimistic date. In Martin's estimation, the odds were strongly against the product's availability for shipping by May 1. As the summer turned to fall several other managers at Jupiter were equally troubled about this ambitious release date.

FALL USER GROUP MEETINGS

One of the rituals at Jupiter was its series of regional user groups meetings each fall. These meetings were usually spread out in the months of October and November. The regional Jupiter user groups were divided as follows: West Coast, Midwest, East Coast, Washington, D.C. (this group catered to Jupiter's many government clients), Canada, and Europe. Thus, there were always six key regional meetings in addition to the international meeting which was held in the spring. It was customary for the product manager and other middle managers to speak at these meetings. This year the focus of the entire user group was on the soon-to-be-released INFORM-3. Attendance would be high since the users were curious about this new product. Besides technical concerns, two questions were uppermost in their minds: Was the development team on schedule? And would they get their copies on May 1 or shortly thereafter?

Despite assurances from Larry Connors, Jeff Bennet, and others, some of the company's most loyal customers joked openly about the May 1 date ("We'll be fooled again by Jupiter!"); many others were skeptical about INFORM-3. Hence Connors knew that these user group meetings were pivotal for Jupiter's survival. He could not afford to lose a substantial portion of his customer base, since he depended so heavily on the maintenance fee revenues. These customers also continued to purchase training, consulting services, and so forth which were also a major source of revenues for Jupiter. In addition, the company's reputation would be further damaged by more defections to other products. At this point INFORM-2's sales were almost nonexistent except for an occasional sale in Europe or the Far East. The fall maintenance money would give Jupiter enough resources to hang on until May when the sales staff could begin selling a state-of-the-art database product, INFORM-3. Thus, it was critically important to instill confidence in the users regarding the May 1 release date.

In September, as Jupiter prepared for the user group meetings, Connors called a meeting of the management committee including Jeff Bennet, Warren Clemens, Joe Casey, Richard Martin, and Louise Cassidy. He told them it would be vital to assure Jupiter's customers that May 1 was INFORM-3's release date and that there had been no slippage in the schedule. He emphasized the importance of being definitive and exuding confidence. The future of Jupiter depended on their ability to convince customers that they could have a new product in their hands by May 1990. If they could convince most customers to hold on, Jupiter could count on a high maintenance renewal rate.

The meeting grew tense as Martin and others protested Connor's injunction. Martin said: "Well, Larry, I realize how important it is to keep our customers but we don't have a lot of confidence in the release date. At the Monday meeting yesterday I learned of delays and serious setbacks with two key modules. Also, the input screens haven't even been designed yet. It's already mid-September—how can we possibly have a saleable product by May 1?" Cassidy concurred, "I'm hesitant about sounding so confident. My group has very little knowledge about INFORM-3. Even if we shipped in May could we support 2,500 customers with a new product? I just don't think so!" Jeff Bennet, Jupiter's marketing VP, voiced a mild protest but wasn't nearly as strident as the other managers at the meeting. Bennet had a reputation for being politically savvy and resisted what he regarded as a challenge to Larry Connor's authority.

Connors listened soberly and carefully to his managers but then responded: "We have no choice. There are *no* other sources of cash besides this maintenance revenue—if we lose a big piece of it we're finished as a company. I know there are some problems with INFORM-3, but we can fix them even if I have to do it by myself! We'll get that product out the door by May! This is no time to lose faith. We all just have to work harder to make it happen. Warren and the other engineers are committed to making it happen, and I need your commitment too. As a company we have to be in lock step on this issue and sing from the same hymnal: INFORM-3 will be available May 1! If you don't think so, maybe I should look for some new managers who have the commitment we need to get the job done."

Martin and his colleagues were duly chastened by Connor's speech. They reluctantly agreed to do everything in their power to convince the user group community that May 1 was a realistic release date. Later that evening at the local bar they talked about what they would be doing. "Maybe INFORM-3 will be ready?" said Casey, "It's a long shot, but it's not impossible." "Well," responded Martin, "I would say there's about a 10 percent chance that it will be finished. Those aren't very good odds." "Look," injected Cassidy, "other software companies around here do this all the time. You guys have heard of vaporware, haven't you! Companies are always announcing products even when they're unsure about the release date. We're no better or worse than they are." "Yeah" pondered Martin, "if the product is a few months late who will be hurt. I don't see the harm. On the other hand, if we're ambivalent and lose customers there might be no Jupiter Software next May. Then the customers will really be hurt—no bug fixes, no new product releases, no customer support." "None of us like it," remarked Casey, "but what choice do we have? If we don't go along with this, our jobs will certainly be at stake."

A MORAL QUAGMIRE

As Martin flew back to Burlingame, he recalled that conversation. He also took from his briefcase and reread Connors's recent memo to the whole company exhorting everyone to cooperate for the common good (see Exhibit 2, p. 189). On the surface, things were beginning to improve. As Connor's memo indicated, the product was beginning to shape up, and there was a tentative plan to get a beta release by March 15. Nonetheless, despite the positive tone of Connors's memo, Martin still thought that this was a real long shot. He had, however, concealed his doubts and won over many "doubting Thomases" among the East Coast users. Martin's speech and the product demo were quite convincing. The slick product demo had been prepared by several of Jupiter's engineers who were able to simulate pieces of the product which had not even been coded yet; these were interspersed with modules that were completed and to the audience the new product came across as a seamless whole. It undoubtedly left the impression that the product was on the brink of completion.

Martin also had gone out of his way to talk with all the major customers at the meeting to assure them that they would have the new product in May. He had known many of these clients for several years since he had been to many of the key sites on the East Coast as a trainer and consultant. Most customers liked Martin and felt he was a man of his word. If he made them a promise or a commitment, he always delivered. Thus, as Martin meandered through the user group meeting, greeting and encouraging Jupiter's various customers, he relied heavily on his credibility to dispel any doubts about INFORM-3 and Jupiter's future. And judging from the reactions to his speech and the product demonstration, Martin felt quite sure that he had succeeded. As he left the meeting he got a pat on the back from Jeff Bennet who told him that "Larry would be very pleased."

But now as Martin's plane approached the San Francisco airport, he considered future meetings. There were several more coming up in the next few weeks. Was he willing to give the same speech and the phony product demonstration to these other groups? Was he prepared to put his credibility on the line once again? Shouldn't he at least qualify the statements about the May 1 release date—let unsuspecting clients know that it was possible but not a sure thing? Martin realized, however, that any sort of ambivalence would be interpreted by Connors as treason and that his job would surely be at risk. He wondered too about the ethical questions involved here. After all, there was a slim chance Jupiter would make the May 1 release date. Technically, then, his statements were not lies. But did he have a moral obligation to reveal the whole truth? Software developers were almost always wrong when they announced release dates so most customers would be forgiving and understanding even if the product was late. Wasn't vaporware standard industry practice? Why should Jupiter set new ethical standards?

As Martin's plane prepared to land, he gazed at the bright lights of the San Francisco airport. He could find no easy answers to these perplexing questions. Nor was he sure what he should do at the Canadian user group meeting the week after next. If he gave the same speech that was such a hit in Boston, it would be another long flight home.

Exhibit 2

Jupiter Software, Inc.
One Northern Blvd.
Burlingame, California

Office of the President

Memorandum

To: Jupiter Managers and Staff
From: Larry Connors
Subject: INFORM-3 Update
Date: Sept. 30, 1989

I spent the day yesterday reviewing Product Development's progress on INFORM-3 with Wayne and Richard. We reviewed the symbol table handler, the low levels, the standard file interface, the screen handler, the data dictionary, the data file editor, the report writer, the output screens and the commands. The progress to date is really outstanding, and the whole engineering staff deserves a great deal of credit. We also discussed upcoming efforts on the transaction processing facility and the data input screens along with the conversion utility. We reached tentative agreement on a schedule to bring us to the March 15 beta release date.

As each of you are aware, in every position, you are now being called on to overcome and rise above your personal limitations. In the next six months, with limited staff, we have to continue to operate our daily business and maintain our current products, while at the same time producing all of the elements required for a successful launch of what is substantially a new product. We can only do this with an all-out effort on the part of each individual and 100 percent team work. We have a great opportunity to turn things around and make this work, but success will require everyone's total commitment and dedication.

Case 7.7 Chicago

> Vaporware: A term used sarcastically for promised software that misses its announced release date, usually by a considerable length of time.[34]

OVERVIEW

"Chicago" was the code name for a new version of Microsoft's Windows operating system. The company announced in 1993 that this new operating system would be available to its users by the end of 1994. It then postponed the product introduction to the first half of 1995. And in December 1994 the company postponed the product launch once again, stating that it would not be available until August 1995, about nine months after the initial due date. Were these delays unavoidable or was Microsoft deliberately much too optimistic about its delivery date?

In a 1995 antitrust case federal Judge Stanley Sporkin had criticized Microsoft for its past practices of promoting vaporware. He cited Microsoft's announcement of Quick Basic 3.0 (QB3), a programming tool for Windows developers. It was alleged that Microsoft preannounced this product in order to impede the sales of a competing product of Borland know as Turbo Basic. The judge cited an internal memo from CEO William Gates saying, "the best way to stick it to Philippe is preannounce . . . to hold off Turbo buyers."[35] Microsoft denied these allegations, and they were never pursued by the Justice Department as Judge Sporkin had requested.

Now Windows 95 can be added to the list of well-known vaporware products. But how do we assess Microsoft's intentions in preannouncing this product? Was it a strategic ploy to avoid losing customers to companies such as IBM and Apple or was this practice more benign, a way of dealing with customer demand for more information?

THE MICROSOFT CORPORATION

The Microsoft Corporation was founded in 1979 in Seattle, Washington as a small upstart software computer company. Its founder and president William Gates was convinced that the personal computer market had enormous potential which could easily be exploited by Microsoft.

Gates proceeded to make a deal with IBM to supply the giant computer company with an operating system for its new personal computer. Gates purchased for $50,000 an outdated operating system known as 86-DOS from a small company called Seattle Computer Products. He revised the 86-DOS program and called it MS-DOS. He licensed this product to IBM in 1981 but wisely retained ownership. As a result when other vendors (such as Compaq and Dell) decided to clone the IBM PC, they had to license their operating systems from Microsoft. By 1994 MS-DOS was used in over 70 million IBM and IBM-compatible computers, and, as a result, Microsoft had over 90 percent of the world market for operating system software. The company also generated significant revenues from its applications software products such as its spreadsheet (Excel) and its word-processing package (Microsoft Word), which were initially written for Apple's proprietary operating system.

In just 15 years Microsoft grew into a $5 billion company with a 25 percent net profit margin and a market value of over $40 billion. In the mid-90s it employed 16,400 people working in 49 countries. Although its revenues were not as substantial as other high-tech companies such as IBM and Apple, no one could doubt Microsoft's clout in the marketplace. As a *Time* magazine article observed, "In some respects, the power Microsoft wields over the computer industry may exceed IBM in its heyday."[36]

A BRIEF HISTORY OF WINDOWS

Windows is the name of the operating system created by Microsoft to succeed its very popular MS-DOS system. An operating system is essentially the heart of the computer, allowing it to communicate with peripheral devices such as printers and disk drives. It also controls the movement of data within a computer. Despite its popularity and widespread use, MS-DOS had many problems such as its lack of user-friendliness. It was frequently contrasted unfavorably with Apple Computer's proprietary operating system which was much more intuitive and easier to use. Hence, Microsoft decided to construct a new state-of-the-art operating system that would provide a graphical user interface similar to the one used by Apple. Windows is still a DOS-based operating system but, unlike DOS, it is not command driven, relying instead on icons, pull-down menus, and simpler instructions.

The first version of this product was known as Windows 1.0, and it was announced in November 1983 for availability in June 1984. But Microsoft ran into development problems and pushed out the release date to June 1985. It finally began shipping this product in November 1985. But despite this long gestation period, Windows 1.0 had many deficiencies and drawbacks such as memory barriers, and hence it did not receive a warm welcome in the marketplace. In May 1990 Microsoft introduced an improved version known as Windows 3.0, which did a much better job of overcoming the limitations of DOS. Since the launch of Windows 3.0, Microsoft has sold over 40 million copies. It should be pointed out that Windows 3.0 was shipped before it was a stable product. The numerous bugs were fixed in version 3.1, but the company's reputation was unquestionably damaged by this hasty release of Windows 3.0.

A subsequent version of the product, known as Windows NT, a high-end system that incorporated networking technology and allowed users to link PCs together. NT could be installed on a powerful PC with copious memory so that it could function as a server in a client/server network. Although Gates estimated that sales of Windows NT would exceed one million copies in its first full year (1994), actual sales were much more modest. Windows NT gained popularity slowly but Gates was confident of its ultimate success.

MICROSOFT'S STRATEGY

Part of the reason for Microsoft's extraordinary success with Windows and other products has been a consistent reliance on its core competence. The company has been extremely well focused and has adroitly leveraged its technologies. For the most part it has eschewed the strategy of bigger computer firms such as IBM and DEC which offer a full range of products and service to their clients including hardware, software, consulting services, service contracts, and so forth. But up to this point in its history Microsoft had concentrated on operating systems and applications software. It had also encouraged developers to invest in these technologies and this led to the wide spectrum of software that runs on its systems.

In short, the company avoided the perils of spreading itself too thin and thereby losing the edge in its core technologies. Observers note that this changed as major clients insisted that Microsoft provide substantial technical assistance with Windows NT; in some cases this meant designing and implementing a full network system. Also, Microsoft began to expand into the information and entertainment business.[37]

But it has continued to dominate the market for PC software with an expanding and loyal base of customers. According to the *Economist*, Microsoft's "PC-software strategy centers on brand loyalty: Lure customers in with operating systems, sell them applications software, keep them sweet—and the cash flowing in—with regular upgrades."[38] Given the rapid pace of technological change, this strategy, of course, depends on both noteworthy and *timely* upgrades to avoid any erosion of the customer base through the migration of customers to competitive products with more advanced technological features.

CHICAGO BECOMES WINDOWS 95

One such upgrade that generated a new round of controversy for the Microsoft Corporation was the version of Windows originally code-named "Chicago." Chicago or Windows 4.0 was another major upgrade that included built-in networking, the capability of 32-bit processing,[39] built-in electronic mail and faxing capabilities, and a program that allows direct access to remote files. The product also included the most complete "plug-and-play" support ever offered by Microsoft.[40] In addition, this new operating system provided sophisticated multitasking, the ability to run several programs simultaneously.

When the company first began discussing Chicago in 1991, its original plan was to finish the product specification by October 31, 1991, release a beta version of the product one year later, and have the final product finished by December 1993. Microsoft officials quickly realized, however, that this ambitious plan was way off the mark. Indeed, the spec for the product was not actually finished until November 1992. It revised the release schedule substantially and announced that this new version of Windows would be ready for shipping by the end of 1994. This was still an aggressive schedule that called for a beta release in June 1994. Also, "the company shortened the original beta schedule for Chicago by 10 months in order to meet the company's long promised end-of-year deadline, . . ."[41] The reduced beta cycle worried many users; if the product was not adequately tested by knowledgeable customers, it could mean that it would be shipped prematurely with many bugs and problems.

In February 1994 Microsoft announced a beta schedule to the public that had been divulged to developers at a meeting in December. This schedule called for a limited beta test of a few hundred users that would begin in late March or April and a more widespread beta set for June. The June beta testing was to involve several hundred thousand users, an abnormally large beta pool. There was speculation that the reason for the large beta test was "to drown out any noise that rival IBM intends to make later this year when it delivers OS/2.2 to beta testers."[42] The reference was to IBM's new version of its rival operating system OS/2 which had many of the same features as Windows. Microsoft remained insistent that the final release of the product would still occur by the end of 1994, despite this obviously compressed development schedule.

But the December 1994 release date for Windows was an overly optimistic target. By late summer of 1994 the company announced what its skeptical user base had feared but anticipated: Chicago would not be ready by December. Microsoft announced that the new operating system would be ready for the market in "the first half of 1995." It also aptly renamed the product to Windows 95. Shortly after the delay was communicated to the public, there was another announcement specifying that the product would be available by late April 1995.

However in December 1994 the company announced again that the product would be delayed even further. Microsoft then maintained that the product would be shipped in August 1995. This was the product's third delay and the news caused Microsoft's stock to fall $2.75 to $59.875. There was no indication of the specific problems behind this delay, but according to some press reports, the problems involved compatibility between the operating system and some of the hardware components and peripheral products which it was supposed to control. In subsequent communications the company attributed the delay to the need for a more prolonged testing phase in order to ensure product stability.

In the fall of 1994, IBM began shipping its new operating system called OS/2 Warp, a 32-bit operating system, that many regarded as a worthy competitor of Windows. IBM viewed Microsoft's delays as fortuitous, hopeful that users would buy computers with OS/2 Warp and that developers would work on compatible software in order to reach those users. IBM estimated that its 1994 sales of OS/2 Warp would be about 800,000.

VAPORWARE?

Most users have learned to take delays such as these in stride since they have become so common in the software industry. Microsoft, like some of its competitors, has developed an infamous reputation for failing to meet its production schedules. Hence most users and developers have become weary of the company's promises and skeptical of its commitments. Many trade journals took the company to task for this latest example of vaporware, but most noted that they really did not expect Chicago to ship on time anyway.

But did Microsoft make a good faith effort to announce a realistic delivery date for Chicago? Were these delays unavoidable, attributable to the unpredictable nature of software development? Or is this another example of vaporware, a practice of announcing a product too far in advance of its availability in order to lock out competitive products? Was Microsoft seeking to freeze the market to keep users from migrating to IBM's OS/2 system?

Many in the computer industry press seemed to think so. At least one editor intimated that the Chicago preannouncement strategy was similar to the tactics used by IBM in its heyday.[43] IBM's overriding goal in the 1960s and 70s was to maintain market share at all cost. During the early 1960s IBM dominated the mainframe market with its 1400 system. But despite IBM's dominance, its technology was vulnerable. Also, it charged exorbitant prices and made huge profits, and this attracted considerable competition. Honeywell, for example, pursued the 1400 line with its H-200 system that processed data faster than the IBM and sold for much less.

Honeywell was initially successful with this machine as its sales began to erode IBM's market share. But IBM dealt with the popular H-200 by prematurely announcing its competitive system known as System/360 in order to freeze the market and avoid losing customers. According to Richard DeLamarter,

> IBM rushed its System/360 in to the breach to stop Honeywell, Control Data, and other competitors. It was the mere promise of that family of computers, as much as their actual installation, that saved the day for IBM. IBM's telling customers about the System/360 helped it corner an overwhelming share of the fast-expanding market for computer systems, even though several models of it did not make it into customer's hands until almost two years after their April 1964 introduction. . . .[44]

Was Microsoft to some extent mimicking the strategy of IBM in order to avoid losing customers to competitors (ironically one of whom is IBM) with better operating systems? Microsoft too was obsessed with market share, and what better way to retain one's users than to lock them in with expectations about the imminence of a new and more powerful operating system?

Microsoft responded directly to these innuendoes and accusations by writing an industry White Paper entitled "Vaporware in the Software Industry." In this paper the company claimed that preannouncing products well before their official release date is nothing more than "predisclosure" and not vaporware. Furthermore, it served an important purpose of engaging "customers and the industry in a useful dialogue about products that help customers make better decisions and developers make better products."[45] Microsoft's argument, then, was that the public benefits immensely from early information and so-called preannouncement about products since it helps users make long-term decisions. In addition, if product announcements are too tightly controlled, isn't there a risk that the distribution of legitimate information could be impeded?

AFTERMATH

Windows 95 was finally released on August 24, 1995 to much publicity and fanfare. Microsoft's advertising budget for the product was estimated to be $220 million. Sales were brisk during the first few weeks after the launch, and the product appeared to be stable. Microsoft announced that in addition to strong retail sales it had commitments for over 300,000 Windows 95 units from a number of major corporations. Finally, in the midst of the hype, the company revealed the scope of this project: a staggering 11 million lines of code, 293 person-years of development time, and an estimated cost of $500 million.

NOTES

1. R. Stern, "Microsoft and Vaporware," *IEEE Micro* (April 1995), p. 85.
2. W. R. Collins et al., "How Good is Good Enough?" *Communications of the ACM* vol. 37, no. 1 (January 1994), p. 85.
3. L. Paine, "Prodigy Services Company (A)" (Boston: Harvard Business School Publications, 1993), p. 13.
4. Ibid.
5. *Stratton Oakmont Inc. v. Prodigy Services Co.*, WL 323710, N.Y. Sup. Ct. (1995).
6. Ibid.
7. *Cubby, Inc. v. Compuserve, Inc.*, 776 F. Supp. 135-144, S.D.N.Y. (1991).
8. E. Joyce, "Software Bugs: A Matter of Life and Liability," *Datamation* (15 May 1987), p. 90.
9. N. Leveson and C. Turner, "An Investigation of the Therac-25 Accidents," *Computer* (July, 1993), p. 23.
10. Ibid.
11. The details of Mr. Cox's ordeal are provided in the Joyce article "Software Bugs."
12. Leveson and Turner, "Investigation of Therac-25," p. 28.
13. Ibid., p. 35
14. P. Ross, "The Day the Software Crashed," *Forbes* (25 April 1994), p. 154.

15. Ibid.
16. M. Geyelin, "Doomsday Device: How an NCR System for Inventory Turned into a Virtual Saboteur," *Wall Street Journal*, (8 August 1994), p. A6.
17. Ibid.
18. M. Brandel and T. Hoffman, "User Lawsuits Drag on for NCR," *Computerworld* (15 August 1994), p. 125.
19. Ibid.
20. Ibid.
21. Geyelin, "Doomsday Device," p. A6
22. C. Bartlett and A. Nanda, "Intel Corporation—Leveraging Capabilities for Strategic Renewal," Harvard Business School Case Study (Boston: Harvard Business School Publications, 1994), p. 3.
23. Ibid., p. 5.
24. J. Markoff, "The Chip on Intel's Shoulder," *New York Times*, 18 December 1994, Focus Section, p. 6.
25. "Intel's Chip of Worms?" *Economist* (17 December 1994), p. 65.
26. B. Crothers and R. Framas, "Intel Rushes to Assure Users Pentium Is Safe," *Infoworld* (12 December 1994), p. 3.
27. P. Lewis, "IBM Halts Sales of its Computer with Flawed Chip," *New York Times*, 13 December 1994, p. A1.
28. Ibid.
29. J. Vijayan, "Vendors Rally Behind Intel," *Computerworld* (19 December 1994), p. 4.
30. D. Lyons, "Sun Screen," *Forbes*, (13 November 2000), p. 69.
31. D. Tennant, "McNealy Blames IBM for Sun's Server Memory Flaws," *Computerworld* (3 December 2001), p. 12.
32. J.Vijayan, "Sun Fixes Server Problem, but Controversy Persists," *Computerworld* (3 December 2001), p. 12.
33. This case originally appeared in R. Spinello, *Ethical Aspects of Information Technology* (Upper Saddle River, NJ: Prentice Hall, 1995). It is based on an actual case history but names, dates, and places have been disguised.
34. Entry in the *Microsoft Press Computer Dictionary* (Seattle, WA: Microsoft Press, 1991).
35. The reference is to Phillipe Kahn, the CEO of Borland.
36. P. Elmer-Dewitt, "Master of the Universe," *Time*, (5 June 1995), p. 50.
37. Gates invested in one alliance to make interactive entertainment products and another to make interactive TV systems.
38. "The Future of Microsoft," *Economist* (22 May 1993), p. 27.
39. This means that the computer can process 32 pieces of data at one time.
40. Plug-and-play refers to the capacity to handle various peripheral devices produced by different manufacturers.
41. D. Barney, "Microsoft Cuts Chicago Beta Cycle 10 Months," *Infoworld* 16, no. 26, p. 1.
42. S. Johnston and E. Scannell, "Microsoft Bets Big on Beta Test of Chicago," *Computerworld* (February 28, 1994), p. 1.

43. See Paul Gillin's comments in "Halftime Report," *Computerworld* (11 July 1994), p. 36.
44. R. DeLamarter, *Big Blue* (New York: Dodd Mead & Co., 1986), p. 58.
45. "Vaporware in the Software Industry," White Paper (Seattle, WA: Microsoft Corporation, 1995).

8

Fair Competition and Internet Access

This last collection of cases highlights two separate but interconnected issues: fair competition and access to the Internet infrastructure. Several of these cases involve two icons of the Internet economy, Microsoft and AOL Time Warner, which function as gatekeepers to that infrastructure. Both companies undoubtedly aspire to expand that role in future years, and they have already clashed over issues such as instant messaging and on-line services.

Some economists believe that the nature of the Internet economy makes it a breeding ground for puissant monopolies like these two companies. Familiarity with this concern is fairly widespread thanks to the attention that has coalesced around the Microsoft antitrust trial. That trial has raised many questions about the applicability of industrial age laws, such as the Sherman Act of 1890, to the information age. While some argue that these laws have little relevance, others say that it is more important than ever to ensure their enforcement.

Antitrust policy cannot be abandoned, but it must strive to strike a balance between allowing innovators to profit from their innovations and inhibiting them from abusing their power in a way that stifles competition. This balance is especially hard to achieve in high-technology businesses where network effects prevail and where there are commonly accepted standards. Network effects suggest that any technology (such as an operating system) based on "connectedness" becomes more significant and popular as more people use it. According to the *Economist*, "The notion is that some businesses—Internet access, credit cards and computer software, to name three—differ fundamentally from other economic activities because the desire for compatibility makes certain forms of competition impractical or even unwanted."[1]

The presence of network effects, therefore, tends to bias industries toward a monopoly structure. Markets for products like operating systems have a winner-take-all dynamic, and logic would strongly imply that the winner should not be punished. On the other hand, we should not let monopolies wield their power unfairly, since such anticompetitive activity will most likely dampen innovation, and this hurts consumers in the long run.

In addition to the theme of fair competition, the cases in this chapter address the important theme of open access. Should there be restrictions on companies such as AOL Time Warner which has some control over the *physical, logical,* and *content layers* of the emerging global information infrastructure (i.e., the conduits or "pipes" through which data flows, Internet access software, and movies, music, or Web pages)?

The general question prompted by most of the cases in this chapter is whether or not we can rely on the invisible hand of the market to rectify potential abuses. Or do we need government intervention? And, if so, is current antitrust law the best way to handle these issues?

With these questions in mind, the first case to be considered is the *Microsoft* antitrust case which has major implications for the laws of cyberspace. Has Microsoft violated antitrust law and the norms of fair competition in its effort to preserve its monopoly of personal computer operating systems? Particular attention will be given to the issue of bundling and the integration of Internet Explorer and Windows. The second case is a follow-up and looks at Microsoft's similar tactics with its new operating system Windows XP, released in the fall of 2001. Has Microsoft once again stepped over the line by bundling instant messaging and a video player into this new operating system? According to Dan Carney, "One of the most effective sources of Microsoft's power is bundling—its process of continuously adding features to its Windows operating system."[2] But is this activity anticompetitive and should the company's right to bundle be restricted?

The third case in the chapter, the "AOL Time Warner Merger," turns our attention to a different set of issues. Is there any danger in one company's owning the cable infrastructure as well as so much content?

Will this company have too much control over crucial elements of the information infrastructure? What are the possibilities for conduit or content discrimination and will AOL Time Warner indulge in such discrimination unless government regulators intervene?

The open access theme continues with the case of "AT&T and the City of Portland." In this case we review the arguments for the closed access model advanced by the cable companies such as AT&T. There is a major public policy debate about the suitability of closed versus open architectures and the main elements of that debate come to the surface in this case. Both the AOL Time Warner and the AT&T cases trigger policy and ethical questions about the responsibility of a monopolist to share its property with its rivals.

The final discussion in this chapter, "Note on the Digital Divide," examines the access issue from a much different angle. Many predict that the coming broadband network will be the real information infrastructure of the twenty-first century. What should be done about the disenfranchised in a society where dependence on that infrastructure will be increasingly critical? Should the United States, for example, pursue a national goal of universal broadband access?

Case 8.1 Microsoft Corporation (A): *The United States of America v. Microsoft*

On a bright, crisp fall morning in October 1997 Attorney General Janet Reno and Joel Klein were beseiged with questions by a mob of reporters. They had called a press conference to announce that the Justice Department was seeking an injunction against Microsoft for violating a consent decree by tying its browser to Windows. It was clear from their responses that Reno and Klein meant business. This action was the first step in an epic confrontation between these two goliaths, and the government seemed determined to prevail.

MICROSOFT'S WINDOW'S MONOPOLY

Most economists will admit that the presence of network effects goes a long way to account for Microsoft's dominance in operating system software.[3] Network effects occur when the benefits of using a product for each individual user increase with the number of users. Interconnectivity and compatibility are critical purchasing criteria, since no one wants to be running an operating system that is not widely used. Hence users understandably purchase the same system that other users have. If one is planning to purchase a desktop computer, one will most likely be drawn to the Wintel (*Win*dows and In*tel*) standard: Microsoft's Windows operating system and Intel's Pentium processor chip. One reason for this is that there are more applications written for this system than rival systems such as Apple's Macintosh or IBM's OS/2. Thus, Microsoft currently controls the standard for PC operating systems because network effects along with the high cost of developing a rival operating system created mammoth barriers to entry, making it insuperably difficult for potential competitors to gain any ground. This accounts for the company's extraordinary success and high profitability. During 1998, the year in which the antitrust trial commenced, Microsoft reported $4.5 billion in net profits on revenues of $14.5 billion.

Some economists have argued that in these increasing-returns industries that bias a company to a single-seller status, monopoly power does not lead inevitably to a negative outcome for society. In their estimation this is because the dominant companies like Microsoft are not conventional monopolies. Rather, they are *serial* monopolies where one monopoly (or near monopoly) gives way to another. In other words, these monopolies are inherently transitory. The rate of innovation is so great that market leaders are regularly leapfrogged by new competitors. Consider, for example, how WordStar gave way to WordPerfect, which then gave way to Word. Some economists argue that this is a socially desirable and efficient outcome given our dependence on standards in a network economy where there is a need to communicate or interconnect.[4]

Lawyers at the U.S. Department of Justice, however, did not share this sentiment. Because of Microsoft's status as a monopoly, the Department of Justice (DOJ) kept a watchful eye on the company throughout the 1990s. Officials at the DOJ became especially concerned about the company's aggressive behavior in the famous "browser wars." A browser is a piece of application software that enables a user to examine a collection of information. When the World Wide Web emerged, so did companies offering browsers. A Web browser enables personal computer users to navigate the Web and to display or scan various Web pages. One such company was Netscape Corporation, founded in 1994 by Jim Clark and Mark Andreesen. Netscape's Navigator browser quickly became the early winner in this immature market and by mid-1996 Netscape dominated the browser marketplace. It had distributed over 40 million browsers and had captured an 87 percent share of the market. Netscape had decisively triumphed in round one of the browser wars.

At this point Microsoft, which up to then had paid little attention to the Internet, decided to enter the fray. The company's CEO Bill Gates developed a strategy, articulated in a 1995 memo called "The Internet Tidal Wave," that would "embrace and extend" the Internet across Microsoft's product line. Microsoft soon introduced its Internet Explorer browser, which, according to Gates, "was priced to sell." In an effort to dethrone Netscape from its entrenched position, Microsoft decided to give away the browser to anyone who purchased Windows; the two products were offered as an integrated package. Thanks to this and other strategic moves by Microsoft, Netscape's market share began to plunge. Netscape cried foul, arguing that Microsoft had unfairly leveraged its monopoly power to beat them in the marketplace.

The DOJ also felt that some of these tactics went too far and violated the Sherman Antitrust Act of 1890. The Sherman Act, the bedrock piece of antitrust litigation in the U.S., is quite concise:

> *Section 1:* Every contract, combination in the form of trust or otherwise, or conspiracy, in restraint of trade or commerce among the several States, or with foreign nations, is declared to be illegal.
> *Section 2:* Every person who shall monopolize, or attempt to monopolize, or combine or conspire with any other person or persons, to monopolize any part of the trade of commerce among the several States, or with foreign nations, shall be deemed guilty of a felony.

Subsequent case law has greatly elaborated on what is permissible or impermissible behavior under the Sherman Act, but the boundaries of acceptable behavior are not always clear. In one of the most significant cases in 1911, *Standard Oil v. U.S.*, the Supreme Court set forth a standard embodied in the phrase "the rule of reason." Once this rule was applied, Courts did not find "all combinations in restraint of trade" illegal but only "unreasonable" combinations.[5]

On May 18, 1998 the Justice Department filed a lawsuit charging Microsoft with antitrust violations. The antitrust suit was immediately regarded as portentous: "an antitrust action to close the century, as central to the functioning of the modern economy as was the case against John D. Rockefeller's Standard Oil which opened it."[6]

This historic case commenced on October 19, 1998 in the district court of Washington, D.C. The presiding judge was Thomas Penfield Jackson. The government's legal team was headed by Joel Klein and David Boies. Boies, who handled Al Gore's postelection litigation in 2000, has had an extraordinary record of success and has often been called "the Michael Jordan of the courtroom." At the helm of Microsoft's defense team was William Neukom, the company's senior vice president for law and corporate affairs. He was ably assisted by the law firm of Sullivan & Cromwell. John Warden, a Sullivan & Cromwell partner, was the head litigator.

THE GOVERNMENT'S CASE

The nucleus of the plaintiff's case focused on four distinct but interrelated violations of the Sherman Act:

- Microsoft's monopolization of the market for PC operating systems and its maintenance of monopoly power by anticompetitive means especially in its efforts to combat the threat posed by browser functionality, regarded as a possible "partial substitute" for the operating system. This is in violation of Section 2 of the Sherman Act.
- Unlawful exclusive dealing arrangements in violation of both Sections 1 and 2 of the Sherman Act. (This category includes Microsoft's exclusive deals with Apple Computer and with Internet Access Providers such as America Online.)
- Microsoft's unlawful attempt to monopolize the market for Web browsing software [in violation of Section 2 of the Sherman Act] (in addition to using anticompetitive means to maintain its power in the market for Intel-compatible PC operating systems, Microsoft attempted to illegally amass monopoly power in the browser market).
- Anticompetitive tying or bundling of Microsoft's Internet Explorer (IE) browser with its Windows operating system in violation of Section 1 of the Sherman Act.[7]

In order to prove the first allegation the plaintiff, the Department of Justice, had to demonstrate that Microsoft was a monopoly and that it had abused its monopoly power, since it is not illegal *per se* to be a monopoly. Most monopolies use their power to hurt consumers by charging higher prices, that is, prices in excess of marginal cost, and reducing output. Microsoft, however, had not exhibited this behavior since it was selling the Operating System (OS) to hardware manufacturers at a modest price of $40. However, while merely possessing monopoly power is not itself an antitrust violation, it is a necessary condition for proving a monopolization charge. The Supreme Court has defined monopoly power as "the power to control prices or exclude competition."[8] Since Windows accounted for a 95 percent share of the PC OS market, it was difficult to conclude that it was not a monopoly. If one includes the Mac OS in this category, Microsoft's market share was still around 80 percent.

Also, Microsoft's market power derived from huge barriers to entry. One barrier is the cost of developing a new operating system, estimated at $500 million. Another barrier is the "application barrier to entry" which is based on two features of the OS market—consumers want an OS for which there is an abundance of applications, and software developers prefer to write applications for an OS that has a large installed base. Microsoft clearly benefited from this applications entry barrier. If "middleware" software (such as the browser) were to succeed, it would erode this barrier. The browser runs on top of the operating system and hence it can function as a middle-level platform for which software applications can be written. In technical terms, middleware refers to software like a browser that exposes its own APIs (APIs or Application Programming Interfaces are blocks of code embedded in an operating system that allow applications to "plug in" and function).

Middleware can pose a threat to the operating system. If applications are primarily written for the browser instead of the OS, the underlying operating system would tend to become irrelevant and commoditized. Hence the potential threat to the continued dominance of Windows. According to one legal analysis: "If a consumer could have access to the applications he desired—regardless of the operating system he uses—simply by installing a particular browser on his computer, then he would no longer feel compelled to select Windows in order to have access to those applications. . . . Therefore, Microsoft's efforts to gain market share in one market (browsers) served to meet the threat of Microsoft's monopoly in another market (operating systems) by keeping rival browsers from gaining critical mass of users necessary to attract developer attention away from Windows as the platform for software development."[9]

Microsoft allegedly sought to prevent Navigator from gaining market share and attracting software developers by aggressively promoting its own browser. Microsoft introduced Internet Explorer (IE) version 2 in November 1995. As the product's quality steadily improved, Microsoft sought to encourage third parties to use and distribute IE (beginning with version 3), and some of these arrangements sparked the claim that Microsoft engaged in anticompetitive conduct.

One contention under the first major allegation (that Microsoft sought to maintain its monopoly power by anticompetitive means) concerned Microsoft's dealings with its Original Equipment Manufacturers (OEMs) regarding the required inclusion of the browser. The OEM channel is one of two primary channels for the distribution of browsers. Microsoft allegedly executed deals with computer makers to exclude Netscape's browser and promote Internet Explorer. Manufacturers who refused to go along were supposedly threatened with losing access to Windows. Although there was a sworn deposition from Compaq accusing Microsoft of threatening to "terminate their agreement" for promoting Netscape and giving its icon prominence on the Presario desktop, Microsoft claimed that "it has never restricted any computer manufacturer from shipping Netscape Navigator or any other computer software."[10] These facts, therefore, were somewhat in dispute.

Microsoft did admit, however, that it had prevented deletion of the IE icon in favor of a competitor's browser icon, arguing that the IE browser was an essential feature of the operating system and should not be tampered with. There is a license restriction that prohibits the removal of desktop icons, folders, and Start menu entries; this restriction also forbids OEMs from causing any user interface other than the Windows desktop to launch automatically when the PC system is booted. Microsoft restricted OEMs rights under their license agreements to modify Windows because such modifications could destroy the principal value of Windows as a stable platform. The government held that the provisions of Microsoft's license agreement to limit the "freedom of OEMs to reconfigure or modify" Windows was anticompetitive because it prevented OEMs from altering Windows "in ways that might . . . generate usage for Navigator." In other words, "it thwarts the distribution of a rival browser by preventing OEMs from removing visible means of user access to IE."[11]

On the other hand, Microsoft's licensing agreements have never prohibited OEMs from preinstalling programs (including Navigator) on their PCs and placing icons for those programs in the "Start" menu. Despite this freedom of OEMs to install Netscape on their PCs, the DOJ claimed that OEMs were reluctant to do so since the presence of both a Navigator and IE icon might bewilder consumers and lead to a flood of phone calls to their support lines. OEMs claimed that their customer support facilities could not handle such calls, and so, rather than risk confusing customers, they chose to refrain from preinstalling Navigator in addition to the mandated installation of IE. As a result, the government's case suggested that Microsoft had succeeded in virtually ostracizing Netscape from the OEM distribution channel, since it was impractical for the OEMs to preinstall a second browser.

The second allegation against Microsoft focused on its many exclusionary deals which could potentially violate both Sections 1 and 2 of the Sherman Act. The main concern was the agreements with various Internet Access Providers (IAPs). The IAP category includes both Internet Service Providers (ISPs) which make available Internet access, and Online Service Providers (OSPs) which provide proprietary off-Web content and services in addition to Internet access. America Online (AOL) is considered an OSP. Because of the monopoly position of Windows, IAPs would have a strong interest in having a favorable location on the Windows desktop. Microsoft developed a mechanism to facilitate the process of signing up for an IAP from the desktop. This was called the Internet Connection Wizard, and only selected Microsoft-approved IAPs could be accessed through the Connection Wizard. Microsoft signed distribution agreements with the major IAPs and those agreements specified that in exchange for being included in the Connection Wizard, Internet Explorer would be the preferred and default browser.

By signing these exclusive deals with IAPs, the government alleged that Microsoft foreclosed Netscape's opportunities in the marketplace. The following brief excerpt is from the testimony of Cameron Myhrvold, a Microsoft vice president and a liaison to the IAP community.

> ***Boies:*** Is it the case that what you were trying to do with the ISPs was to prevent the ISPs from presenting Internet Explorer and Netscape Navigator side by side and allowing the consumer to choose between them?
>
> ***Myhrvold:*** What we wanted to do, sir, was to encourage the distribution of Internet Explorer. Especially in the early days when we had no distribution of Internet Explorer through ISPs, when we had very, very small market share. . . . We were very concerned that if the user saw Netscape Navigator side by side with Internet Explorer, and Netscape having all of the mind share and usage share, we would lose all of those, or the majority of, those decisions. So we did specifically ask that ISPs distribute Internet Explorer by itself so that we would not lose all of those side-by-side choices.
>
> ***Boies:*** You were concerned that if you presented the consumer with a choice of the two browsers, side by side, they would pick Netscape rather than yours, right?
>
> ***Myhrvold:*** Yes, that's right.[12]

In 1996 Microsoft also entered into an arrangement with AOL whereby AOL agreed to incorporate IE browsing technology seamlessly into the AOL client software. IE would be AOL's default browser, that is, the one which would automatically be installed. In exchange for this arrangement, Microsoft agreed to place an AOL icon in its OLS folder.[13] And AOL was forbidden to promote or support any non-Microsoft Web browser and not provide software using any non-Microsoft browser except at the customer's request. If AOL members wanted to use Netscape, they would have to locate that product and go through the steps of downloading and installing it. This was a time-consuming process that most AOL members would be inclined to avoid.

Presumably, AOL chose IE because it was technically superior to Navigator, but this fact is in some dispute. David Colburn, a senior vice president for America Online, testified for the government that AOL chose Internet Explorer as its default browser "and agreed to limit its members' use of Netscape, because Microsoft dangled irresistible bait: promotion of America Online's service on every personal computer running the Windows operating system."[14] According to Colburn, IE and Navigator were technically equivalent, but AOL wanted that premium placement on Windows interface. However, in his cross-examination of Colburn, John Warden of the Microsoft defense team produced an e-mail message from Steve Case, the CEO of AOL, written on January 24, 1996, which seems to present a different viewpoint:

> From a pure technology standpoint, it does look like Microsoft may win this one. Couple that with their distribution (OS) muscle, then Netscape clearly faces an uphill battle.[15]

In addition, according to Microsoft, AOL's commitment to use IE did not prevent AOL from complying with a subscriber's request for Navigator. Nonetheless, according to the Justice Department, this was an unlawful exclusive dealing arrangement which excluded Netscape from efficient channels to achieve increases in market share. The Supreme Court ruled in *Tampa Electric Co. v. Nashville Coal* (325 U.S. 320 [1961]) that exclusive contracts do not violate antitrust laws unless the probable effect is to "foreclose competition in a substantial share of the line of commerce affected." The burden fell on Microsoft to defend these exclusive arrangements with IAPs by proving that there was some pro-competitive justification.

The DOJ also charged that Microsoft engaged in exclusionary conduct in its deal with Apple Computer. This agreement required Apple to preinstall or bundle the most current version of IE with the Mac OS and to make IE the default browser. Apple was not allowed to position icons for a non-Microsoft browser on its desktop. In order to force Apple into this arrangement, Microsoft allegedly threatened to cancel its development of the latest version of Mac Office (the major application software program written for the Mac by Microsoft that includes word processing and spreadsheet functionality). According to an internal e-mail from Bill Gates: "I think Apple should be using IE everywhere and if they don't do it, then we can use Office as a club."[16] Gates also reported that he had called Apple's CEO to ascertain "how we should announce the cancellation of Mac Office." Shortly after that phone call, the agreement was signed.

The third allegation involved Microsoft's liability for attempted monopolization of the browser market in violation of Section 2 of the Sherman Act. Case law says that "to demonstrate attempted monopolization a plaintiff must prove (1) that the defendant has engaged in predatory or anti-competitive conduct with (2) specific intent to monopolize and (3) a dangerous probability of achieving monopoly power."[17] It was alleged that Microsoft initially attempted to coerce Netscape to divide the browser market. According to this plan, Microsoft would let Netscape develop browsers for Macintosh, UNIX, and 16-bit Windows systems, while it would develop browsers for the much larger market of 32-bit Windows 95 systems. According to the testimony of Jim Barksdale (the CEO of Netscape at the time): "If we refused to agree, Microsoft made it clear that they would attempt to crush us."[18] Microsoft disputed this claim and said that such a "market allocation proposal" never came up in its deliberations with Netscape. But according to the DOJ, when Netscape refused to abandon the development of browsing software for 32-bit versions of Windows, Microsoft *intentionally* sought to expand Internet Explorer's share of browser usage and to simultaneously depress Navigator's share to an extent sufficient to demonstrate to software developers that Navigator would never emerge as the standard software to browse the Web. The government also claimed that there was a "dangerous probability" that Microsoft would achieve monopoly power in the browser market.

Perhaps the most significant and complicated aspect of the government's case against Microsoft centered on the fourth and final allegation. The DOJ contended that Microsoft was culpable of unlawful technological tying, that is, bundling its Internet Explorer (IE) browser with the Windows operating system. Initially, Microsoft relied upon contracts with its Original Equipment Manufacturers (OEMs) to ensure that its browser functionality was included with Windows. For Windows 98 and beyond, however, the company modified the design of its Windows code to incorporate browser functionality. By commingling the browser code with the code for Windows 98, Microsoft made it infeasible to disable the browser.

A tying arrangement violates the Sherman Act if "the seller has appreciable economic power in the tying product market, and if the arrangement affects a substantial volume of commerce in the tied market."[19] In the Microsoft case the Windows operating system was the tying product and the Internet Explorer browser was the tied product.

There have been many famous antitrust cases involving tying, but one of the more relevant and recent cases to address the issue is *Jefferson Parish Hospital District v. Hyde.* In this case the Court held that a hospital offering hospital services (i.e., surgery) and anesthesiology services as a package was guilty of tying. There was some question in this case about whether or not surgical services and anesthesiology are separate products—the case for separability is certainly not intuitively obvious. According to this ruling, the patients perceived the services as separate products for which they desired a choice, and the package had the effect of forcing patients to purchase an unwanted product. Thus, tying anesthesia services to surgery in *Jefferson Parish* was judged to be anticompetitive because consumers were forced to purchase products from the hospital that they would prefer to get from others. The Court proposed a "consumer demand" test for determining tying: In difficult cases where there is a question of the functional relation between two products, it is necessary to examine the empirical evidence of demand for the tied product separate from the tying product. The Court decreed that "no tying arrangement can exist unless there is a sufficient demand for the purchase of anesthesiological services separately from hospital service."[20]

On the surface the bundling of the two products in this case (the OS and IE) seemed to benefit consumers since IE was given away for free. It was alleged, however, that unsuspecting consumers were being harmed because they were losing an ability to choose between IE and Netscape's Navigator browser. Also, this bundling was problematic because the browser was potentially a partial substitute for the monopoly product, that is, the operating system. As noted, the Web browser can become an alternative platform for which applications are written, which might mean that it would one day usurp the OS's monopoly status. Navigator, for example, supports JAVA, and Microsoft supposedly feared that once introduced on users' systems, this JAVA-enabled platform would attract software developers writing JAVA applets. In the long run, then, it could displace Windows as an attractive platform for new applications and take advantage of that self-reinforcing network effect that made Windows so powerful.

As a result, the DOJ argued that Microsoft tied IE to Windows not for any valid technical purpose, but as another strategic ploy to preserve its current monopoly. Microsoft artificially bolted together these two separate products in violation of the Sherman Act. Late in the trial Microsoft released a video purporting to illustrate 19 benefits resulting from the integration of the browser and Windows 98. But in dramatic cross-examination by Boies, Jim Allchin, senior VP of Microsoft, was forced to admit that those same benefits could be had by running Windows 95 with a stand-alone version of the browser. As Allchin acknowledged this 19 times, he was clearly annoyed and he accused Boies of semantic word games. But Boies had proven his point: It was "entirely practical to deliver these two pieces of functionality separately."

Quite simply, according to the government's case, Microsoft exercised its substantial market power to preserve its "applications barrier to entry" by means of this tying arrangement. By controlling the platforms that software vendors write for, Microsoft sought to maintain the market's dependence on Windows and the applications written for Windows.

MICROSOFT'S DEFENSE

Despite the depth and persuasiveness of the government's case, Microsoft's legal team marshaled a strong defense against these allegations. With regard to the first allegation (that Microsoft is a monopoly and has maintained its power not through competition on the merits), Microsoft steadfastly argued that it did not possess monopoly power and that it did not behave like a monopolist. It did not control output the way a traditional monopolist does. According to Microsoft, there was no evidence that it controlled a significant percentage of the productive assets in the operating system business, so it could not restrict total output of operating systems and thereby raise prices—Linux or IBM, for example, could easily expand their output to meet the entire consumer demand for operating systems. Microsoft further argued that the dominant market position of Windows "was created by and is dependent on consumer demand not the company's control of total output."[21] There was also some question about the relevant market—was it the market for Intel-compatible PC operating systems (as the government claimed) or should it also include non-Intel-compatible operating systems (such as Mac OS)? Even if the broader market definition were adopted, Microsoft still had 80 percent of the market, and the company acknowledged this "predominant" market share. But Microsoft contended that there were no structural barriers to entry that preserved its alleged monopoly power, and it challenged the notion of an applications barrier to entry, observing that approximately 2,500 applications have been written for IBM's OS/2 operating system.

While Microsoft's claim that Microsoft had no monopoly power seemed counterintuitive, some economists did not find this argument so implausible. An economist from MIT, Richard Schmalensee, who testified on Microsoft's behalf, argued that true monopolies maximize profits by charging a price well above marginal cost, that is, a price higher than they would charge in a competitive market. He claimed that if Microsoft were a true monopoly the profit-maximizing price for Windows 98 would be at least $900 and maybe as high as $2,000. As a result, "Since Microsoft is a profit maximizing firm, and since it is not charging the monopolist's profit maximizing price, Mr. Schmalensee deduces that it cannot be a monopoly."[22] The point was that Microsoft could not charge such a price because it faced *long-run competition*. The Microsoft monopoly was not as potent as its market share would seem to suggest, since there were market-based price constraints. Microsoft faced competition from potential future rivals: other operating systems or even non-PC devices like the Palm Pilot or network appliances. The *Economist* suggests that Microsoft faced long-run competition even from itself: "What makes Windows 98 at $2,000 a shot seem preposterous is that nobody would have bought it at that price: They would have stuck with Windows 95."[23]

Some of the allegations regarding anticompetitive behavior were certainly problematic for Microsoft. But its lawyers defended Microsoft's efforts to prevent computer manufacturers from displacing the desktop icon for Microsoft's browser. Microsoft had a right under federal copyright law to prevent unauthorized alteration of its copyrighted operating system. "If intellectual property rights have been lawfully acquired, their subsequent exercise cannot give rise to antitrust liability."[24] Microsoft also pointed out that its OEMs can install a second browser in addition to IE. The company rejected the argument that two browsers would lead to "consumer confusion." Recall that according to the OEMs, this meant that support costs would rise as users who saw two browser icons would be confused and would call for support. But Microsoft observed that some OEMs do install multiple browsers without such adverse consequences. Finally, Microsoft argued that despite the restrictions of the OEM license agreement, Netscape was not blocked from distributing its product. It was relatively easy to download Navigator from a number of different Web sites.

Microsoft also contended that it did not exhibit anticompetitive behavior in its struggle with Netscape but rather "pro-competitive" behavior. It did not prevent a competitor from reaching the marketplace (thus decreasing consumer welfare) but defeated the competitor in the marketplace through improved products, increased distribution, and lower prices (thereby increasing consumer welfare).[25] This is how the competitive marketplace works: Microsoft took on an important rival and through tough competition produced and distributed a superior browser for its customers. Also, Microsoft's design of Windows did not foreclose competition from rival Web browsers. Microsoft did attempt to maximize IE's share of the browser market at Netscape's expense, but this is compatible with a procompetitive intent.[26]

The second allegation regarding the agreements with Internet Access Providers (IAPs) was defended primarily on the grounds that exclusive contracts and cross-marketing agreements are commonplace in a competitive market economy and most especially in the Information Technology (IT) industry. According to one supportive brief, "they represent vigorous competition on the merits, serving the legitimate purposes of facilitating entry into new markets and preventing IAP's from misappropriating the free advertising provided by placement on the Windows desktop."[27] There was convincing (although not undisputed) testimony that AOL chose Internet Explorer because of this product's technical superiority (see Steve Case's e-mail cited above). There was also evidence presented that Netscape was more difficult to deal with than Microsoft. In another internal AOL e-mail Case wrote, "Netscape is breathing its own fumes and needs a wake up call. They need some gravity to bring them back to earth."[28] The bottom line was that these agreements did not deny Netscape access to the marketplace—Netscape had been able to distribute Navigator in the PC marketplace despite Microsoft's IAP arrangements.

Microsoft also countered the allegations about an exclusive deal with Apple Computer. It argued that Apple's agreement to make IE its default Web browser was part of a larger (and voluntary) technology agreement in which Microsoft also agreed to develop new versions of Office over a five-year period. Moreover, "Apple reserved the right to . . . bundle browsers other than Internet Explorer with the Mac OS and, in fact, bundles both IE and Navigator with the Mac OS today."[29]

Microsoft's defense team attempted to refute the third allegation and the charge of attempted monopolization of the browser market with the claim that Microsoft's competition with Netscape was not anticompetitive since it did not foreclose Navigator from the marketplace. Microsoft's lawyers also claimed that the company did not act with a "specific intent" to monopolize but rather sought to prevent Netscape from dominating the browser market. Moreover, there was no "dangerous probability" that Microsoft would achieve domination in this market, which had not even been properly defined. "We cannot just accept the plaintiff's unproven allegation of a 'browser' market," argued the Microsoft defense team.[30]

In response to the fourth and final allegation, Microsoft's lawyers pointed out that freezing the Windows operating system posed a great danger to the future of innovation in the software industry. They argued that the proposal to freeze Windows reflects a view that all beneficial product enhancements have already been developed. As Microsoft's attorneys explained in one of their briefs, "Had Microsoft not added

Internet technologies to its products, it would be an anachronism today, [because] the Internet has become both a major inducement for consumers to buy PC's for the first time and a major occupier of time and attention of PC users."[31] By preventing firms from integrating into their products previously provided stand-alone products, the courts would chill innovation to the detriment of consumers. Thus, Microsoft contended that the government's case suggested a dangerous precedent for other software companies that produce an industry standard—could they too be accused of leveraging their monopoly power just by adding new functionality to their products? Software products are dynamic and must be allowed to evolve; if not, consumers will suffer the consequences of outdated technologies. On the contrary, in this case, consumers enjoyed tangible benefits from Microsoft's integration of IE and Windows. Wouldn't a "browserless version" of Windows be less appealing to consumers, "most of whom want a fully functional computing solution that is simple and easy to use 'right out of the box' without installing additional software."[32]

Microsoft contended, therefore, that it had to have a right to innovate by adding new functionality to its software products. The government argued that the products were really separate and were bundled together not for the sake of efficiency but solely for an anticompetitive purpose. It further maintained that Windows and IE were separate products because "consumers today perceive operating systems and browsers as separate products for which there is separate demand."[33] Microsoft, on the other hand, claimed that this "consumer demand test" for separability cannot be applied to software products and insisted that the evolution of software is a process of bundling a new functionality (i.e., a new product) into an old product, even though it is still possible to provide those products separately. As Microsoft's lawyers argued, word processors now include spell checkers and PCs now include modems, even though both features used to be sold separately as add-on products. Are these, too, examples of unlawful ties? And with regard to Windows 98 the plaintiff had not even been able to identify the software code that is supposedly a separate, tied product.

According to *N. Pacific Ry. v. U.S.*, product ties are illegal only if they coerce buyers to "forego their free choice between competing products."[34] But Microsoft's actions did not preclude consumers from freely choosing a competing Web browser such as Navigator.

In summary, in refuting the fourth allegation Microsoft argued that without the capacity to enhance its core products in this way, those products would become stagnant and ineffectual. For Gates and other Microsoft executives, this was the most crucial principle at stake in this trial: Microsoft, and not the federal government, should be making product design decisions and determining what goes into its integrated software products.

Microsoft consistently maintained that far from violating the antitrust laws, its conduct was procompetitive, producing enormous consumer benefits. It cited the work of scholars like Hazlett who said, "The facts of the 'browser war' lead inexorably to one conclusion: consumers have benefited enormously from the ferocious rivalry between Netscape and Microsoft."[35] The company had not abused its monopoly power. It did not foreclose or ostracize Netscape from the marketplace since Netscape has always functioned on Windows. And it did not compel America Online to favor its browser over Netscape's. From the outset Microsoft had said that its actions and strategies were part of "rough and tumble capitalism" and that the government's case was "wrongheaded because it does not understand the computer industry, especially the necessity of cooperation of companies so that sophisticated technology products work with one another."[36]

CLOSING ARGUMENTS

The testimony ended on June 24, 1999 after 78 court days and 13,466 pages of transcripts. Judge Jackson told the lawyers, "All right gentlemen, it has been almost a pure pleasure. Let's keep it that way." The press awaited both legal teams as they left the courtroom. Microsoft declined to give a statement. Joel Klein simply said that his team had shown that Microsoft "clearly engaged in a broad pattern of illegal behavior" and that this deserved a serious remedy.[37]

Each side was asked to file final briefs for Judge Jackson in which it would summarize the basic facts of the case as it understood them. The core argument of the government's summary brief was that Microsoft was a monopoly in the PC business and that there were huge barriers to entry keeping competitors out, especially its software applications barrier. Also, Microsoft employed a number of coercive tactics to preserve its hegemony. These tactics included exclusionary arrangements with IAPs, the deal with Apple Computer, the tying of Windows and the browser. They were designed for a single purpose: to exclude Netscape from the marketplace and prevent middleware from becoming a new platform for applications.

Microsoft's summary brief, on the other hand, reiterated that the government had failed to demonstrate any appreciable harm to consumers, who were receiving the Windows operating system and browser functionality at a very affordable price. Even the government's key witnesses could not dispute this claim. As Ken Auletta reports, when the government's chief economic witness, Franklin Fisher, was asked if Microsoft harmed consumers, he replied, "On balance, I would think the answer was no up to this point."[38] Microsoft's attorneys also posed these questions: "If Microsoft was a monopoly, why did it spend so many billions each year on R and D? Why does each copy of Windows cost so little? . . . [Shouldn't] Microsoft's design choices be respected as long as there is plausible claim that this brings some advantage?"[39] Finally, Microsoft's attorneys insisted that there was no evidence that the bundling of IE and Windows prevented Netscape from distributing its product to consumers.

Was the government's case off the mark and "wrongheaded" as the company suggested, or had Microsoft stepped over the line and competed unfairly even by the standards of the "rough and tumble" world of capitalism?

Case 8.2 Microsoft Corporation (B): Windows XP

Microsoft's antitrust saga will probably not end with the government's 1998 case for its Windows monopoly. In October 2001 Microsoft launched Windows XP, a major new upgrade of the Windows operating system. It is undoubtedly the most important product release for the company since Windows 95. According to Microsoft, Windows XP is a more stable product than earlier versions of Windows. It also does a superior job of handling pictures, video, and music.

With Windows XP, Microsoft is also attempting to deliver an array of new Internet or Web services for individuals and corporations. In keeping with its past strategy which leveraged Windows as much as possible, the Windows operating system is once again a major platform for the delivery of these services. Hence Windows XP is designed to work well with XML (Extensible Markup Language) and SOAP (Simple Object Access Protocol), two technologies considered vital for Web services. Windows XP also includes Passport, an on-line identification system essential for the secure data exchanges that will be part of Web services.

In addition, Windows XP incorporates a sophisticated instant messaging system along with software for playing digital music and watching videos. Once again this is consistent with Microsoft's basic strategy of relying on its dominant Windows operating system to leverage its way into new markets. By bundling a media player and an instant messaging system into Windows, Microsoft is open to the same accusations that led to the antitrust trial chronicled in the previous case. Like the browser, both of these products are offered or sold separately by Microsoft competitors. Is Microsoft once again using its operating system to extend its monopolistic power? Let us consider each of these controversial XP features.

- **Instant Messaging:** This functionality is similar to the browser since it will probably expand to support new services and low-level applications (e.g., programs that would enable engineers in different locations to work together on the same blueprints). While instant messaging does not qualify as middleware, it does support other innovative products such as game software that would allow users to play against each other. The leader in this technology is AOL with almost 61 million users worldwide (as of February 2002). As a result, according to Mike France, "Microsoft is clearly trying to leverage its Windows monopoly to build a customer base for its messenger system rather than those produced by rivals."[40] By embedding its instant messaging service into Windows XP, Microsoft seeks to thwart AOL's growing dominance in this arena.
- **Media:** As digital music and DVDs become more popular, video players will also become more important to computer users. Windows media player, which allows users to play music and video, is designed to function as a platform for digital forms of entertainment. A user simply clicks on a Web music file from the Start menu, loads a CD, and then invokes Windows Media Player to play the music. RealNetworks, Inc.'s product, RealPlayer, is the leading software for these applications. It has over 215 million consumers signed up for its services. Real has finalized deals with five of the seven major PC manufacturers to include its software on their machines. But according to *Business Week,* "even when Real is an alternative, Microsoft's media player is easier to find on Windows XP screens and menus."[41]

Consumers can still download and use competing products such as RealPlayer, but Microsoft is obviously encouraging them to use its own services which are conveniently preloaded and prominently displayed.

Is all of this more of the same from Microsoft? Is it illegally leveraging XP to extend its dominance into new markets such as instant messaging? Are these legitimate enhancements or is Microsoft continuing to arbitrarily stretch the definition of an operating system? Finally, is Microsoft continuing to create obstacles for competitors and for the freedom of consumers?

In its defense Microsoft argues that these enhancements and improved features benefit users—it is simply developing better technology for its customers and preventing its operating system from becoming anachronistic in a fast-changing world. Thus Microsoft continues to insist that its bundling efforts are not anticompetitive because they create value for consumers. It hopes the court of public opinion will finally accept this argument and that its future will not be mired by additional antitrust lawsuits. As Gates has repeatedly said, there is no magic line between an application and an operating system. But is there no limit to what should be included in the operating system, and, if there is a limit, who should determine it?

Case 8.3 The AOL Time Warner Merger

INTRODUCTION

In the spring of 2000 two media giants, Time Warner and Disney, became embroiled in a controversy that led Time Warner to drop the ABC network (owned by Disney) from 11 of its cable markets including New York City. Viewers were outraged but they had no alternative but to wait things out. The contract dispute was soon resolved and ABC was back on the air within two days. There is an old saying that "content is king," but this dispute shows that the real power is with those who control the "pipes," the cable lines or conduits through which the content is delivered to the customer. Disney's concerns as a content provider were magnified when a merger was announced between America Online and Time Warner. Would independent content providers be left out or disadvantaged by conglomerates that controlled cable TV, Internet access, and their own content? Would this new colossus become a powerful gatekeeper over the distribution of content? If a giant company like Disney had misgivings about this merger, maybe it really wasn't in the public interest.

THE PROPOSED MERGER

Under the leadership of CEO Steve Case, America Online (AOL) has become a phenomenally successful company. By 1996, after just three years of operations, they had "emerged from nowhere to become the Goliath of cyberspace."[42] AOL succeeded by offering users a convenient and "low-tech" way of getting Internet access. According to Frank Rose, "their weapon was price—cut-rate, flat-fee connections offering unlimited access for US$19.95 a month or less—and they're targeting the lucrative, high-usage subscribers whose triple-digit monthly bills have kept AOL's bottom line black."[43] As a result, AOL is the world's leading Internet Service Provider (ISP) with over 25 million users at the time of the merger. This includes four million users of CompuServe, which was purchased by AOL in 1998. It has a 45 percent share of all households that use a dialup connection for Internet access. It also offers several Internet products such as AOL Instant Messenger and Netscape, which it acquired in 1999 in a deal valued at nearly $9 billion. Its other Internet properties include MapQuest, Moviefone, and Digital Cities. Estimates are that about 35 million people a month visit at least one of AOL's properties.

AOL also functions as a portal and its portal business is exceptionally strong, accounting for more than 20 percent of its revenues in 2000. Companies pay millions to be promoted on AOL's properties. In recent deals, "Amazon.com paid $19 million to serve as the preferred book seller on AOL.com, and Barnes & Noble agreed to pay $40 million to become the 'exclusive' bookseller within AOL's proprietary network."[44]

With AOL version 6.0 the company introduced its "AOL anywhere strategy." The goal is to allow users to get AOL mail, content and other features from devices other than computers such as pagers, set-top boxes, or Palm Pilots. According to AOL's executives, "[Version 6.0] is the hub of the AOL Anywhere experience. It's the key bridge to what is going to happen to the Internet in the next couple of years."[45]

AOL's partner in the new merger, Time Warner, owns and operates a broad conglomeration of media businesses including magazines, music, movies, and television. It owns the *Time, People* and *Sports Illustrated* magazine franchises; the Warner Bros. Records, Atlantic Records, and Elektra Entertainment recording labels; the Warner Brothers and New Line Cinema movie studios; the WB network and various cable networks such as HBO, Cinemax, CNN, TNT, and TBS. Time Warner is also the second largest cable company in the United States with 12.6 million cable subscribers at the time of the merger.

This $103.5 billion merger, which was first made public in January 2000, was heralded in the press as a marriage of entertainment and the Internet. According to one popular perspective, the merger also represented "the long-awaited convergence of the analog present and the digital future."[46] In the waning years of the analog era, content is still closely tied to its delivery systems. The owners of television stations, for example, have firm control over content and services; they produce the shows and send them over the air waves to their viewers. But with digital technology all forms of content, including voice, data, and video, can be converted into simple bits of data (1s and 0s). Also, the digital conduits or pipes that carry this data, such as cable lines or telephone lines, can do so indiscriminately and without regard for the particular content. The Internet, of course, greatly facilitates the global distribution of this digital data.

The combination of AOL and Time Warner came at an opportune time, as cable companies were just beginning to offer their customers high-speed Internet access through a modem attached to cable lines. The AOL Time Warner merger is expected to accelerate this trend toward broadband[47] Internet access. Once the Internet's capacity is increased, it will become the universal, low-cost delivery system for all types of digital information. With broadband, AOL and other ISPs will be able to offer real-time video streaming of motion pictures or videos of live events.

Many media critics lauded the merger, expecting this new media conglomerate to become an "entertainment machine." Others had many questions. Would the merger really bring about a revolution in on-line content and entertainment? "Will Time Warner, faced with a constant and instant audience, find new ways to deliver content? Could the combined pair, for example, create and release an entire movie, or book, or musical work online?"[48]

Regardless of these doubts and questions, the media giant was expected to have a strong bottom line. At the time of the merger it was estimated that the combined company would generate over $40 billion in revenues in 2001 with half of that money coming from AOL and cable TV. Cash flow (earnings before interest, taxes, depreciation, and amortization) was projected to be about $11 billion.

ECONOMIC BENEFITS AND RISKS

It is obvious that this marriage of entertainment and the Internet has many opportunities for synergy, such as cross-promotion and marketing. In one early promotion AOL disks were included in *Sports Illustrated* magazines, while the magazine's famous swim suit issue was heavily promoted on AOL. New Line Cinema, a smaller unit of Time Warner, worked closely with AOL on Web-based promotions to increase sales for its films such as *Lord of the Rings*. Some of the more unconventional promotions include fan chat rooms and on-line auctions of movie memorabilia. And in the summer of 2000 the Warner Brothers movie *The Perfect Storm* was heavily promoted on AOL through advertisements, sneak previews, and other promotions. AOL also began promoting *Time* magazine and signed up several hundred thousand subscribers, while the magazine mailed millions of AOL startup disks to its subscribers.

These arrangements point to the logic underlying this merger: bring together different media platforms under one roof so the same content can be delivered in different ways and be promoted in a synergistic fashion. In some respects the merger of Time Warner and Turner Broadcasting System had already demonstrated that this content sharing principle was workable. The union of AOL and Time Warner enables AOL to serve as another way of promoting and distributing Time Warner's diverse content. The main economic case for the merger, then, appears to the durability of this cross-promotional power.

A merger of this magnitude is also risky. There is the obvious risk of merging companies with very different cultures. The pace of change at AOL is alien to how things are done at Time Warner, where the organizational structure has been far more bureaucratic. Time Warner's different content units have been described as insular fiefdoms, each with a unique style and culture. According to Sharon Walsh, "The chemistry seems lethal. On one side are the hard-driving, khaki-wearing masters of the networking universe who have been king makers only since the mid-1990s. On the other are the more conservative media masters who've been around for 77 years and deep down, may feel like they're behind the times."[49]

More significant perhaps are the risks inherent in the strategy of vertical integration. According to the *Economist*, the principal danger is that "the content does not get the best distribution, or the distribution network does not get the best content."[50] Or one flawed piece of content could end up damaging multiple distribution outlets. However, while this combination of content and delivery has some perils, it also has great promise and in the eyes of many economists, the merger is well worth the risk.

In some respects, however, the merger seems to be going against the de-integration trend in this industry which began in the 1990s. As the worlds of telecommunications, entertainment, and computing begin to converge, the multimedia industry was being restructured, "moving from a set of three vertical businesses to a collection of five largely independent, horizontal industry segments."[51] These segments are content, packaging (e.g., AOL, Yahoo, or Bloomberg are considered "packagers" of content), transmission networks (companies in this segment like AT&T provide the physical infrastructure that helps distribute information), manipulation infrastructure (e.g., software that performs interactive network tasks), and terminals. But this merger represents the return of a vertical integration strategy that brings together owners of digital conduits or pipes with content providers. It remains to be seen whether or not this strategy will really add value for both of these companies.

Will this vertically integrated Internet/media organization be nimble enough to compete with more specialized rivals? Was this merger really necessary? Why not a more contingent relationship such as a partnership or a strategic alliance?

REGULATORY CONCERNS

The union of AOL and Time Warner faced immediate opposition not only from Disney, but also from many other players in related industries. The merger needed the approval of two U.S. regulatory agencies: the Federal Communications Commission (FCC) and the Federal Trade Commission (FTC). After holding public hearings, both agencies articulated their own concerns. Would the merger yield any anticompetitive effects especially in the market for broadband Internet access? Regulators were particularly apprehensive about the possibility of content and conduit discrimination.

As noted, AOL dominates the "narrowband" ISP marketplace with over 24 million users. This customer base positions AOL to be a dominant ISP broadband leader as well. Time Warner also provides broadband Internet access through a partially owned subsidiary called Road Runner. According to the FTC's Consent Order, "the relevant broadband ISP markets are likely to become highly concentrated as a result of the merger, and the merger will increase the ability of the combined firm to unilaterally exercise market power in Time Warner cable areas and throughout the United States."[52]

How could AOL Time Warner exercise such power? They could insist that Time Warner cable users be required to use AOL as their ISP or make it expensive and inconvenient for customers to adopt rival ISPs. The combined company could exclude nonaffiliated ISPs to the detriment of consumers. In this form of conduit discrimination AOL Time Warner could prevent rival services such as an ISP or portal from access to its conduit.

There are other possible forms of conduit discrimination, such as "insulating its own conduit from competition by limiting its distribution of affiliated content and services over rival platforms."[53] In other words, AOL Time Warner could deny its content to other distributors. For example, the company could simply refuse to deliver a premium piece of content over any other competing cable system.

A second concern was that AOL Time Warner would engage in *content discrimination*, that is, discriminate against content that does not originate from Time Warner by blocking that content all together or degrading it in some way. It would not be difficult to configure its platforms to be predisposed to Time Warner content by manipulating caching technology, "which allows popular websites to be stored closer to the end user, possibly at cable headend, in order to avoid backbone delays."[54] For example, according to Daniel Rubinfield and Hal Singer, AOL Time Warner content could be given preferential caching treatment: "A combined AOL Time Warner could provide preferential caching service to its affiliated CNN-Sports Illustrated site, while providing inferior caching support to the Walt Disney Corporation's ESPN site."[55]

A final concern focused on AOL's Instant Messaging (IM) network. IM programs work as follows: "Users have a list of other people's IM handles, and they click on a name to initiate a chat session; then the two or more people write text messages that are delivered almost instantly and persist in a window on one another's machines."[56] AOL's popular IM system has 61 million users, but it is proprietary and remains closed to members of competing systems such as Yahoo Messenger and Lotus Sametime. Thus, for example, AOL users cannot converse with users of Yahoo Messenger.

Competitors such as Microsoft and Yahoo have expressed concerns with this system's lack of openness and others worry that AOL's dominance in instant messaging could give it leverage in the competition for Internet telephony. Critics contend that AOL does not have a good track record in opening up its systems. For example, AOL has not made its IM software compatible with the software of rival text software such as iCast. According to iCast's testimony in front of the FCC: "The only barrier to the explosion of new innovations and uses in the instant messaging market is AOL's insistence that a large part of the market be off limits to other segments of the same market."[57]

THE "END-TO-END" PHILOSOPHY JEOPARDIZED

During their deliberations both agencies were lobbied heavily by advocates of open access who believed that information or data should be able to travel from one end of the global information infrastructure to the other unimpeded. Open access advocates claimed that this merger represented a potent threat to the future of that concept. They stressed the need to preserve the Internet's basic design principle of end-to-end (or "e-to-e"), whereby an unintelligent, simple network processes packets of data indiscriminately, that is, without regard for their content. The Internet's simple structure was designed for wide and open access and any sort of preferred access goes against this basic principle. The

Internet must remain, they argued, an open and neutral space, which welcomes innovation and does not discriminate on the basis of content. In their view, allowing bundling of cable and ISP services would compromise this key architectural principle of end-to-end design, since cable-owned ISPs would heavily influence the use of broadband technology. In all likelihood the range of services available to broadband cable users would be determined by these ISPs. Thus, for example, an ISP such as AOL would control whether broadband customers could be purveyors of their own Web content or whether full-length streaming video would be permitted. In the past the ISP Excite@Home has made its users sign a contract forbidding streaming video with a duration of more than 10 minutes.

But there is another side to this issue. Some economists argue for a balance between the need for openness with respect for private property rights and an appreciation of investment incentives. Are nonaffiliated ISPs the equivalent of free riders, as some cable companies or conduit owners have suggested? How should cable companies be compensated for sharing their property? If we do allow cable companies to favor their own ISP, will that provide an incentive to implement broadband more speedily? The need for investment incentives is particularly acute in this capital intensive industry, but allowing companies to gain that incentive by monopolizing the market for ISPs may not be a welfare-maximizing solution.

DECISIONS

The AOL Time Warner merger was studied for 11 months. Regulators were keenly aware that the stakes were high. During the middle of the government's study, AOL publicly promised that they would open up their systems. But in exchange for access to other ISPs they asked for 75 percent of subscription revenues. They also required that Time Warner have veto power over what is on the welcome screen, and they also wanted a permanent ad on that screen.

As regulators grappled with this merger, they faced many tough choices. Should they require AOL Time Warner to open its cable system to rival ISPs? What are reasonable terms for such access? Should they also require it to open its system to rival content? And should they demand that AOL's Instant Messenger become an open system? U.S. federal officials were not about to block this merger, but they needed to think carefully about the right conditions. What restrictions, if any, should be imposed upon this new company?

Case 8.4 AT&T and the City of Portland

Making efficient use of the Internet requires access to the network, which can be implemented over several different types of conduits such as telephone lines or cable wires. Most agree that broadband access either through cable lines or through DSL[58] will give users the highest caliber Internet access. Broadband providers fighting for customers and revenues to cover their mammoth investments have been engaged in a number of conflicts over the scope of control of their broadband infrastructures.

In the late 1990s AT&T decided to make a bold strategic move. It spent almost $110 billion to transform itself from a long distance phone company into a cable-based communications network. One of its key moves was the $48 billion acquisition of Tele-Communications Inc. (TCI), a major cable company with 17 million customers. Since the acquisition, AT&T has been upgrading TCI's network where necessary so it can handle two-way phone calls and Internet traffic in each market it serves. AT&T's goal is to offer a full package of broadband services through this cable network. The assimilation of TCI was followed by the acquisition of MediaOne and the potential for its 8 million subscribers. As of 2002, AT&T is the largest U.S. cable company with 16 million cable subscribers. AOL Time Warner follows with 13 million subscribers.

The TCI acquisition also gave AT&T control over Excite@Home, an Internet Service Provider and a portal that enables Internet access for cable TV subscribers. With the TCI and MediaOne acquisitions AT&T had positioned itself to become a major player in the delivery of broadband services. AT&T now offered cable broadband through Excite @Home to its many new customers. These customers have access to @Home, the Internet Service Provider linked to the portal Excite, which provides e-mail services and search functionality and some content. AT&T's subscribers cannot purchase cable broadband access separately from another IAP (such as AOL). Through 2002 @Home had exclusive rights to deliver high-speed Internet access over segments of AT&T's cable network.

When AT&T purchased TCI, the Federal Communications Commission (FCC) declined to impose any restrictions on AT&T, nor did it insist upon any open access requirements for the giant telecom, despite its substantial share of the cable market. Many public interest groups voiced concerns, arguing that restricting cable broadband access to Excite@Home was anticompetitive and harmful to consumers since it limited their choices.

After the merger, AT&T began the process of transferring the TCI cable franchises to its cable operations. This step required the approval of local franchising authorities in certain local districts. TCI's franchises with Portland allowed the city to "condition any transfer upon such conditions, related to the technical, legal and financial qualifications of the prospective party to perform according to the terms of the Franchise, as it deems appropriate." The regulatory commission queried AT&T about certain matters including its intentions for bundling Internet service provider and cable services. AT&T indicated that Excite@Home would be used exclusively over its cable broadband network and that this proprietary product was "not subject to common carrier obligations." The local telephone company, US West, and others objected on the grounds that AT&T's decisions negatively impacted consumer welfare, since consumers would be deprived of a choice for their ISP.

Portland's regulatory commission agreed with these concerns and hence it voted to approve the transfer from TCI to AT&T but only subject to certain conditions. Specifically, AT&T was to grant unrestricted access to its cable broadband transmission facilities for Internet service providers. According to the ruling, AT&T had to provide "non-discriminatory access to . . . [its] cable modem platform for providers of Internet and on-line services."[59]

AT&T, however, refused to accept these restrictive terms. Subsequently it initiated legal action arguing that the open access condition violated the Telecommunications Act of 1996. It argued that according to that act cable broadband access does not fall within the definition of cable service. The federal district court rejected AT&T's argument and concurred with the City of Portland's right to impose the condition of open access.

But in the summer of 2000 that ruling was reversed by the Ninth Circuit Court of Appeals. That court rejected the categorization of cable broadband access as a cable service and accordingly concluded that Portland had no right to regulate that service under the franchise agreement. According to the appeals court, broadband Internet access was a unique, hybrid service, composed of the pipes or cable lines along with the service provider. Hence it could not be regulated by the cable franchising authority, in this case, the City of Portland. The Appeals Court's conclusion was unambiguous:

> We hold that subsection 541 (b) (3) [of the 1996 Telecommunications Act] prohibits a franchising authority from regulating cable broadband access, because the transmission of Internet service to subscribers over cable broadband facilities is a telecommunications service under the Communi-

cations Act. Therefore, Portland may not condition the transfer of the cable franchise on nondiscriminatory access to AT&T's cable broadband network.[60]

CLOSED VERSUS OPEN ACCESS

Despite the ruling in AT&T's favor, the debate about open access continues unabated. Many argue that the federal government, Congress, or the FCC should step in and mandate open access for all cable networks. But the cable companies argue that the market, not local government regulators, should dictate cable Internet access arrangements.

For the most part cable companies like AT&T continue to embrace the closed access model which is epitomized by the "old AT&T" telecommunications network. The closed model entails one integrated system operated by a single company that has the sole discretion of determining the products and services that will be made to consumers. Since the emergence of "Community Antenna Television" (CATV) in the 1950s, cable television has always operated as a closed system and this closed-model approach is being extended to broadband Internet access. Internet users looking for broadband access require two services from cable companies: (1) the last mile connection which feeds directly into people's homes and provides the physical link to an ISP, and (2) affiliation with an ISP which provides direct Internet access to the Web and other features. The extension of the closed model to broadband means that both of these services are provided by the cable company and that its customers must use an affiliated ISP and not one of their own choosing.

Cable companies put forth several arguments on behalf of the perpetuation of this closed model. They note that if consumers do not like this arrangement, they have other options. For example, they could choose a broadband Internet connection through DSL (Digital Subscriber Line), a service provided by local telephone companies (such as Qwest or Verizon) that can also deliver video and high-speed Internet access. Cable companies also contend that they are more likely to invest in technological and system upgrades if they can maximize return on their investment. If these companies cannot get an adequate return on their investment, they will not have a strong incentive to invest in new infrastructure. And if open access is required, shouldn't cable companies receive adequate compensation for sharing their private property with competitive ISPs? Those ISPs are the equivalent of free-riders, piggybacking on these upgraded cable networks.

Finally there is the technical argument against open access. According to one report, "Because of the way cable systems are designed, allowing multiple Internet providers to use cable networks would lead to slowed data speeds and other glitches. Cable networks differ in architecture from telephone systems, which can accommodate thousands of competing Internet providers without mutual interference."[61] While the technical argument is persuasive to some, critics of the cable industry point out that cable companies could simply adopt a different technology, that is, use modems that will accommodate other ISPs more readily.

For AT&T and other cable companies, this sort of "forced access" demanded by the City of Portland could have a harmful effect on an industry that must still make major investments to provide consumers across America with high-speed Internet access. Those who agree with AT&T also point to the confusion that would ensue if we end up with a "patchwork quilt" of Internet access policies formulated by different jurisdictions. Opponents of closed access argue that AT&T's stance is problematic since the cable company is emerging as the single gatekeeper controlling broadband Internet access for most individuals.

Case 8.5 Note on the Digital Divide

> There is a growing digital divide between those who have access to the digital economy and those who don't, and that divide exists along the lines of education, income, region and race.
>
> —President Bill Clinton[62]

The global information infrastructure is rapidly transforming virtually every area of human life—business, entertainment, politics, and even romance. We live in a "network society," where connection to the network is critically important to one's social and economic advancement. Therefore we should be especially concerned about "social exclusion." If, as Tom Friedman suggests, "the Internet has become an essential tool of life," what do we do about those who are excluded from this medium through poverty and ignorance?[63] Those who are excluded from this technology could become more marginalized and severely handicapped in the network economy. As a United Nations report recently warned, "The network society is creating parallel communications systems: one for those with income, education, and literally connections, giving plentiful information at low cost and high speed; the other for those without connections, blocked by high barriers of time, cost, and uncertainty and dependent upon outdated information."[64] There is good reason, therefore, that some policy leaders have become preoccupied with this problem.

Furthermore, when the broadband economy finally becomes a reality, the cost of social exclusion from the information infrastructure will be even more substantial, since those who remain unconnected will miss out on even more opportunities. Broadband, the term used for high-capacity and high-speed data networks, will allow for more efficient delivery of video and other multimedia forms of information.

The so-called digital divide takes two forms. There is the global divide between developed and developing countries. Consider, for example, that Internet usage is heavily concentrated in developed countries, especially the United States. The United States has only 5 percent of the world's population but it has 50 percent of the world's personal computers linked to the Internet.

There is also a problem *within* developed countries like the United States, where many individuals and households are still not connected, and this represents the national divide. The axis of discussion in this Note will be the national social divide and not the global divide. Both of these problems are serious but the former is more manageable and perhaps an appropriate initial focus for U.S. policy makers. The national social divide involves the disparities within the United States between those who have access to information resources and those who lack access to those resources. Those who have solid computer skills, Internet access, and information literacy are much better positioned to achieve economic, social, and political success in the information age.

The "divide" is usually based on socioeconomic lines, that is, patterns of Internet use mirror present patterns of wealth and privilege. The main question is what should be done to resolve this problem and what are the implications of allowing the market to handle such social issues over time. Should the United States be more proactive and should its policy makers set an aggressive goal of universal broadband access?

DIVIDING LINES

Various studies conducted in both the private and public sectors have attempted to measure the extent and severity of the digital divide. One such study conducted by the Department of Commerce, called "Falling through the Net," found that households with incomes of $75,000 and over are 20 times more likely to have Internet access than those at lower income levels, and 9 times more likely to have computer access.[65] Even in the midst of prosperous and well-educated communities, such as Silicon Valley, the disparity between the information "haves" and "have nots" is glaring.

Other studies suggest that while the goal of digital inclusion is advancing rapidly, there is still a division along racial lines. Certain racial minorities are not using the Internet enough. For example, while 50.3 percent of whites and 49.4 percent of Asian Americans have Internet access, data reveals that only 29.3 percent of African Americans have such access, and the number drops to 23.5 percent if one looks at households.[66] Thus, Susan Kretchmer and Rod Carveth conclude that "while African Americans may not feel completely excluded from cyberspace, they may not feel included either."[67] There are several reasons for this—for one thing, according to the authors, African Americans see cyberspace as lacking color, and this is "a big negative" for them.[68]

The digital divide is not confined to racial lines. Other factors include family status and geography. Only 28.1 percent of nonfamily households have Internet access, but that number increases to 60.6 percent for families. And urban areas are more likely to have Internet access than rural areas, where only 38.9 percent have such access.[69] Also, it is no surprise that another key demographic variable is income. According to Manuel Castells, "91 percent of households with incomes of 75,000 dollars per year had computers in 2000, while the proportion dropped to 22 percent for children whose family income was less than 20,000 dollars. Moreover, low-income households were less likely to have Internet access, even when they had computers."[70] Finally, it might appear that the more education one has, the greater the likelihood of PC ownership and Internet usage. However, according to a study conducted by Donna Hoffman and others, "these levels are higher for Whites than for African Americans and these race differences persist even after adjusting for education. In fact, the gaps for access and usage are largest for those with a college degree." This data leads the authors of the study to conclude that differences in educational background do not account for the digital divide.[71]

SOLUTIONS

Closing this divide will arguably yield significant social and economic dividends as more and more citizens become connected to this "marketplace of ideas." Those in rural and low-income communities who currently lack access will be able to enjoy the convenience and security which is provided by technology and network connections. The Clinton administration seemed predisposed to advancing this goal as indicated in its National Information Infrastructure (NII) initiative. The core of the NII initiative is explained in the principles and goals articulated in the "Agenda for Action." These include the following: extend the "universal service" concept to ensure that information resources are available to everyone at an affordable price. The Agenda served a useful purpose. It endorsed the private sector's lead in NII development and it asserted that government action would do no more than complement that leadership. However, as Brian Kahin points out, the policy problems in some of the Agenda's "ambitious items," such as universal service, "were never fully articulated let alone resolved."[72]

There are several possible remedies for closing the digital divide. Some argue that in the long run market forces will ultimately reduce the gulf between digital haves and have nots. The impersonal marketplace, however, is often an inadequate forum for drawing attention to noneconomic issues including the inequities implicit in this well-documented digital divide. Is it possible to achieve the goal of universal Internet access envisioned by the Clinton administration through government intervention?

The problem is reminiscent of the need to provide citizens across the country with a telephone connection. We have obviously succeeded in achieving the goal of universal telephone service, since 94 percent of Americans have a telephone connection. What precisely is meant by the notion of "universal service"? Eli Noam defines universal service as "a public policy to spread telecommunications to most members of society, and to make available, directly or indirectly, the funds necessary."[73] But can we broaden the concept of universal service to Internet access?

Alexander Graham Bell invented the telephone in 1876, but few people saw the need for this device until many years later. However, in the early twentieth century its commercial success created a growing need for telephone service, and the United States Congress wanted to make sure that such service was available in all areas of the country and affordable even to those with low incomes. The 1934 Communications Act laid the groundwork for the principle of universal telephony service, a policy that was scrupulously followed by AT&T until its breakup in 1982. AT&T was a heavily regulated monopoly and it was responsible for providing universal service at a reasonable cost. Various cross-subsidies were also implemented for the purpose of achieving the goal of universal telecommunications. For example, businesses and long distance callers paid higher fees so that everyone could afford to make local telephone calls. Similarly, those in urban areas subsidized the higher costs associated with providing service in remote rural areas.

There are some relevant lessons in how universal telephony was accomplished. The free market did not resolve the need for universal telephony. Rather, once this *community need* became evident, the government carefully intervened to ensure that the need was met. But it should also be noted that the government did not provide any direct subsidies to AT&T.

Could this model work for universal Internet service? It's possible, but many questions will need to be addressed. What's an affordable price for Internet access? Are cross-subsidies a realistic option? In other words, can we charge a higher price for certain Internet-related services to ensure that everyone who wants it has an Internet connection? Manipulating rates in order to cross-subsidize will obviously be more difficult without the benefit of an AT&T-like monopoly. Or will the government need to provide funds for this purpose? For example, the federal government could provide investment credits to telecom companies that introduce high-speed data lines into rural or remote areas. This type of government assistance is sure to meet strong political resistance. Direct government subsidies would also make network services subject to political control.

Another problem is the difficulty of defining an "essential service." In the case of the telephone, it was straightforward to conclude that at a minimum everyone needed a telephone and a connection to make local or long distance calls. But what does universal service mean for computer users? Should the provision of universal service include a standard phone connection or should it include a broadband connection for high-speed access? If the latter, is it sufficient to ensure that high-speed Internet access is available everywhere, including rural areas? Or does universal service also mean that everyone should be able to *afford* that high-speed Internet connection? Does it even imply that everyone should be given the means to own a computer, without which connectivity is useless? Personal computers have come way down in price (and substitutes are emerging), but these devices are far more expensive than a telephone. What about the problem of computer literacy—how will all these new users, many of whom are quite naïve about technology, be educated so they can feel comfortable enough with a personal computer system? Some states, like Illinois, have funded community technology centers where new users can receive basic training in computer technology. The reach and success rate of such experimental programs, however, are still unknown.

Because of these and other difficulties, some advocate a cautious approach to universal access. But the ideal of universal service, however it is defined, is not without strong advocates. Castells, for example, argues that policy makers must summon the political will to rectify this problem. Otherwise, he writes, "more of the same leads to the broadening of the digital divide, a divide that may ultimately engulf the world in a series of multi-dimensional crises."[74]

Leslie Simon, fully cognizant of the challenges enumerated here, also maintains that the goal of universal service should not be abandoned. He argues that this can be accomplished through competition among telecommunications firms and other infrastructure providers: "If government policies increase competition, the flow of new products and services and lower prices that make universal access possible will roll out at an even faster rate." But as a "backup system," according to Simon, we also need "limited and temporary government intervention measures to jump-start universal access in institutions such as schools, hospitals, libraries, community centers, and assisted living and nursing facilities."[75]

Simon, Castells, and other optimists believe that the government can work with the private sector to ensure that the Net's economic and social benefits are distributed as widely as possible. Skeptics claim, however, that while this goal is laudable, it is unrealistic: The universal service formula, once employed so successfully by AT&T, is an old solution that cannot be transported to the digital age.

NOTES

1. "The Economics of Antitrust," *Economist* (2 May 1998), p. 64.
2. D. Carney, "The Microsoft Case: Tying It All Together," *Business Week*, (3 December 2001), p. 68.
3. An operating system is software that controls the execution of programs on a computer system.
4. See, for example, S. Liebowitz and S. Margolis, *Winners, Losers, and Microsoft* (Oakland, CA: Independent Institute, 1999).
5. T. Morgan, *Modern Antitrust Law and Its Origins* (New York: West Publishing, 1994).
6. "Microsoft Accused," *Economist* (23 May 1998), pp. 21–23.
7. Case law has established that Section 1 of this Act prohibits certain tying arrangements as a restraint of trade.
8. *United States v. E.I. du Pont de Nemours & Co.*, 351 U.S. 377 (1956).
9. U.S. Court of Appeals, *United States of America v. Microsoft Corporation*, 253 F. 3d 34 D.C. Cir. (2001).
10. "The Justice Department v. Microsoft: The Evidence and the Answers," *New York Times*, (27 October 1997), p. D5.
11. U.S. Court of Appeals, *United States of America v. Microsoft Corporation*.
12. Quoted in K. Auletta, *World War 3.0* (New York: Random House, 2001), p, 198.

13. This folder appears on the Windows desktop and contains the icons of proprietary client software of online service providers; clicking on one of these icons initiates the process of signing up for the OLS's services.
14. J. Brinkley and S. Lohr, *U.S. v. Microsoft* (New York: McGraw-Hill, 2001), p. 193.
15. Ibid, p. 57.
16. *United States of America v. Microsoft Corporation*, 84 F.Supp. 2d 9 D.D.C. (1999) [Findings of Fact].
17. *Spectrum Sports Inc. v. McQuillan*, 506 U.S. 456 (1993).
18. E.Wasserman, "A Defeat for Microsoft," *Industry Standard* (November 15, 1999), p. 68.
19. *Eastman Kodak Co. v. Image Technical Servs., Inc.*, 504 U.S. 451 (1992).
20. *Jefferson Parish Hospital District v. Hyde* 466 U.S. 21 (1984).
21. Microsoft Brief on Appeal, *United States of America v. Microsoft Corporation*, 87 F. Supp. 2d D.D.C. (1999). (Hereafter "Microsoft Brief.")
22. "Big Friendly Giant," *Economist* (January 30, 1999), p. 72.
23. Ibid.
24. *United States of America v. Microsoft Corporation*, quoted in 253F. 3d 34 D.C. Cir. (2001).
25. Microsoft Brief.
26. See *The Browser Wars, 1994-1998*, Harvard Business School case for more background on the competitive dynamics between Microsoft and Netscape. (Boston: Harvard Business School Publications, 1998).
27. Association for Competitive Technology and Computer Technology, Amicus Curiae Remedies Brief re *United States of America v. Microsoft* 97 F. Supp. 2d 59 D.D.C. (2000).
28. Microsoft Brief.
29. Ibid.
30. Ibid.
31. Ibid.
32. Ibid.
33. Quoted in Microsoft Brief.
34. *N. Pacific Ry. v. U.S.*, 356 U.S. 1 (1958).
35. T. Hazlett, "Microsoft's Internet Exploration," 29 *Cornell J. L. & Pub. Policy*, 52 (1999).
36. J. Brinkley and S. Lohr, *U.S. v. Microsoft* (New York: McGraw-Hill, 2001), p. 38.
37. Ibid., p. 257.
38. K. Auletta, *World War 3.0*, p. 284.
39. Ibid.
40. M. France, "Get Ready for Windows XP. Trustbusters Are," *Business Week*, (30 July 2001), p. 37.
41. J. Greene, "Rob Glaser Is Racing Upstream," *Business Week*, 3 September 2001, p. EB 16.
42. F. Rose, "Keyword: Context," *Wired* (December 1996), pp. 254–257.
43. Ibid.
44. G. Rivlin, "AOL's Rough Riders," *Industry Standard* (30 October 2000), p. 142.

45. James Fallows, "The Next Great Power," *Industry Standard* (13 November 2000), pp. 51–52.
46. C. Yang et al., "Show Time for AOL Time Warner," *Business Week,* (15 January 2001), p. 57.
47. Broadband is the industry term for sending a lot of information through a single wire; with broadband a consumer's Internet connection, phone service, and cable TV can all move through one "superfast connection." That connection ordinarily comes from one of two sources: a modem connected to the cable lines, which can handle much more data than copper phone lines, or a Digital Subscriber Line (DSL) from a telecom company which converts voice and other data signals into digital packets which can move more efficiently through phone networks. (See R. Blumstein, "A Road Map through the Bewildering World of Telecommunications," *Wall Street Journal,* 18 September 2000, p. R4.
48. K. Swisher, "Playing Nice," *Grok* (September 2000), p. 119.
49. S. Walsh, "Do You Time Warner Take AOL . . . ," *Industry Standard* (October 30, 2000), p. 165.
50. "One House, Many Windows," *Economist* (19 August 2000), pp. 60–61.
51. W. Bane et al., "The Converging Worlds of Telecommunication, Computing, and Entertainment," in *Sense and Respond,* ed. S. Bradley and R. Nolan (Boston: Harvard Business School Press, 1998), pp. 31–62.
52. Federal Trade Commission "Analysis of Proposed Consent Order to Aid Public Comment." Washington, D.C., 2000.
53. D. Rubinfield and H. Singer, *Open Access to Broadband Networks: A Case Study of the AOL/Time Warner Merger,* 16 Berkeley Technology Law Journal 631 (2001).
54. "Communications Daily Notebook," *Communications Daily,* (11 May 2000).
55. Rubinfield and Singer, *Open Access to Broadband Networks,* p. 636.
56. M. Schwartz, "The Instant Messaging Debate," *Computerworld* (7 January 2002), p. 40.
57. Comments of iCast Corp. In re Applications for Consent to Transfer of Control of Licenses by Time Warner Inc. and America Online, Inc., January 22, 2001.
58. Digital Subscriber Line (DSL) transforms a computer's digital signals into sound waves so that they can move more quickly through the copper wires that make up the phone network.
59. Cited in *AT&T v. Portland,* 216 F. 3d 871 9th Cir. (2000).
60. Ibid.
61. L. Lessig, "The Cable Debate, Part II," *Industry Standard* (2–9 August 1999), p. 22.
62. President William Jefferson Clinton, speech delivered in Anaheim, California, July 8, 1999; available at http://www.whitehouse.gov.
63. T. Friedman, *The Lexus and the Olive Tree* (New York: Farrar Straus Giroux, 1999), p. 118.
64. "United Nations Development Report," UNOP, 1999, p. 63.
65. See http://www.ntia.doc.gov.ntiahome/fttn99.

66. M. Castells, *The Internet Galaxy* (New York: Oxford University Press, 2001), p. 249.
67. S. Kretchmer and R. Carveth, "The Color of the Net: African Americans, Race, and Cyberspace," *Computers and Society* (September 2001), pp. 9–14.
68. Ibid.
69. Castells, *Internet Galaxy,* p. 250.
70. Ibid., p. 251.
71. D. Hoffman et al., "The Evolution of the Digital Divide," in *The Digital Divide,* ed. B. Compaine. (Cambridge, MA: MIT Press, 2001), pp. 47–98.
72. B. Kahin, "The U.S. National Information Infrastructure Initiative: The Market, the Web, and the Virtual Project," in Kahin and Wilson, eds., *National Information Infrastructures* (Cambridge, MA: MIT Press, 1997), pp. 150–189
73. E. Noam, "Beyond Liberalization: Reforming Universal Service," *Telecommunications Policy* 18, no. 9 (1994), p. 687.
74. Castells, *Internet Galaxy,* p. 271.
75. L. Simon. *NetPolicy.Com* (Baltimore, MD: John Hopkins University Press, 2000), pp. 172–173.

Selected References

Arranged by Subject Matter

INFORMATION TECHNOLOGY ETHICS AND POLICY—GENERAL BACKGROUND READINGS

Castells, Manuel. *The Internet Galaxy.* New York: Oxford University Press, 2001.

Edgar, Stacey. *Morality and Machines: Perspectives on Computer Ethics.* Sudbury, MA: Jones & Bartlett, 1997.

Ermann, David M., Claudio Guitierrez, and Mary B. Williams, eds. *Computers, Ethics and Society.* New York: Oxford University Press, 1990.

Forrester, Tom, and Perry Morrison. *Computer Ethics: Cautionary Tales and Ethical Dilemmas in Computing.* 2d ed. Cambridge, MA: MIT Press, 1994.

Gould, Carol, ed. *The Information Web: Ethical and Social Implications of Computers.* Boulder, CO: Westview Press, 1989.

Grillo, John P., and Ernest Kallman. *Ethical Decision Making and Information Technology.* Watsonville, CA: Mitchell McGraw-Hill, 1993.

Johnson, Deborah. *Computer Ethics.* 3d ed. Upper Saddle River, NJ: Prentice Hall, 2001.

———, and Helen Nissenbaum, eds. *Computers, Ethics, and Social Values.* Upper Saddle River, NJ: Prentice Hall, 1995.

Kling, Rob, ed. *Computerization and Controversy.* 2d ed. San Diego, CA: Academic Press, Inc., 1996.

Laudon, Kenneth. "Ethical Concepts and Information Technology." *Communications of the ACM* (December 1995), pp. 33–39.

Langford, Duncan, ed. *Internet Ethics.* London: Macmillan. Ltd., 2000.

Lessig, Larry. *Code and Other Laws of Cyberspace.* New York: Basic Books, 1999.

O'Reilly and Associates, eds. *The Internet and Society.* Proceedings of Harvard Conference on the Internet and Society. Cambridge, MA: Harvard University Press, 1997.

Rogerson, Simon, and Terrell Ward Bynum. *Information Ethics: A Reader.* Cambridge, MA: Blackwell Publishers, 1998.

Rosenberg, Richard. *The Social Impact of Computers.* New York: Harcourt Brace Jovanovich, 1992.

Severson, Richard. *The Principles of Information Ethics.* Armonk, NY: M.E. Sharpe, 1997.

Simon, Leslie. *NetPolicy.Com.* Baltimore, MD: John Hopkins University Press, 2000.

Spinello, Richard. *Ethical Aspects of Information Technology.* Upper Saddle River, NJ: Prentice Hall, 1995.

———. *Cyberethics: Morality and Law in Cyberspace.* Sudbury, MA: Jones & Bartlett, 2000.

———, and Herman Tavani. *Readings in Cyberethics.* Sudbury, MA: Jones & Bartlett, 2001.

FREE EXPRESSION

Camp, Jean, and K. Lewis. "Code as Speech." *Ethics and Information Technology* 3, no. 1 (2001), pp. 21–33.

Carroll, Michael. "Garbage In: Emerging Media and Regulation of Unsolicited Commercial Solicitations." 11 *Berkeley Technology Law Journal* (Fall 1996).

Electronic Privacy Information Center. *Filters and Freedom.* Washington, DC: Electronic Privacy Information Center, 1999.

Fogelman, Martin. "Freedom and Censorship in the Emerging Electronic Environment." *Information Society* 10 (1994), pp. 295–303.

Fried, Charles. "Perfect Freedom or Perfect Control." 114 *Harvard Law Review* 606 (2000).

Godwin, Michael. *CyberRights: Defending Free Speech in the Digital Age.* New York: Random House, 1998.

Lessig, Larry. "Tyranny in the Infrastructure." *Wired* (March 1997), p. 96.

Rosenberg, Richard. "Free Speech, Pornography, Sexual Harassment, and Electronic Networks." *Information Society* 9 (1993), pp. 285–331.

———. "Controlling Access to the Internet: The Role of Filtering." *Ethics and Information Technology* 3, no. 1 (2001), pp. 35–54.

Sunstein, Cass. "The First Amendment in Cyberspace." 104 *Yale Law Journal* 1757 (1995).

Turner, William B. "What Part of 'No Law' Don't You Understand? A Primer on the First Amendment and the Internet." *Wired* (March 1996), pp. 104–112.

Wallace, Jonathan, and Mark Mangan. *Sex, Laws, and Cyberspace.* New York: Henry Holt & Co., 1996.

PRIVACY ISSUES

Agre, Philip, and Marc Rotenberg, eds. *Technology and Privacy: The New Landscape*. Cambridge, MA: MIT Press, 1997.

Brandeis, Louis, and Samuel Warren. "The Right to Privacy." 4 *Harvard Law Review* 193 (1890).

Brin, David. *The Transparent Society*. Reading, MA: Addison-Wesley, 1998.

Cespedes, Frank, and H. Jeff Smith. "Database Marketing: New Rules for Policy and Practice." *Sloan Management Review* (Summer 1993), pp. 7–22.

Chalykoff, John, and Nitin Nohira. "Note on Electronic Monitoring." Boston, MA: Harvard Business School Publications, 1990.

DeCew, Judith. *In Pursuit of Privacy*. Ithaca, NY: Cornell University Press, 1997.

Dempsey, J. "Communication Privacy in the Digital Age: Revitalizing the Federal Wiretap Laws to Enhance Privacy." 8 *Albany Law Journal of Science & Technology*, 43 (1997).

———. "The Fourth Amendment and the Internet." Testimony before the Subcommittee on the Constitution of the House Judiciary Committee, April 6, 2000.

Doss, Erni, and Michael Loui. "Ethics and the Privacy of Electronic Mail." *Information Society* 11 (1995), pp. 223–235.

Electronic Frontier Foundation (EFF). "The Fourth Amendment and Carnivore." Testimony before the House Judiciary Committee on the Constitution, July 28, 2000.

Etzioni, Amitai. *The Limits of Privacy*. New York: Basic Books, 1999.

Flaherty, David. *Protecting Privacy in Surveillance Societies*. Chapel Hill, NC: University of North Carolina Press, 1989.

Gandy, Oscar. *The Panoptic Sort: A Political Economy of Personal Information*. Boulder, CO: Westview Press, 1993.

Gavison, Ruth. "Privacy and the Limits of the Law." 89 *Yale Law Journal* 421 (1984).

Garfinkel, Simson. *Database Nation*. Cambridge, MA: O'Reilly & Associates, 2000.

Lyon, David, and Elia Zureik, eds. *Computers, Surveillance, and Privacy*. Minneapolis: University of Minnesota Press, 1996.

Mason, Richard, and Mary Culnan. *Information and Responsibility: The Ethical Challenge*. Thousand Oaks, CA: Sage Publications, 1995.

James Moor. "Towards a Theory of Privacy in the Information Age." *Computers and Society* (September 1997), pp. 27–32.

Regan, Priscilla. *Legislating Privacy: Technology, Social Values and Public Policy*. Chapel Hill: University of North Carolina Press, 1995.

Rosen, Jonathan. *The Unwanted Gaze*. New York: Random House, 2000.

Sipior, Janice, and Burke Ward. "The Ethical and Legal Quandary of Email Privacy." *Communications of the ACM* (December 1995), pp. 48–54.

Smith, Jeff. *Managing Privacy: Information Technology and Corporate America*. Chapel Hill: University of North Carolina Press, 1994.

Smith, Robert Ellis. *Ben Franklin's Web Site: Privacy and Curiosity from Plymouth Rock to the Internet*. Providence, RI: Sheridan Books, 2000.

Solveig Singleton. "Privacy as Censorship: A Skeptical View of Proposals to Regulate Privacy in the Private Sector." Cato Institute, Washington DC, 1998.

Spinello, Richard. "E-Mail and Panoptic Power in the Workplace." In L. Hartmann, ed. *Perspectives on Business Ethics*. New York: McGraw-Hill, 2002.

Tavani, Herman. "Internet Search Engines and Personal Privacy." In *Proceedings of Conference on Computer Ethics: Philosophical Enquiry*, ed. Jeroen van den Hoven. Rotterdam, The Netherlands: Erasmus University Press, 1997, pp. 169–178.

Ware, Willis. "The Digital Persona and Its Application to Data Surveillance." *Information Society* 10 (1994), pp. 77–92.

Westin, Alan. *Privacy and Freedom*. New York: Atheneum, 1967.

Wright, Marie, and John Kahalik. "The Erosion of Privacy." *Computers and Society* 27, no. 4 (December 1997), pp. 22–26.

INTELLECTUAL PROPERTY

Alderman, John. *Sonic Boom: Napster, MP3 and the New Pioneers of Music.* Cambridge, MA: Perseus Publishing, 2001.

Band, Jonathan, and Masanobu Katoh. *Interfaces on Trial.* Boulder, CO: Westview Press, 1995.

Barlow, John. "The Economy of Ideas: A Framework for Rethinking Copyrights and Patents." *Wired* (March 1994), pp. 47–50.

Boyle, James. *Shamans, Software, and Spleens.* Cambridge, MA: Harvard University Press, 1998.

Burk, Dan. "The Trouble with Trespass." 4 *Journal of Small and Emerging Business Law* 27 (1999).

Clapes, Anthony Lawrence. *Softwars: The Legal Battles for Control of the Global Software Industry*. Westport, CT: Quorum Books, 1993.

Davis, G. Gervaise. "War of the Words: Intellectual Property Laws and Standardization." *IEEE Micro* (December 1993), pp. 16–22.

Ginsburg, J. "Copyright Legislation for the 'Digital Millennium.'" 23 *Columbia-VLA Journal of Law and the Arts* 137 (1999).

Goldstein, Paul. *Copyright's Highway*. New York: Hill & Wang, 1994.

McCuaig, David. "Halve the Baby: An Obvious Solution to the Troubling Use of Trademarks as Metatags." 18 *John Marshall Journal of Computer and Information Law* 643 (2000).

Moore, Adam, ed. *Intellectual Property: Moral, Legal and Intellectual Dilemmas.* Lanham, MD: Rowman & Littlefield, 1997.

O'Rourke, Margaret. "Defining the Limits of Free-Riding in Cyberspace: Trademark Liability for Metatagging." 33 *Gonzaga Law Review* 227 (1997).

Samuelson, Pamela. "How to Interpret the Lotus Decision (And How Not To)." *Communications of the ACM* (November 1990), pp. 30–33.

———. "Software Compatibility and the Law." *Communications of the ACM* (August 1995), pp. 15–22.

———. "Good News and Bad News on the Intellectual Property Front." *Communications of the ACM* (March 1999), pp. 19–24.

Shirky, Clay. "Where Napster is Taking the Publishing World." *Harvard Business Review* (February 2001), pp. 143–148.

Stallman, Richard. "GNU Manifesto." 1985. http://www.gnu.org/gnu/-manifesto.html.

Stefik, Mark. *The Internet Edge*. Cambridge, MA: MIT Press, 1999.

SECURITY AND COMPUTER CRIMES

Bainbridge, D.I. "Hacking—The Unauthorized Access of Computer Systems: The Legal Implications." *Modern Law Review* (March 1989), pp. 236–245.

Bellovin, Steve. "Network and Internet Security." In Dorothy Denning, ed., *Internet Besieged.* New York: ACM Press, 1998, pp. 117–136.

Branscomb, Anne. "Rogue Computer Programs and Computer Rogues: Tailoring the Punishment to Fit the Crime." 16 *Rutgers Computer and Technology Law Journal,* 61 (1991).

Denning, Dorothy. "The U.S. vs. Craig Neidorf." *Communications of the ACM* (March 1991), pp. 24–30.

Froomkin, Michael. "It Came from Planet Clipper: The Battle over Cyrptographic Key Escrow." 15 *University of Chicago Legal Forum* 69 (1996).

Garfinkel, Simspon, and Eugene Spafford. *Web Security and Commerce.* Cambridge, MA: O'Reilly Publishing, 1997.

Levy, Steven. *Hackers: Heroes of the Computer Revolution.* Garden City, NY: Doubleday, 1984.

———. "Battle of the Clipper Chip." *New York Times Magazine*, 12 June 1994, pp. 35–43.

———. *CRYPTO.* New York: Viking, 2001.

Spafford, Eugene. "Are Computer Hacker Break-ins Ethical?" *Journal of Systems Software* (January 1992), pp. 41–47.

Tavani, Herman. "Defining Computer Crime: Piracy, Break-Ins, and Sabotage in Cyberspace." In R. Spinello and H. Tavani, eds. *Readings in CyberEthics.* Sudbury, MA: Jones & Bartlett, 2001.

LIABILITY, SAFETY, AND RELIABILITY

Brooks, Thomas. "Catching Jellyfish in the Internet: The Public Figure Doctrine and Defamation on Computer Bulletin Boards." 21 *Rutgers Computer & Technology Law Journal* 461 (1995).

Charles, Robert. "Computer Bulletin Boards and Defamation: Who Should Be Liable? Under What Standard?" *Journal of Law and Technology* 2 (1987), pp. 121–150.

Collins, Robert W. "How Good is Good Enough." *Communications of the ACM* (January 1994), pp. 76–86.

DiCato, Edward M. "Operator Liability Associated with Maintaining a Computer Bulletin Board." 4 *Software Law Journal* 147 (1990).

Godwin, Michael. "Libel Law: Let it Die." *Wired* (March 1996), pp. 116–118.

Jensen, Eric C. "An Electronic Soapbox: Computer Bulletin Boards and the First Amendment." 39 *Federal Communications Law Journal* 217 (1987).

Johnson, Deborah, and John Mulvey. "Accountability and Computer Decision Systems." *Communications of the ACM* (December 1995), pp. 58–64.

Joyce, Ed. "Software Bugs: A Matter of Life and Liability." *Datamation* (May 1987), pp. 15–20.

Leveson, Nancy, and Clark Turner. "An Investigation of the Therac-25 Accidents." *Computer* (July 1993), pp. 18–41.

Mullen, L. "The Fourth Circuit has Ruled in Zeran v. America Online: Absolute Immunity for the Internet Service Provider?" 1997. http://www.law.-stetson.edu/courses/computerlaw/papers/mullen97.htm.

Nissenbaum, Helen. "Computing and Accountability." *Communications of the ACM* (January 1994), pp. 32–43.

Raquillet, R. "The Good Samaritan: The Exclusion of Liability of ISP's for Third Parties Defamatory Conducts." 1999. http://www.lclark.edu/~loren/-cyberlaw99fall/projects99.

Ross, Philip E. "The Day the Software Crashed." *Forbes*, 25 April 1994, pp. 142–156.

Stern, Richard. "Microsoft and Vaporware." *IEEE Micro* (April 1995), pp. 6–7; 84–85.

FAIR COMPETITION AND ACCESS ISSUES

Auletta, Ken. *World War 3.0: Microsoft and Its Enemies*. New York: Random House, 2001.
Brinkley, Joel, and Steve Lohr. *U.S. v. Microsoft*. New York: McGraw-Hill, 2001.
Clinton, William, and Albert Gore. "A Framework for Global Electronic Commerce." 1997. Available at: http://www.iitf.nist.gov.
Compaine, Benjamin. *The Digital Divide: Facing a Crisis or Creating a Myth.* Cambridge, MA: MIT Press, 2001.
Digital Divide Network. http://www.digitaldividenetwork.org.
Heileman, John. *Pride before the Fall.* New York: HarperCollins, 2001.
Kahin, B. "The U.S. National Information Infrastructure Initiative: The Market, the Web, and the Virtual Project." In B. Kahin and E. Wilson, eds., *National Information Infrastructures.* Cambridge, MA: MIT Press, 1997, pp. 150–189.
Lemley, Mark, and Larry Lessig. "The End of End-to-End: Preserving the Architecture of the Internet in the Broadband Era." 48 *UCLA Law Review* 925 (2001).
Liebowitz, Steven, and Joseph Margolis. *Winners, Losers, and Microsoft.* Oakland, CA: Independent Institute, 1999.
McKenzie, Richard. *Trust on Trial: How the Microsoft Case is Reframing the Rules of Competition*. Cambridge MA: Perseus Publishing, 2000.
Rubinfield, D., and H. Singer. "Open Access to Broadband Networks: A Case Study of the AOL/Time Warner Merger." 16 *Berkeley Technology Law Journal* 631 (2001).
Viscusi, W., et al. *Economics of Regulation and Antitrust.* 2d ed. Cambridge, MA: MIT Press, 1998.
U.S. Government Digital Divide Website. http://www.digitaldivide.gov.
Yang, C., et al. "Show Time for AOL Time Warner." *Business Week,* 15 January 2001, pp. 57–59.

Index